A University in Troubled Times

A University in Troubled Times

Queen's Belfast, 1945–2000

L.A. CLARKSON

FOUR COURTS PRESS

This book was set in 10.5 on 12.5 pt Ehrhardt
by Mark Heslington, Northallerton, North Yorkshire for
FOUR COURTS PRESS LTD
7 Malpas Street, Dublin 8, Ireland
Email: info@four-courts-press.ie
and in the United States for
FOUR COURTS PRESS
c/o ISBS, 920 N.E. 58th Avenue, Suite 300, Portland, OR 97213.

A catalogue record for this title is available from the British Library.

ISBN 1–85182–862–1

Printed in Great Britain by
MPG Books, Bodmin, Cornwall

Foreword

As befits an institution founded in 1845, Queen's University Belfast has been
the subject of several histories. In addition to histories of its faculties, schools,
departments, clubs and societies, the University has been chronicled in three
major general histories: the monumental two-volume work by J.C. Beckett and
T.W. Moody, covering the period 1845–1950; the more popular and accessible
history by Brian Walker and Alf McCreary, covering the period 1845–1995; and
the present work by Leslie Clarkson, covering the period 1945–2000.

Leslie Clarkson's history differs from those of his predecessors in its scope
and in its approach. He restricts its scope to the second half of the twentieth
century, and he adopts the approach of the social historian, playing down the
activities of individuals and stressing the importance of the social context. Such
an approach is particularly appropriate for describing and analysing the history
of Queen's, because it has a closer connection with its local community than any
other university in the United Kingdom or Ireland. Indeed, as Leslie Clarkson
points out, this connection gives the story of Queen's its unique characteristic.

Northern Ireland has a highly distinctive regional identity, and the local
community has looked to Queen's, particularly when it was the region's only
university, to supply its educated elite and to provide teaching and research that
contribute directly to the wealth and welfare of the community. More important, Queen's local community is a divided community. The University has tried
to remain a civilising influence above the community divisions. But balancing
the competing claims of Protestants and Catholics and Unionists and
Nationalists, and at the same time balancing these claims with its intellectual
obligations to the international world of scholarship, has often proved difficult.

This balancing act was particularly difficult during 'the Troubles', the civil
war that occurred in Northern Ireland between the 1960s and the 1990s. By
analysing the interplay between the University's development and its social context during these troubled times, Leslie Clarkson makes a significant contribution to our understanding of both Queen's and Northern Ireland.

Professor Sir George Bain
President and Vice-Chancellor
Queen's University Belfast

Contents

LIST OF ILLUSTRATIONS   xi

LIST OF GRAPHS AND TABLES   xiii

ABBREVIATIONS   xv

PREFACE   xvii

1   A 'COLLEGE FOR STUDENTS IN ARTS, LAW, PHYSIC, AND OTHER
    USEFUL LEARNING'   1
    Universities: liberal or vocational?   2
    Northern Ireland, 1945–2000   8

2   QUEEN'S, BELFAST   12
    Prelude: 1845–1945   12
    1945–2000: some statistics   15
    Post-war recovery   16
    The 1950s: expansion and a widening reputation   19
    1960–75: missed opportunities and political problems   21
    1975–95: austerity and anguish   22
    1995–2000: renaissance?   24

3   QUEEN'S, STORMONT, AND WESTMINSTER   26
    Policy before Robbins and Lockwood   26
    Robbins and Lockwood   29
    Life after Lockwood: Chilver, Butler, and beyond   37
    The Dearing Report   43
    Conclusion   44

4   WHO PAYS?   46
    Government grants   46
    Student fees   53
    Research grants and contract income   55
    Other income   57
    Spending the money   58
    Conclusion   61

5   MANAGERIAL AND BUREAUCRATIC DEVICES   63
    Foundations: charters, statutes, structures, members, and officers 64
    The 1982 charter and statutes   66
    A Registrar: to have or not to have?   69
    Creating a camel   73

Caging the camel   81
Conclusion   83

6   BRICKS, MORTAR AND SOME CONCRETE   85
    Pre-war legacies and post-war difficulties   86
    Building in the 1950s and 1960s   86
    Consolidation and retrenchment: the 1970s and 1980s   95
    Queen's and conservation   100
    Rationalization and renewal in the 1990s   103
    Conclusion   104

7   STAFF – ACADEMIC AND OTHERS   105
    Counting heads   105
    Some scholars: some survivors, and some newcomers   107
    Academic appointments, 1945–2000: a profile   112
    The professoriate   118
    Gender   119
    Religion   122
    The non-academic staff   125
    Conclusion   126

8   STUDENTS   128
    Student numbers   129
    Gender and denomination   131
    Faculty and subject distribution   134
    Student support   136
    The Students' Union and student participation   140
    Conclusion   147

9   SCHOLARSHIP   149
    Introduction: purpose revisited   149
    Undergraduate studies   151
    The quality of teaching   158
    Postgraduate training   162
    Research   163
    Conclusion   167

10 QUEEN'S AND COMMUNITY   169
    Extra-mural studies, continuing education, and outreach   170
    Public lectures, the Arts, and the Festival at Queen's   173
    Troubled times   175
    Discrimination, the National Anthem, and Irish language signs   184
    Conclusion: Into the light   191

11 CONCLUSION   193

Appendices   195
1.1 Senior officers of the University   195
1.2 Full-time academic staff by faculty (teaching and research)   197
1.3 Annual full-time lecturing appointments (excludes research staff)   199
2.1 Student numbers (pre-1997 faculties)   201
2.2 Percentage distribution of students (pre-1997 faculties)   203
2.3 Totals of male and female students (post-1996 faculties)   205
2.4 Percentage distribution of male and female students (post-1996 faculties)   207
2.5 Full-time, part-time, and postgraduate students   209
3.1 Sources of income (£s)   210
3.2 Sources of income (per cent)   211

BIBLIOGRAPHY   213

INDEX   221

Illustrations

Illustrations occur between pages 110 and 111.

1 Queen's University, *c.*2000
2 The Quadrangle, *c.*2000
3 Old Library
4 Great Hall
5 The Old Queen's Elms, demolished in 1964
6 The New Student's Union in 1970
7 Sir David Lindsay Keir, Vice-Chancellor (1939–49)
8 Sir Eric Ashby, Vice-Chancellor (1950–9)
9 Dr Michael Grant, CBE, Vice-Chancellor (1959–66)
10 Sir Arthur Vick, Vice-Chancellor (1966–76)
11 Sir Peter Froggatt, Vice-Chancellor (1976–86)
12 Sir Gordon Beveridge, Vice-Chancellor (1986–97)
13 Sir George Bain, Vice-Chancellor (1998–2004)
14 Senator George Mitchell, Chancellor since 1999
15 Mary McAleese (Law). President of Ireland since 1997
16 J.C. Beckett, MRIA (History). Professor of Irish History, 1958–75
17 Brenda McLaughlin, CBE (Geography and Social Studies).
    Senior Pro-Chancellor of Queen's University since 1999
18 Seamus Heaney (English), Nobel Laureate. Poet
19 Estyn Evans, MRIA. Professor of Geography, 1945–66
20 Sir David Bates, FRS. Professor of Applied Mathematics and Theoretical
    Physics, 1951–74
21 John Blacking, Professor of Social Anthropology, 1970–90
22 John McCanny, CBE, FRS. Professor of Microelectronics Engineering since
    1988
23 Edna Longley, MRIA. Professor of English, 1991–2003
24 Dame Ingrid Allen, MRIA. Professor of Neuropathology, 1978–97
25 Elizabeth Meehan, MRIA, Professor of Politics since 1997
26 Margaret Mullett, FSA. Professor of Byzantine Studies since 1998
27 Entering the Heaney Library
28 Computer Suite
29 School of Music
30 Pharmacy Laboratory
31 Gaelic football
32 Hockey
33 Netball

34 The Rowing Club
35 Relaxing
36 The Union shop
37 Coffee time
38 Student crèche
39 Graduating
40 After the ceremony
41 The garden party
42 Champagne bar
43 Queen's University of Belfast at Armagh
44 The Cardinal Daly Library, Armagh
45 The Art Gallery, Lanyon Building
46 Festival at Queen's (Pure Movement, 2003)
47 Young aeronautical engineer
48 Young doctor
49 Young scientist
50 Young in heart. Jazz in the cloisters
51 President Clinton, June 2000
52 Prince of Wales, January 2002

Graphs and tables

GRAPHS

7.1 Full-time academic staff (teaching and research), 1945–2000   112
7.2 Annual full-time permanent lecturing appointments, 1945–2000   113
7.3 Proportion of academic staff qualifications from QUB   115
7.4 Annual average female full-time appointments   120
8.1 Student numbers, 1945–2000   129
8.2 Percentage of students by sex, 1945–2002   132
8.3 Roman Catholic students as a percentage of total students   132
9.1 Proportion of 1sts and 2.1 degrees (all subjects)   160
9.2 Proportion of 1sts and 2.1 degrees (humanities and pure and
     applied science)   160

TABLES

2.1 Summary statistics (five-yearly averages)   15
4.1 Sources of income, 1945–99   47
4.2 Breakdown of expenditure, 1945–99   59
7.1 Categories of staff in 2000   106
7.2 Categories of staff, 1944–99 (five yearly averages)   107
7.3 Religious composition of staff, 1987–2000   123
7.4 Representation by religion in each employment category (per cent)   124
8.1 Distribution of students by faculty   135
9.1 Research assessments results, 1989–2001   165

Abbreviations

AUT	Association of University Teachers
CVCP	Committee of Vice-Chancellors and Principals
DENI	Department of Education, Northern Ireland
ESRC	Economic and Social Research Council
HEFCE	Higher Education Funding Council, England
MRC	Medical Research Council
NERC	Natural Environment Research Council
NIWP	Northern Ireland Working Party
NUI	National University of Ireland
NUS	National Union of Students
NUU	New University of Ulster
QUB	Queen's University, Belfast
RAE	Research Assessment Exercise
SERC	Science and Engineering Research Council
SRC	Students' Representative Council
SRCSU	Students' Representative Council of the Students' Union
SSR	Student-Staff Ratio
SU	Students' Union
TCD	Trinity College, Dublin
THES	*Times Higher Education Supplement*
TQA	Teaching Quality Assessment
UCC	University College, Cork
UCD	University College, Dublin
UFC	Universities Funding Council
UGC	University Grants Committee
UCG	University College, Galway
UU	University of Ulster
WSH	Women Students' Hall

Note on Vice-Chancellors

Every Queen's Vice-Chancellor received a civic honour while in office with the exception of Dr Grant. Throughout I have used the title they held when they left office. Until the appointment of Professor Sir George Bain it was not the practice to give the Vice-Chancellor a professorial title.

Preface

Sir Gordon Beveridge invited me to write this volume a decade ago. He had previously commissioned Brian Walker, the Director of the Institute of Irish Studies, and Alf McCreary, the Information Officer, to write what he called the 'people's history' of Queen's, which appeared in 1994 under the title, *Degrees of excellence*. Sir Gordon also wanted a book that had the space to explore issues more deeply. I am sorry that other commitments delayed the completion of this study and Sir Gordon is not alive to see the result.

Since his arrival in 1998 the present Vice-Chancellor, Sir George Bain, has been most encouraging. He has read various drafts of the manuscript but has not attempted to impose any sort of official line, except to tell me I have been too kind about Vice-Chancellors. Although I was invited by one Vice-Chancellor and encouraged by another, I have been free to write what I like. Sir Gordon initially appointed a committee to advise me. It met once, possibly twice; otherwise we have not bothered one another: the best kind of committee.

The University has generously provided a subsidy for publication. I am extremely grateful for the help I received from the staff of the Library's special collections. I am grateful for assistance from the staff in the offices of the Registrar and the Academic Registrar and for their tea, coffee and biscuits. Jim Swann in the Planning Office seemed to delight in finding statistics in obscure places. Ivan Ewart and Shan McAnena have been of great help with the illustrations. Alf McCreary was kind enough to pass on to me the transcripts of interviews he conducted when writing *Degrees of excellence*. Tom Collins, Gerry Power and Anne Langford have been helpful in various ways. Dr Margaret Crawford cast her needle eye over my text and statistical appendices and asked some awkward questions.

There are two other sets of obligations to acknowledge. The first is to my wife and family who have had to share me with Queen's for almost forty years. The other is to all those men and women who have worked and studied in Queen's over the last half century. It is they who have made Queen's and this is their story. I hope they will not find it wanting.

A 'college for students in arts, law, physic, and other useful learning'

In January 1882, thirty-seven years after the foundation of the Queen's University in Ireland and two years after the Queen's University had been restructured into the Royal University, the Revd Josias Porter, President of the Queen's College, Belfast wrote to the Chief Secretary of Ireland complaining of a lack of money:

> A college placed like this, in the centre of a great manufacturing popula-
> tion, should have the power of adapting itself to the educational wants of
> the community. In addition to intellectual culture it should give all facili-
> ties for instruction in those departments of science which would serve to
> develop local industries. Belfast is the capital of Ulster, indeed I may say
> of Irish, commerce and manufacture. It is the Manchester of Ireland. It
> therefore requires a college somewhat on the model of Owens College,
> with a full scientific staff, and complete scientific apparatus and laborato-
> ries ... We want systematic training; and the vast majority of our people
> care nothing for degrees except when preceded by such training.[1]

The President's plea for more money reflected two concerns that have run throughout the history of Queen's ever since: function and funding. The two are connected. The first may be simply restated in the form of a question: What are universities for? Are they places, as Newman argued thirty years earlier, for 'the training of the mind'? Or are they, as Porter maintained, institutions for educating men (and women) for the economic well-being of the local community? If the former, there is no compelling reason why universities should be paid for by the state, which is not to say that there are no reasons at all. But if the purpose of universities is to fit men and women to occupy positions of leadership and to enrich society economically and intellectually, then perhaps the state has some obligation to support them.

The question of function has engaged universities throughout the ages. In Ireland it has a special dimension because the Queen's University in Ireland was established by royal charter in 1845 to solve a particular problem: how to provide university education for the population beyond the very restricted facilities available in Trinity College, Dublin. Most of the income for the three Queen's

---

1 T.W. Moody and J.C. Beckett, *Queen's Belfast, 1845–1949: the history of a university* (London, 1959), ii, 780–1. Owens College became part of the University of Manchester.

colleges came from the state (the rest came from fees). The position did not change when the college in Belfast gained its independence in 1908–9. After Partition the financing of Queen's became the responsibility of Stormont, and it remained so after the Second World War. The Northern Ireland government then had the benefit of advice from the University Grants Committee, but the Stormont ministers were naturally concerned whether they were financing a university for the advancement of learning in the abstract, or whether they were investing in the welfare of Northern Ireland.

UNIVERSITIES: LIBERAL OR VOCATIONAL?

The American educational philosopher, J.S. Brubacher, has characterized the competing purposes of universities as the epistemological and the political. A similar but more familiar distinction is between the liberal and vocational. The first stresses learning for its own sake: 'people seek to understand the world they live in as a matter of curiosity'. Knowledge has its own justification and it does not need a purpose beyond itself. This is in contrast to the political purpose of knowledge, which holds that universities transmit knowledge that has practical application for the professions and therefore for the society at large. Universities on this argument are required to train men and women in vocational skills need-ed for the proper workings of the community.[2]

Other issues lie beneath these views. The liberal philosophy carries with it the implication that universities constitute a commonwealth of scholarship unbounded by geography. The location of any particular university is a matter of indifference. In practice modern universities do not become situated by chance. A college was built near to Belfast in 1845 because the city had grown rapidly dur-ing the first half of the nineteenth century and was on the threshold of even faster growth. From its inception it was the needs of the population and the north of Ireland that determined what was taught in the college. These requirements, it may be noted, included Greek and Latin, as well as vocational subjects much as mathematics, medicine, law and engineering, and room was made also for mod-ern languages essential for commercial intercourse in the modern age.

The high priest of 'knowledge for its own end' in the mid-nineteenth centu-ry was John Henry Newman. He expounded his ideal before the Catholic University of Dublin in 1852, a foundation set up by the Irish Catholic bishops when Belfast and the other Queen's colleges were still in their fledgling years. According to Newman, a university was a place where:

> An assemblage of learned men, zealous for their own sciences, and rivals of each other, are brought, by familiar intercourse and for the sake of intellectual peace, to adjust together the claims and relations of their

2 J.S. Brubacher, *On the philosophy of higher education* (London, 1978), 12–14.

respective subjects of investigation. They learn to respect, to consult, to aid each other. Thus is created a pure and clear atmosphere of thought, which the student also breathes, though in his case he only pursues a few sciences out of the multitude. He profits by an intellectual tradition, which is independent of particular teachers, which guides him in his choice of subjects, and duly interprets for him those which he chooses. He apprehends the great outlines of knowledge, the principles on which it rests, the scale of its parts, its lights and its shades, its great points and its little, as he otherwise cannot apprehend them. Hence it is that his education is called 'Liberal'. A habit of mind is formed which lasts through life, of which the attributes are, freedom, equitableness, calmness, moderation, and wisdom; or what ... I have ventured to call a philosophical habit.[3]

Having defined the nature of knowledge, Newman went on to ask: 'What is the *use* of it?' He answered his own question by arguing, 'knowledge is capable of being its own end. Such is the constitution of the human mind, that any kind of knowledge, if it really be such, is its own reward.'[4] Newman believed the intellectual world to be a rational, ordered place, and knowledge was similarly rational and ordered.[5]

Any one acquainted with a modern university might wonder whether it truly is an assemblage of men (and women) united in intellectual peace and respectful of the claims of rival subjects. The competition for reputation, students, staff, money, and equipment, creates a climate sometimes more akin to a cattle auction. As the boundaries of knowledge have expanded, so scholars have found it more comfortable to remain corralled in their own corners than to wander through the broad meadows of learning. Students are more likely to demand guidance from lecturers on how to pass examinations than on how to lead them in the search for knowledge in that 'pure and clear atmosphere of thought' generated by a harmony of learned men and women.

Knowledge for its own sake is an appealing ideal for scholars, most of whom who prize how their peers regard their scholarship more than whether it has practical application. 'Ask yourself which judgement matters most to the young physicist', wrote Sir Eric Ashby, Vice-Chancellor of Queen's during the 1950s, 'the judgement of the Vice-Chancellor and senate and students of the university, or the judgement of physicists in the Royal Society and on the committees which distribute grants from the Science Research Council?' The answer was self-evident. But modern Vice-Chancellors have to take a wider view. Vice-Chancellors of Queen's, more than most, with a Stormont minister at the end of the telephone, were aware that taxpayers met most of the bills and therefore had legitimate claims to be interested in what the University was doing.

3 J.H. Newman, *The idea of a university*, ed. I.T. Ker (Oxford, 1976), 95–6.   4 Newman, *The idea of a university*, 97.   5 Brubacher, *Higher education*, 70–1.

Even when the belief in liberal education seemingly has full reign, it is constrained by the needs of society for vocational training. No university has ever pursued a pure liberal agenda unsullied by vocational requirements. In the words of Brubacher:

> Just to understand, let alone to solve the intricate problems of our complex society would be next to impossible without the resources of college and university. Problems of government, industry, agriculture, labour, raw materials, international relations, education, health, and the like – once solved empirically – now demand the most sophisticated expertise. The best place to procure such expertise and people trained in its use is in our higher institutions of learning.[6]

During his first months as Vice-Chancellor, Sir Eric Ashby wrote, 'ever since the twelfth century it has been the business of universities to train students for the professions, and this business is in no way incompatible with the acquisition of general intellectual health'.[7] The medieval universities trained canon and secular lawyers, physicians and administrators, bishops and senior clergy. During the sixteenth and seventeenth centuries, Oxford and Cambridge educated young men to become gentlemen, a status that carried responsibilities as well as deference. Gentlemen owned land, administered estates, dispensed local justice, and were the keystone of a hierarchical society. In the late Middle Ages they had taken over the reins of administration that had once been in the hands of the church. For this they required training in law, grammar, rhetoric, Greek and Latin. These skills could be acquired in the grammar schools, the inns of court, or from tutors, but the universities were essential for their development and preservation.[8] In Dublin in 1734, students at Trinity were reminded that the college was 'a publick nursery, from whence, once grown up, you are to be removed and planted out for the Ornament and Good of the Kingdom'.[9] Just over a century later, the charter of Queen's College, Belfast described it as 'one perpetual college for students in arts, law, physic, and other useful learning'.[10]

Throughout the nineteenth century British universities provided useful learning for a tiny minority of society. Their graduates were intended for the church (usually the Church of England) or to go to the Empire as colonial administrators. Others joined the home civil service, moved into the professions, or entered the world of business and commerce, although less often that of manufacturing.[11] Queen's was no different. In 1907 President Hamilton, President

6 Brubacher, *Higher education*, 13–14. 7 *Q: A literary magazine*, 1 (1950), 4, (QUB archives P/876) 8 L. Stone, *The crisis of the aristocracy, 1558–1641* (Oxford, 1965), 672–92. 9 Quoted in C.H. Holland (ed.), *Trinity College Dublin & the idea of a university* (Dublin, 1991), 10–11. 10 Moody and Beckett, *Queen's Belfast*, ii, 730. 11 There is a large literature on the relationship between universities and business in nineteenth-century Britain. See, for example, D.C. Coleman, 'Gentlemen and players', *Economic History Review*, 2nd series,

of the Queen's College and about to become the first Vice-Chancellor of the independent university, claimed:

> In Belfast and all over Ireland its sons are everywhere – in the pulpit, in the solicitor's office, at the bar, on the bench, in the consulting room, in the merchant's counting house, in the schoolroom, in the professor's chair. In London, there is a colony of them of absolutely marvellous numbers, some of whom have risen to high positions in the medical world, at the bar, on the press, in the church ... Nor have the narrow seas which wash the shores of the British Isles been able to restrain them ... They are to be found occupying high positions in the United States from New York to San Francisco. They have penetrated the icy regions which lie within the Arctic Circle. Under the burning sun of India they help to rule for its Emperor our dusky fellow-subjects. One of them is the most powerful European in China, another is the Chief Justice of Hong Kong, two are professors in Peking, and in Japan they have done a large work in the development of that western civilisation which is fast revolutionising the domains of the Mikado.[12]

Even in Newman's mind, knowledge for its own sake was not empty of purpose. For him, all knowledge bore witness to God's creation. Theology therefore occupied a prime position within his vision of a liberal education. It was 'the first among equals', although he was careful to distinguish between the study of theology for 'the purposes of the pulpit' and of its being 'cultivated as a contemplation'.[13] He went so far as to argue, 'in laying down that intellectual culture is its own *end*, ... has its *use* in itself also.'[14]

During the twentieth century the requirements that universities should offer vocational education has grown enormously as the pace of social and technical change quickened. The Second World War demonstrated the importance of universities for the war effort, and after the war the part that universities should play in advancing science and technology was widely discussed.[15] In 1945 the Rector of King's College, Newcastle defined the task of universities as meeting 'the post war demand for an expanded production of scientists and technologists.' Two decades later, the Duke of Edinburgh told the University of Salford (itself a product of a technological age), 'a university should measure its success just as much by the number of millionaires as by the number of Nobel Prize winners which it produces.' Queen's can muster a millionaire or two, and among its graduates there are a couple of Nobel Prize winners, although it is a fair guess that the Duke had not been thinking of Nobel laureates in literature and peace.

28 (1973), 92–116; R.D. Anderson, *Universities and elites in Britain since 1800* (London, 1992). **12** *The book of the fete: Queen's College Belfast* (Belfast, 1907), 114–15. **13** Newman, *The idea of a university*, lx–lxii and 101. **14** Ibid. 142. Italics in original. **15** M. Sanderson, *The universities and British industry, 1850–1970* (London, 1972), 339–59.

A more authoritative statement came from the University Grants' Committee in 1967. 'There is no doubt that it would be valuable if the universities collectively made a further deliberate effort to gear a larger part of their "output" to the economic and industrial needs of the nation.'[16]

A major voice in the debate was that of Sir Eric Ashby. He used his graduation addresses at Queen's to advocate the expansion of science and technology in the university curriculum, although not at the expense of the humanities.[17] By the end of the twentieth century the place of the natural and applied sciences in the University had been established more firmly than ever. Vocational training extended well beyond science and technology, for example into the social sciences where there had been an explosion of courses in accounting, business studies and related subjects. Even in the humanities, language degrees were now likely to include translation skills or be combined with subjects such as finance or law.

The demand for vocational education is closely related to the concept of relevance. This is not a straightforward issue. The advocates of a liberal education regarded knowledge for its own sake as relevant to society. The reflective study of ideas underpinning human behaviour and the natural world is a worthwhile and necessary activity in its own right. The nineteenth-century universities taught the classics because they provided mental stimulation and revealed the foundations of western civilization. This way of thinking underpinned the report of Robbins committee in 1963 into the future of higher education in Britain. The committee identified four purposes of higher education. The first was to offer 'instruction in skills suitable to play a part in the general division of labour'. The second was 'to promote the general powers of the mind'. The third was to advance learning. And, finally, the task of universities was 'the transmission of a common culture and common standards of citizenship'.[18] This last point, for most people involved in higher education, neatly resolved any conflict between the liberal and vocational duties of universities. The 'common culture' was most obviously studied through the humanities, although it was found, too, in the values that underpinned the applied, natural, medical and social sciences.

Societies need universities to provide an education that possesses direct vocational relevance. Medicine is an obvious example, but careers in accounting, law, psychology, and social work all now require relevant first degrees. Employment in architecture, computer science, the pharmaceutical and chemical industries, food processing and many other occupations are all but closed to students who have not studied these subjects as undergraduates. At the end of the twentieth century courses in the humanities possessed – or were supposed to possess –

16 All three quotations will be found in Sanderson, *The universities and British industry*, 349 and 360. 17 H. Silver, 'The making of a missionary: Eric Ashby and technology', *History of Education*, 31: 6 (2002), 557–70. 18 *Report of the Committee on Higher Education* [*The Robbins report*] (London, 1963).

clearly identifiable 'transferable skills', such as those of communicating clearly and logically, of distinguishing between the relevant and the irrelevant, and writing correctly and, if possible, elegantly. The supporters of the humanities, in the tradition of Newman, maintained their disciplines had always done these things.

Newman's vision of a university it did not embrace research. The task of a university, he wrote, 'is the diffusion and extension of knowledge, rather than the advancement'. And again: 'there are other institutions far more suited to act as instruments of stimulating philosophical inquiry, and extending the boundaries of knowledge, than a University.'[19] These institutions included observatories, learned societies, the Royal Society and the British Academy. His view was in marked contrast to the tradition in German universities, but it persisted in Britain well into the twentieth century; traces of it can still be found in the careers of one or two academics in Queen's after 1945. After the war universities accepted without question that research was an essential activity.[20] By the end of the twentieth century any scholar who suggested that there might be too much research and there were too many vacuous and unreadable publications, ran the risk of being cast out of the academic temple.

The pressures on universities to engage in research come from several directions. Research is implicit in the nature of a university as a place for the advancement of learning. Society depends on knowledge generated in university laboratories and libraries. Industry carries out some of its own research, usually of the kind relevant to their own needs, but it less commonly engages in 'blue-sky' research. If universities do not undertake research that may or may not have immediate practical applications, there are few other bodies that are able or willing to do so. In the case of the humanities, the universities are almost the only institutions where such research is possible. Most scholars choose to work in universities because of the opportunities they provide for pushing out the frontiers of knowledge.

During the 1980s and 1990s government funding of universities in the United Kingdom became linked explicitly with the quantity and quality of their research. It was important for universities to have plenty of productive researchers on the staff capable of carrying out work judged by independent assessors to be of international standard. University managers began to scrutinize the research performance of individual academics in a fashion unthinkable earlier in the century and Vice-Chancellors, like frenzied football managers, competed fiercely with one another to recruit the best researchers.

What is occasionally disputed is not whether universities should be involved in research but whether their research should be abstract or directed towards the solution of particular problems. The case for abstract research in the

19 Newman, *The idea of a university*, 5 and 7.   **20** For a discussion see H. Silver, *Higher education and opinion making in twentieth-century England* (London, 2003).

universities is that industry is not well equipped to undertake fundamental investigations. It also fits in with the ideal of knowledge for its own sake. The distinction between the abstract and the applied brings us back to the alleged tension between the epistemological and the political philosophies of higher education. Can a university pursue liberal and vocational studies at the same time? Most universities contrive to do both, but Brubacher has suggested that the two philosophies clash in a more fundamental sense. The epistemological, or liberal, view is that knowledge is value-free. The political, or vocational, approach is that education is for a particular purpose and is therefore based on a set of values that derive ultimately from the society in which the university is located. Queen's has never agonized much about such niceties. Over the years its staff have got on with their research projects according to their fancies and – more recently – with an eye for where the research grants might come from. And they have taught students liberal values and vocational skills to the best of their abilities.

Circumstances determined that Queen's should have a foot in both the liberal and the vocational camps. The University had been founded in 1845 to serve its region. This remained the position when Belfast became part of the Royal University in 1879–80. Its elevation to an independent university in 1908–9 did not alter the fact, and Partition further strengthened the connections between the University and its region. Queen's was also part of the United Kingdom network of universities and it had justifiable aspirations to be part of the inter-national community of scholarship. But it was, and remains, a provincial university in the literal meaning of that phrase.

NORTHERN IRELAND, 1945–2000

What sort of society was Northern Ireland in the second half of the twentieth century? When President Porter asked for more money for the college in 1882, he was able to argue that Belfast was the industrial and commercial capital of Ireland. The underpinnings of the Northern Ireland economy, then part of a larger entity, were the linen and shipbuilding industries, and an agricultural sec-tor restructured after the Famine and exporting its products to the towns and cities of Britain. Belfast was the great industrial centre of Ireland and rivalled Dublin in size and prosperity.

Much had changed during the ensuing decades and was to change even more by the end of the twentieth century.[21] Forty years after Porter wrote, Northern

21 The following paragraph, unless otherwise stated, are based on K.S. Isles and N. Cuthbert, *An economic survey of Northern Ireland* (Belfast, 1957), and R.I.D. Harris, C.W. Jefferson, and J.E. Spencer, *The Northern Ireland economy: a comparative study in the economic development of a peripheral region* (London, 1990).

Ireland had become a political region separated from the rest of Ireland and was a part of the United Kingdom. The political arrangements did not please a significant minority of the population and this led to community tensions that at times made the work of the University difficult. Economically, the old staple industries of linen, shipbuilding and agriculture were in decline. The population in 1945 was approximately 1.4 million; fifty years later it had grown to nearly 1.6 million. The rate of natural increase was among the highest in Western Europe, and although the rate was declining by the end of the century, it remained substantially greater than in other regions of the United Kingdom. In 1951, 16 per cent of the population was aged between five and the school-leaving age, which was then set at fourteen. By 1981 the proportion had risen to 20 per cent (the leaving age was now sixteen), although by 1986 it had fallen back slightly. Even so, Northern Ireland had a substantially higher proportion of young people than other parts of the United Kingdom. To make the point in a slightly different way, in 1991 nearly a half of the population of Northern Ireland was aged between five and twenty-nine. This was higher than any other country in the OECD with the exception of Turkey.[22]

The age structure had implications for the size of the age cohort from which university entrants were traditionally drawn. The large number of young people generated a rising demand for university places that needed to be satisfied either from within the Province, or by students seeking places in England, Scotland or Wales (or in the Republic of Ireland). The Lockwood report in 1965 forecast that Northern Ireland would require between 12,000 and 13,000 additional university places by 1980–a considerable underestimation as it turned out.[23] During the 1970s there were worries that the number of eighteen-year olds in Great Britain would peak in 1983 (at 919,000) and then decline by eighteen per cent by 1991. The Northern Ireland trend was expected to be similar.[24] The Chilver committee in 1982 estimated the demand for university places would rise to a maximum of between 13,000 and 14,000 by the mid-1980s, and then fall to between 10,500 and 12,500 by 1995, before rising again.[25] In the event Queen's experienced no fall in demand from school leavers, notwithstanding the creation of a second university in the Province and the continuing outflow of students to universities and polytechnics in Great Britain.

The relatively high rate of growth of population generated substantial numbers of young men and women seeking jobs. They entered a labour market undergoing major structural changes. Northern Ireland's three traditional industries, shipbuilding, linen, and agriculture had provided 43 per cent of total employment in 1951, but only 11 per cent in 1981. The service industries were

22 R.D. Osborne, *Higher education in Ireland North and South* (London, 1996), 8.   23 The Government of Northern Ireland, *Higher education in Northern Ireland [The Lockwood report]* (Belfast, 1965), 16.   24 *Senate minutes 1974–5*, appendix F, 7.   25 Osborne, *Higher education in Ireland*, 18.

now the largest sector of the economy. They employed one-third of the work-force in 1951 and more than two-thirds thirty years later. Within this sector the biggest increase was in public services. Economic growth in the Province was fuelled by government expenditure, which created a demand for civil servants and similar workers, many of them university educated. The size of the total workforce hovered around 550,000 throughout the period, of which females accounted for 31 per cent in 1961 and 43 per cent in 1986. The supply of labour was greater than the growth of demand, with the result that unemployment remained consistently higher than in other regions of the United Kingdom.

Queen's had a responsibility to provide the human capital needed in Northern Ireland. The University offered courses that equipped men and women – increasingly women – for employment in the professions, particularly in areas such as education, law, social work, medicine, management, accounting and administration. Many postgraduate courses were part-time and these explain much of the growth in part-time numbers at the end of the century. By then Queen's had also established outreach centres in Armagh and Omagh to make university training available in the outlying parts of the Province.

Northern Ireland also needed men and women who could enrich the cultural life of society. This was primarily the role of in the Faculty of Arts where the teaching was directed more to the inculcation of liberal values than to transmitting professional skills. But it was not theirs alone. The training of the mind occurred in all faculties – education, engineering, science, theology, medicine, agriculture, and law – and these added to the common good of the community.

A distinctive feature of society in Northern Ireland is an acute awareness of the denominational split between Protestants and Roman Catholics. These labels indicated not so much strict religious devotions as perceptions about the attitudes possessed by an individual in relation to their political allegiances. In the years following the Second World War the Roman Catholic/Protestant division in Northern Ireland was approximately one-third/two-thirds, but with the passage of time the proportion of Roman Catholics in the population increased to over 40 per cent. There was an even greater increase among the age-cohort most likely to supply university entrants. The Roman Catholic population of Ulster was becoming better educated, more prosperous, and more ambitious. Increasing numbers were seeking higher education and they were coming to Queen's in greater numbers. Their presence brought home a truth: that Queen's was a university for the whole Province, but the Province was far from homogeneous in its political thinking and aspirations.

The economic and social characteristics of the Province would have mattered less had Queen's been a different kind of university. Neither Oxford nor Cambridge had to take much account of the nature of the regions in which they were situated. The great metropolis of London had survived for centuries without a university, and when it acquired colleges in some number during the nineteenth century they made little difference to the capital. The English provincial universities were sometimes closely associated with their localities; several had emerged as the result of local initiatives. Scottish universities such as Edinburgh and St Andrews are likely to have as many English as Scottish students, although newer universities such as Strathclyde have strong regional links. But no British university by reason of its history has been so intimately related to its local community, as was Queen's. The University was sometimes too close to the community for comfort. Nevertheless, its task was to provide both liberal and vocational education for the population. It aspired also to be part of an international community of scholarship. It has had several masters to serve, but the Province has been close by looking over its shoulder. The problem with this metaphor is that the Province is not really a master. Queen's is an autonomous institution and is the master of itself.

Queen's, Belfast

This book tells the story of Queen's during the second half of the twentieth century. The first one hundred years have been the subject of a monumental two-volume study by Moody and Beckett published in 1959 and there is no attempt to emulate their work here.[1] Still, as a prelude to this present study of the University during the second half of the twentieth century, and as an encouragement to readers to turn to Moody and Beckett, a short excursus through the first century is offered. This is followed by a synoptic account of the years between 1945 and 2000, which are dealt with thematically in subsequent chapters.

PRELUDE: 1845–1945

There were mixed reasons for setting up the Queen's University in Ireland in 1845. There was then only one university in Ireland serving a population of eight and a half million people. This was 'the College of the Holy and Undivided Trinity near Dublin' founded in 1592 to provide 'education, training and instruction of youths and students in the arts and ... that they may be better assisted in the study of the liberal arts and the cultivation of virtue and religion'.[2] The religion in question was of the Protestant, Anglican, kind. Trinity was not open to Roman Catholics and other dissenters until 1793–4. Even then the full privileges of the College were denied to Roman Catholics, and they remained few in numbers. It was only from the 1920s that they became a significant minority among students in Trinity.[3]

Since emancipation in 1829, the Roman Catholic middle classes had become more prosperous and Ireland required 'a well-educated and middle order ... for its intellectual and moral progress'.[4] Neither the syllabuses nor the Protestant ethos of Trinity satisfied their needs. University reform was in the air in other

---

1 *Queen's, Belfast 1845–1949* (London, 1959). There is also the illustrated history by Brian Walker and Alf McCreary, *Degrees of excellence: the story of Queen's, Belfast, 1845–1995* (Belfast, 1994), covering the period 1845–1994.   2 R.B. McDowell and D.A. Webb, *Trinity College, Dublin, 1592–1952* (Cambridge, 1982), 3.   3 Ibid., 503–4; Moody and Beckett, *Queen's Belfast*, i, xxxvii.   4 Sir Thomas Wyse, MP for Waterford City and a strong advocate for the extension of university education in Ireland, quoted in J.A. Murphy, *The College: a history of Queen's University/College Cork, 1845–1995* (Cork, 1995), 1. See also Moody and Beckett, *Queen's Belfast*, i, liii–liv.

parts of the United Kingdom, particularly in England where the University of London and Durham University were challenging the hegemony of Oxford and Cambridge. The time was ripe for an expansion of university education in Ireland.

There were other pressing issues in Ireland. Political and sectarian tensions were never far below the surface after the Act of Union and during the 1830s and early 1840s there was a strong movement for repeal. It was important for the United Kingdom government that Ireland should remain peaceable, and Sir Robert Peel, who became Prime Minister in 1841, introduced several measures intended to mollify Catholics. These included an increase in the annual grant to the seminary at Maynooth, the passing of the Charitable Bequests Act that made it easier for the Catholic Church to benefit from bequests, and the Colleges (Ireland) Act introduced into the House of Commons in May 1845.[5]

The act proposed setting up provincial colleges as part of a Queen's University in Ireland. Belfast, Cork, and Galway were the eventual locations of the colleges, but other places had been considered, including Dublin. The colleges were to be strictly non-denominational and they immediately ran into opposition from the clergy. The Protestant churches were not enthusiastic, but the hostility was strongest among the Catholic bishops led by Archbishop McHale of Tuam. Nevertheless the bill went through and the act was passed in July 1845 creating a university with colleges in Belfast, Cork and Galway.

The colleges commenced teaching in 1849. They got off to an uncertain start. Galway and Cork struggled to achieve respectable numbers. Belfast did rather better, with 195 entrants in the first year, 93 in the second year and 82 in the third. Thereafter enrolments fell away, although they recovered during the 1860s.[6] There were many difficulties besetting the infant colleges. They had been set up during the devastating famine and began teaching in 1849 when the country still had not recovered. The famine did not directly affect the middle classes, but it depressed general economic activity. More important for the health of the colleges, there was no satisfactory system of secondary education preparing students for higher education. And all of the colleges, although Belfast less so than the others, struggled against the hostility of the churches.

The college in Belfast prospered modestly over the next thirty years. But the University as a whole did not achieve its purpose of providing higher education for the Catholic middle classes. The colleges drew their students primarily from the Protestant population and only about a quarter of the students attending the University were Roman Catholics (the proportion was lower still in Belfast).

5 The background to these developments is summarized by G. Ó Tuathaigh, 'The establishment of the Queen's Colleges: ideological and political background', in Tadhg Foley (ed.), *From Queen's College to National University: essays on the academic history of QCG/UCG/NUI, Galway* (Dublin, 1999), 1–15. 6 Ó Tuathaigh, 'The establishment of the Queen's Colleges', 14–15; Murphy, *The College*, 52–3 and 76–7; Moody and Beckett, *Queen's Belfast*, ii, 661.

Trinity College had introduced scholarships in 1854 open to Roman Catholics and these took a few students away from the Queen's colleges. A crucial difficulty was that the Roman Catholic hierarchy objected to public money being used to support non-denominational colleges where Catholic students should not go (a few went, nevertheless). In Dublin the response of the bishops had been to set up a Catholic University in 1852 with the future Cardinal Newman as its rector.

The bishops wished their university to be funded by the government in the same way as it financed the Queen's colleges, but they insisted it could not be 'godless'. The implication of their position was that if the government were to fund both the Queen's colleges and the Catholic University, none of them should be godless. The administration in Dublin Castle saw the problem rather differently. It could modify the constitution of the University to permit religious teaching. Or it could allow students to enter for the university's examinations without attending any of the three colleges; instead students should be free to study in godly or godless colleges as they chose.

After many twists and turns, the Westminster government chose the second course in 1879.[7] The Irish University Education Act of that year did away with the Queen's University in Ireland, although not the colleges. In its place it created the Royal University of Ireland. This was an examining body, not unlike the University of London, and the colleges lost much the independence they had originally enjoyed. The examinations of the Royal University were open to students wherever they had studied. The compromise satisfied no one. The colleges lost status, students, and income. In Belfast the numbers of students enrolling in Queen's College Belfast declined as schools such as Victoria College, Belfast prepared pupils for the examinations of the Royal University.

The Royal University was a recognition that the 1845 initiative had failed to solve the sectarian problems besetting higher education in Ireland. But neither did the new arrangements. The eventual solution in 1908 was the creation of two separate universities. The Catholic University of Dublin, together with the Queen's colleges in Cork and Galway (and also Maynooth), were amalgamated into a National University of Ireland, which was soon comfortably assimilated into society. It was in ethos Roman Catholic and it served the needs of a predominantly Roman Catholic population. Trinity remained in Dublin to cater initially mainly for Protestants and after independence for the whole population. The Queen's College, Belfast became independent as the Queen's University of Belfast and began teaching in 1909. It was a non-denominational university and it did not provide teaching in theology from public funds. Nevertheless, it presented a staunchly Presbyterian face to the population of the north of Ireland. That population, however, was divided along sectarian lines. Queen's grew into

7 For details of the discussions between 1850 and 1879 see Moody and Beckett, *Queen's Belfast*, i, 277–87.

a university of solid worth offering higher education mainly to the Ulster middle classes. After 1920 it became increasingly identified with the new state and this raised an uncomfortable question: Was it a university for the whole community or merely for one part? This question was seldom articulated during the 1940s and 1950s, but it was asked with increasing stridency from the mid-1960s.

Table 2.1 sets out the bare bones of the University between 1945 and 1999.[10] It reveals a seven-fold increase in student numbers accompanied by an eight-fold increase in the number of academic staff.[11] At the end of the century the student-staff ratio (SSR) was better than it had been immediately after the war when the University was short of staff, but worse than it had been since 1950. The SSR had improved continuously until the late 1970s but worsened throughout the 1980s and 1990s. The explanation is hinted at in the last three columns of the table, which show the income of the University in three different ways. There

1945–2000: SOME STATISTICS

Table 2.1: Summary statistics (five-yearly averages)

	Students	Academic staff[8]	Student/staff ratio	Current income ($\pounds$s)	Deflated income ($\pounds$s)[9]	Deflated income/ student ($\pounds$s)
1945–9	2441	173	14.1	227,323	218,581	90
1950–4	2651	241	10.9	404,689	311,839	118
1955–9	2798	313	8.9	694,224	429,987	154
1960–4	4145	433	9.6	1,335,518	736,166	178
1965–9	5891	591	10.0	3,107,047	1,431,707	243
1970–4	6689	703	9.5	6,516,375	2,202,245	329
1975–9	6627	785	8.4	15,952,342	2,737,240	413
1980–4	7406	840	8.8	34,536,654	3,290,759	444
1985–9	8842	939	9.4	53,004,444	3,827,278	433
1990–4	11,603	1047	11.1	98,177,200	5,358,383	462
1995–9	16,153	1350	12.0	126,400,200	6,140,496	380

8 The annual staff figures are presented in appendix 1.2. Staff are defined as full-time teaching and research staff. The University did not publish statistics of academic staff until 1969 but from that date they were included in the Vice-Chancellor's annual reports. The figures from 1945 to 1968 have been constructed from the annual calendars. See the notes to appendix 1.2. 9 The deflator used is that used by the Association of University Teachers. 10 Student numbers include undergraduates and postgraduate students studying for degrees or similar qualifications. They do not include students in the Institute of Life-Long Learning (previously known as Continuing Education and, before that, as Extra-Mural Studies) except for those reading for the BA (General Studies) degree. Also excluded are students enrolled at Stranmillis and St Mary's colleges. 11 The five-yearly averages employed in table 2.1 understate the increase in student numbers that were increasing rapidly at the end of the century.

was a huge increase in annual funding at current prices. Even when adjusted for inflation – a chronic feature of the period – there was a twenty-eight-fold increase in income. The final column demonstrates that funding *per* student increased more than four-fold in real terms over the fifty years, but it had reached its peak at the beginning of the 1980s and then declined until the end of the century.

Nevertheless, more was being spent per head of students during the 1990s than had been the case half a century earlier. However, two points need to be remembered. The first was that in 1945 Queen's was seriously under-funded compared to all British universities. Second, not all the additional money was spent on lecturing staff who were the main point of contact for students. A growing proportion was being used for the administrative support necessary for the running of a large university and on research staff. Research was absorbing large sums of money and much of income was tied specifically to research projects and was not available for teaching students.

The table suggests the history of the University during the second half of the twentieth century may be divided into five sub-periods. The first was half a decade of post-war recovery, of Queen's getting back to normal. Then followed a decade of expansion when many new staff were appointed and the international reputation of the University grew. This led from about 1960 into a period of missed or frustrated opportunities and the beginnings of political turmoil that lasted for the next thirty years. From the mid-1970s to the mid 1990s the years were made extremely difficult by the continuing political conflict in the Province, high rates of inflation, and the financial squeeze imposed on the University by successive governments. Finally in the second half of the 1990s Queen's entered into a period of rapid change.[12] By examining these sub-periods in turn we can put flesh on the bones displayed in the table. Closer consideration of the issues will follow in later chapters.

POST-WAR RECOVERY

Unlike other universities in the United Kingdom, there had been an increase in student numbers during the Second World War. At its end there were over 500 more students in Queen's than there had been when it started. Four chairs and seven full-time lectureships were unfilled. There were also many men still serving in the armed forces. The student-staff ratio was high by conventional standards and the University depended heavily on temporary teaching assis-

---

12 B. Walker and A. McCreary have used a different periodisation: The Golden Years 1950–59; Consolidation 1959–66; Surviving the Troubles 1966–76; Hurricanes of Change 1976–86; The Old Order Changeth ... 1986– (Walker and McCreary, *Degrees of excellence*). How historians divide the past into periods is always a matter of judgment.

tants. There were vacancies among the administrative staff, but even at full strength the administration was barely able to cope with the enlarged University. There was an immediate need to augment the teaching staff, provide more teaching space, and increase the University's income.

Three lectureships were raised to chair status in 1945 and a chair of jurisprudence created in 1946. During 1945 and 1946 the University made 59 full-time academic appointments. Another five lectureships were created in 1947. By 1948, 59 of the 85 lecturers were post-war appointments, as were 17 of the 34 professors. Lecturers now outnumbered professors by more than two to one, whereas in the 1930s professors had been in the majority. As Moody and Beckett commented, the changing proportions shifted the social mix and the power structures in the University. Before the war the academic business of Queen's was in the hands of the professors who met in regularly in the Academic Council and often socially as well. Now professors were a minority and they needed to take account of the opinions of lecturers. Among the new professors were men of high scholarly achievement. Much of the talent among the lecturing staff remained untested, but it is important to stress that Queen's was not regarded by aspiring academics from outside Northern Ireland as a provincial outpost to be avoided if at all possible.[13]

There remained the constraints of cramped premises and straitened finances. A building programme had commenced in the 1930s but had been suspended during the war. There was an urgent need for teaching, laboratory and library space, and student residences. Additional teaching accommodation was provided by the purchase of houses in University Square and elsewhere. Temporary buildings were erected and existing ones modified; at times the campus looked like a hutted encampment. By 1948 building restrictions had eased somewhat and during the next two years several major projects got underway. This activity added up to 'a large-scale programme, comparable to that which had marked the early years of the university'.[14]

Following a visit from the University Grants Committee, the Ministry of Education doubled its grant to Queen's in 1945–6, pushing its contribution to total income up from 43 to 59 per cent of the total in a single year. In 1944–5 the University derived 20 per cent of its income from fees but this proportion fell as the government's contribution increased. Even so, income per student was only half the level in British universities of comparable size. As the Vice-Chancellor later remarked, 'it was unacceptable that an Ulster student should have to be educated at half the cost of an English or Scottish student'.[15]

Two areas of teaching immediately concerned the University. The first was to provide short courses for members of the armed forces still serving in

13 Moody and Beckett, *Queen's Belfast*, ii, 532 and 576–621; Walker and McCreary, *Degrees of excellence*, 53–90, passim. For a fuller discussion see chapter seven. 14 Moody and Beckett, *Queen's Belfast*, ii, 531. 15 Reminiscences of Lord Ashby, recorded by Mr Alf McCreary, Information Officer, QUB, 1990.

Northern Ireland. This was the task of the Department of Extra-Mural Studies.[16] The second was to educate returning ex-servicemen who shared the lecture theatres with fresh-faced youngsters straight from school. Within the confines of limited resources the University offered a widening range of courses. New courses in geography, mathematics and physics, music, and education were introduced in 1947. In the following year there were academic developments 'of a kind which imposes little or no additional financial strain'. In 1949 new degrees were instituted in music, education and dentistry.[17] The foundations were being laid for more prosperous times.

In 1948 the Vice-Chancellor, Sir David Keir, outlined a fundamental duty for the University, which was to contribute to post-war reconstruction:

> The main lines of the problem facing all universities are by now sufficiently clear. The United Kingdom, having through the war sacrificed most of what still remained of its formerly commanding material advantages, must for its recovery rely to a greater degree than for many generations on the trained intelligence of its people, its command of scientific skills, and the character and resourcefulness of its educated classes in particular. These needs as they are being placed before the universities amount first to a substantial increase in the university population: second, to an increase of one hundred per cent in the output of graduates in the scientific schools, and at the same time an intensification of that fundamental research without which industrial research and industry itself must stagnate and decay: third, to the maintenance of a just balance between studies of all kinds, scientific and humane, so that the mind and work of the nation may be guided by men who bring to the task not only the specialised professional skill but also such qualities, evenly shared among them, as breadth of vision, respect towards things of the intellect and spirit, integrity of judgment and sensitive devotion to duty. Having in the past aimed, and not without success, at the cultivation of such purposes as these but only for a small section of the community and under conditions far less exacting than those of today, we now find ourselves obliged to do the same on an immensely greater scale and in the midst of a national emergency.[18]

The Vice-Chancellor continued, 'thus far Queen's has managed to do its part'. By the time he left Queen's in 1949 to become Master of Balliol College after a decade of guiding the University through the war and post-war reconstruction, Queen's was getting into good shape. Student numbers had increased by 28 per

16 *Vice-Chancellor's reports, 1944–45*, 154–5; *1945–46*, 163–4; *1946–47*, 195–6; *1948–49*, 206.   17 *Vice-Chancellor's reports, 1946–48*, 193; *1947–48*, 202; *1948–49*, 188.   18 *Vice-Chancellor's report, 1947–48*, 210.

cent since the end of the war, staff numbers by nearly 60 per cent, and income had doubled. The symbol of recovery was the formal opening of the Whitla Hall in February 1949.

THE 1950S: EXPANSION AND A WIDENING REPUTATION

During the 1950s, under the leadership of an outstanding Vice-Chancellor, Sir Eric Ashby, the University broke the bonds of post-war shortages of materials and loosened the financial constraints. Student numbers went up by 17 per cent. Even so modest an increase had not been expected. In October 1953 the Vice-Chancellor wrote, 'we can reasonably expect that the student population may remain for some time at about its present level'. (At some point the Secretary of the University had written 'wrong!' in the margin of the minutes.) In 1959 full-time student numbers stood at 2700; the total, including part-time students, was over 3000.[19] Real income was rising but Queen's remained a poor relation among universities. In 1951–2 its *per capita* income was 65 per cent of that of its comparator universities; in 1955–6 it had increased to 70 per cent.[20]

Rising income enabled Queen's to enlarge the academic staff by 90 per cent during the 1950s. The Vice-Chancellor set about recruiting promising young academics to chairs. His philosophy was, 'Appoint the right academic staff and administrative staff and you are home and dry. You needn't do anything else except to go round and be nice to people.' He later recalled, the Board of Curators, the body responsible for academic appointments:

> settled on a procedure that, in retrospect, turned out to be gratifyingly successful. The Vice-Chancellor was given discretionary power to discover whom the bright young scholars and scientists were and to invite one or other of them to come to Queen's to meet the Curators ... My method was to visit three leaders in the field in which we were searching and to ask each of them to give me three names of potential candidates who are not yet distinguished but who would be likely to do distinguished work in the next ten years. I found that in science the three referees all came up with the same name and in arts subjects this rarely happened. In this way we attracted to Queen's a number of young men who were astonished to have been invited. I used to say to them, 'If you haven't been invited to leave Queen's for another chair in five years (though I hope you'd not accept the invitation), we shall think we made a mistake.'[21]

19 *Senate minutes, 1953*, 175; *1959*, 254. **20** *Vice-Chancellor's report, 1950–51*, 198; *Senate minutes, 1956*, memorandum to UGC quinquennium 1958–63. The comparator universities were Aberdeen, Bristol, Nottingham and Sheffield. **21** Reminiscences of Lord Ashby.

The policy – it would not have been possible in Northern Ireland in the 1990s – worked and Queen's became renowned as 'Britain's nursery for good professors'. Many of Ashby's appointees moved on to other universities, taking with them good reports of Queen's.

Queen's shared with all universities the problems of a growing burden of administration. In 1949 Professor Newark, acting Vice-Chancellor before the arrival of Ashby, reflected ruefully on the problem. The University was operating with an administrative structure virtually unchanged since 1908. There had been a multiplication of committees, each with 'its own paraphernalia of agenda, minutes and reports'. Newark deplored the 'intolerable delays on the carrying through of business to its completion', and asked the question that the University was still trying to answer half a century later: how to balance 'the tradition of democratic government' through committees with the equally strong tradition that 'those who fulfil the primary function of a University – teaching and research – must also take their share in the government of the place.'[22] He had no answer. The Vice-Chancellor took up the theme the following year:

> There is a jealously guarded tradition among us that academic affairs should be managed by academic people. It is essential for the health of British universities that this tradition should be maintained, and one of the major problems facing us (and other British universities) is how to maintain the tradition without clogging up a professor's day with bureaucratic trifles. We all know that the solution does not lie in relieving professors of responsibility for academic affairs; some of us think it does lie in separating what could be called academic strategy from academic tactics, with academic staff responsible for the first and administrative officers responsible for the second. It is quite clear that no administrative officer should have to decide whether there is to be a school of architecture or a chair of Russian; it is not equally clear that no professor should have to decide whether his colleague should have a wastepaper basket or a typist.[23]

He returned to the subject in his last report to Senate in 1959. With the growth of the University, 'some academic bureaucracy is inevitable'. Academics should originate academic policy but 'the translation of policy into action is another matter: in general professional administrators are better at it than academics'.[24] He had touched on a subject that concerned the University for the rest of the century.

During the 1950s major building projects eased the problems of accommodation. The biggest of these was the David Keir building. There were

22 *Pro-Vice-Chancellor's report, 1949–50,* 211.   23 *Vice-Chancellor's report, 1950–51,* 204–5.
24 *Vice-Chancellor's report, 1958–59,* 254–5.

extensions to existing premises, including Queen's Chambers and a reconstruction of the Library. There remained, however, an urgent need to provide halls of residence for students. Queen's could not shed its image of a 'nine-to-five' university while most of its students lived at home or in lodgings. These problems remained to be solved in the future.

By the end of the decade Queen's had been transformed from a respectable provincial university into one noted for the quality of its academic staff. The transformation had been helped by ministers at Stormont who listened sympathetically to requests for money (and even tried to meet them), and by the fact that the government interfered little with the affairs of universities. The Vice-Chancellor was a major thinker on university education who believed in the importance of liberal and vocational education and the power of universities of to enrich the whole community.[25]

1960–75: MISSED OPPORTUNITIES AND POLITICAL PROBLEMS

Queen's entered the 1960s in a healthy condition and the future looked bright. Nevertheless, the new Vice-Chancellor, Dr Michael Grant, used his first annual report in 1960 to sound a downbeat note by pointing to the inadequacies of the Library and the unsatisfactory amenities available for students.[26]

All this was true, but it did not set a cheerful tone for the future. University thinking in the decade was dominated by two important reports, one written by Lord Robbins and the other by Sir John Lockwood. The Robbins report inquired into the future of higher education in Great Britain. It argued in favour of the wider benefits to society as well as to the economy of a liberal education, and believed that there were many young men and women who could benefit from it if given the opportunity. The Lockwood report examined higher education in Northern Ireland and identified a growing demand for higher education, most of which would have to be met by a new university and a polytechnic. Throughout its deliberations, Queen's viewed the prospect of any substantial growth with suspicion. In direct contradiction to his predecessor, Dr Grant believed it was difficult to attract first-class staff to Northern Ireland. He doubted also whether there were a sufficient number of qualified school leavers able to benefit from an enlarged university sector. When the Lockwood committee proposed the creation of a rival university, Queen's protested it could have expanded had it been given the chance. But the opportunity was missed.

Dr Grant left after six years to devote his life to writing histories of classical civilization. Sir Arthur Vick became Vice-Chancellor in 1966. The tenor of his

25 Eric Ashby, *Adapting universities to a technological age* (London, 1974); H. Silver, 'The making of a missionary: Eric Ashby and technology', 557–70. **26** *Vice-Chancellor's report 1960*, 268.

first two annual reports to the Senate was optimistic. The first praised the attitudes of students at a time when student unrest was rampant in many British universities. This was as much a message to a wider audience as to Senate. The second highlighted the work of the University's staff in contributing 'to the stock of knowledge and understanding upon which future generations may draw'.[27] There were academic developments to report including three-year honours degrees in the Faculty of Economics. These were precursors of a wider move away from the historic pattern of three-year pass and four-year honours degrees. The entry requirements for Queen's were brought into line with those of other universities in the United Kingdom as Queen's was trying to extend its appeal to students from beyond the Province. But for the Troubles it might have succeeded.

A less prominent passage in the Vice-Chancellor's report in 1969 struck an ominous note. The deans of residence reported, 'although it has been a most difficult year with the increase of tension in the Province and the student involvement in this, it has led to a new openness between the different religious groups in the University'.[28] Four years later the Vice-Chancellor referred to the Troubles depressing applications from students from outside Northern Ireland. Still, Queen's was expanding modestly. Between 1967 and 1973 student numbers increased by 10 per cent and income doubled in current prices (57 per cent in real terms). Thirteen new chairs had been established and ninety-one new lectureships.

The Vice-Chancellor's report in 1974 reflected a marked switch in mood. In the previous year he had looked forward to 'good prospects of healthy and sustained development leading to approximate parity in terms of grants per student with comparable universities in Great Britain'. But now an 'economic blizzard [has begun] to blow in the United Kingdom'.[29] The blizzard blew unabated for several years, obliterating the financial signposts that had guided policy. Sir Arthur's final report in 1978 stressed the necessity for strict financial prudence. In addition, the political situation in Northern Ireland had worsened. From 1975 Queen's faced a quarter of a century of austerity, turmoil, and a rival university.

1975–95: AUSTERITY AND ANGUISH

Sir Peter Froggatt succeeded Sir Arthur Vick as Vice-Chancellor in 1978. His first report chronicled the collapse of the quinquennial system of university funding that had operated since the war. Sir Arthur Vick had arranged with the University Grants Committee for the University's grant to be increased year by year until it was on a par with universities in Great Britain. For a few years

27 *Senate minutes, 1968*, appendix F, 3. 28 *Senate minute, 1969*, 28. 29 *Senate minutes, 1974*, appendix I, 5.

Queen's was cushioned from the severe financial restrictions afflicting many British universities in the early 1980s. Then, in the mid-1980s, the government calculated that Queen's was more than 10 per cent *over-funded* and the University was faced with an abrupt reduction in grant income of 13 per cent.

Real income per student remained virtually static during Sir Peter Froggatt's tenure of office. Staff numbers increased by 10 per cent, but student numbers went up by almost 30 per cent. The result was a worsening of the student-staff ratio. The government regarded the increase in teaching loads as a sign of rising productivity, but for universities they threatened to undermine scholarly standards. To counter this interpretation the UGC (and later the University Funding Council) established two methods of scrutinizing the activities of universities: what ultimately became known as the Research Assessment Exercise (RAE) to measure the quality of research, and the Teaching Quality Assessment (TQA) to perform a similar function for teaching. RAEs and TQAs came to dominate the lives of administrators and academics alike. Meanwhile Queen's was becoming caught up in terrible political violence. Over the next two decades, terrorist bombs damaged buildings, two academic members of staff were murdered, several students were killed, and union politics reverberated with the rancour beyond the walls.

Against bleak financial and political landscapes there were four important areas of academic development. The move to three-year honours degrees in all faculties except medicine continued. The move was paralleled by the introduction of the BA (General Studies) programme that offered a part-time degree in a wide range of disciplines studied over a period of five or six years. Thirdly, in the early 1990s the University moved from the traditional three terms (Trinity, Hilary, and Michaelmas) to a two-part teaching year (semesters). Finally, Queen's had to adjust to the emergence of a powerful rival, the University of Ulster formed in 1982 out of a merger between the New University of Ulster and the Ulster Polytechnic.

Sir Peter Froggatt resigned in 1986 and was succeeded by Sir Gordon Beveridge. He had to wrestle with financial problems that seemed to grow greater with every passing year. True, total real income rose by 64 per cent between 1986 and 1997, but now the government was driving towards mass higher education without fully funding it and the student population increased by 77 per cent. Staff numbers grew by only 6 per cent (indeed they fell for several years after 1986) and the student-staff ratio rose to the levels of the austerity days immediately following the war.

The new Vice-Chancellor also had to cope with major social and political changes in the Province. The worst of the street violence was over but Queen's was forced to recognize the truth that in the eyes of a significant minority of the population it was a bastion of Unionism. The perception coalesced around the issue of employment when 1989 Queen's was accused of discriminating against Roman Catholics. For the next six years the University was buffeted by charge and counter-charge. The issue did not affect academic life directly but it distracted the attention of the Vice-Chancellor and the Senate away from the need to reform the administrative structure of the University and how to find alternative sources of income.

1995–2000: RENAISSANCE?

In 1995 the University celebrated its 150th birthday. It marked the event in traditional manner by distributing honorary degrees in appropriate directions and wining and dining those whom it perceived to be the great and the good. It opened its doors to the citizens of Belfast and beyond, enticing them with a range of exhibitions and public lectures. Some of the staff went up to London to visit the Queen (the President of Ireland was there too) and purred over the canapés. The University did not launch a public appeal for money, although it had planned to do so.

The early 1990s had not been good years for Queen's. The University of Ulster was grabbing the best headlines whilst Queen's was defending itself from charges of discrimination. The financial balance sheet had been kept in the black by a rigorous policy of holding expenditure down within the bounds of diminishing *per capita* income. The economies took their toll. Academic standards remained high, especially in teaching, but morale and resources were worn thin as a result of continual financial restrictions.

Sir Gordon Beveridge resigned in 1997. He had been the second longest serving President and Vice-Chancellor in the history of the University, and none of his predecessors had experienced such difficult times. His proudest achievement was the establishment of the Queen's University at Armagh in 1995. After a brief interregnum Sir George Bain, an ebullient Canadian who had been Principal of the London Business School, succeeded him. The welcomes had scarcely subsided when the University found itself on embarking on a new academic plan costing £25 million designed to raise teaching standards still further and enhance research performance. The University's administration was restructured, a new communications office was put in place to improve public relations, an appeals office was opened to raise money from private sources, and the Queen's stationery was given a new logo. The front of the Lanyon Building received a face-lift and the Great Hall was restored at a cost of £2.5 million to a grandeur of which Charles Lanyon could only have dreamed.

If investments in timber and stone were a guide, the auguries for an academic renaissance were good. By the end of 2001, indeed, the results of the academic plan were showing through. Queen's stood nineteenth among more than a hundred universities in the research league table (league tables had become standard accoutrements of universities by the end of the twentieth century) and its teaching ranking fifteenth.

The new Vice-Chancellor had an easier ride than his predecessor. There was a 'peace process' in Northern Ireland and Belfast no longer looked quite such as an off-putting place to newcomers as it had been during the 1970s and 1980s. There was now a chance that Queen's could attract and retain good staff. Was there a renaissance? It will be the task of a future historian to decide whether the developments in Queen's at the end of the twentieth century qualify for the description.

3

Queen's, Stormont, and Westminster

All universities in the United Kingdom enjoy a corporate independence, but all are affected by government policies towards higher education and all depend, to a greater or lesser extent, on the government for their income. In the case of Queen's the reliance on the state has been particularly great. The Queen's University in Ireland was established by the government in 1845 and was funded principally from the public purse. When Queen's became independent in 1908–9 its financial dependence on the state remained. When the state of Northern Ireland was created, the responsibility for supporting the University passed to Stormont. This continued to be so after the Second World War, although Westminster became increasingly involved. The level of government was determined by its higher education policies. This chapter is concerned principally with the evolution of policies; their effects on funding are the subjects of the chapter that follows.

POLICY BEFORE ROBBINS AND LOCKWOOD

During the two decades following 1945, higher educational policy was based on largely unspoken assumptions about the purposes of university study and there was no blueprint, either in London or Belfast, setting out what universities should do. Queen's received an annual grant from Stormont, the size of which was determined after considering advice received from the University Grants Committee in London. In 1945 the grant was substantially increased. The Vice-Chancellor accepted it gratefully, adding:

> With these feelings of satisfaction and gratitude there mingles a deep sense of obligation. Greater opportunity means greater responsibility, in particular towards the Province which has so fully placed its trust in its own University. The Government and people of Northern Ireland may feel well assured that no effort will be lacking on our part to justify their support.[1]

In 1952, when Queen's prepared its funding submission to the UGC for the next five years, it rested its case on two grounds. The first was an appeal to the

---

1 *Vice-Chancellor's report, 1944–5*, 149.

national interest. The second was a plea that Queen's should be treated in the same way as other universities in the United Kingdom:

> The University has two reasons for confidence in making the following proposals: the first, that skilled and enlightened citizens, essential for this country's struggle for national recovery, are not being produced in sufficient quantity, and are not taking sufficient part in industrial and commercial life ...; the second, that Queen's has not had anything like its share of the opportunities for rehabilitation afforded since the war to its sister universities ... The University believes that even in the present emergency [i.e. post-war austerity] there is a strong case for affording the young men and women of Ulster opportunities for university education not inferior to those already available in similar universities in Great Britain; and in that belief, as a further step towards parity with other British universities, it puts forward the following proposals.[2]

Both arguments assumed the University was essential to the well being of the Province. Three of its faculties – medicine, agriculture, and applied science – had strong vocational links with the community. The major hospitals in Belfast and the Queen's medical school had long enjoyed a close association, which was strengthened following the introduction of the National Health Service into Northern Ireland in January 1949. By an agreement between the University and the Northern Ireland Hospitals' Authority, clinical staff in the Faculty of Medicine were appointed by the University, but they held appointments jointly with the Hospitals' Authority and both bodies contributed to their salaries. This was a different arrangement from those in other parts of the United Kingdom where the staff of university medical schools held honorary appointments in the teaching hospitals. The University and the Hospitals' Authority believed that this was not the best system for Northern Ireland because there was only one university and one medical school.[3] The Ulster pattern was later to puzzle research assessment panels trying to evaluate the quality of research in medicine and dentistry because of the difficulty in separating out work done in University time from that done in hospital time.

The Faculty of Agriculture's connections with the Northern Ireland government dated back to 1924. The Ministry of Agriculture provided the money, but the staff were appointed jointly by Queen's and the Ministry. The faculty was responsible for supplying scientific services for the farming community,

---

2 *Senate minutes, 1952: Memorandum to the University Grants Committee*, para. 2.0. 3 *Senate minutes, 1950*, 23–9. There is some evidence that the peculiar Northern Ireland arrangement was introduced because the dean of medicine, Professor Biggart, opposed the British system of honorary appointments. See J.A. Weaver, 'John Henry Biggart 1905–1979: a portrait in respect and affection', *Ulster Medical Journal*, 54: 1 (April 1985), 14.

then still a large sector of the economy, as well as for teaching undergraduates. This unusual arrangement emerged following Partition because there was no institution in the new jurisdiction providing education or research in agriculture, and the Ministry of Agriculture was anxious to encourage agricultural development.[4]

The arrangements for the teaching of engineering had evolved piecemeal over the years and were closely related to Belfast's traditional industries. The Faculty of Applied Science and Technology had been established in 1920 and teaching was shared between the University and the Municipal Technical Institute, later known as the College of Technology. The Belfast Corporation controlled the Institute and appointed its staff, some of who were appointed as recognized teachers of the University.[5] The Institute taught most of the courses in mechanical and electrical engineering and the University provided most of the tuition in civil engineering. Several courses at the Institute were available part-time in the evenings and so were accessible to people seeking a technical education at a high level. In 1951 the University and the Belfast Corporation agreed that there should be a concentration of degree work in a new building currently being planned at Queen's, and the engineering staff in future should be appointed by the University under normal academic conditions of employment. The College of Technology continued with some degree teaching for a while but it devoted most of its energies to HND courses. The work of the University and College of Technology was co-ordinated by a Joint Authority for Higher Technological Studies.[6]

The Faculty of Law educated men and women for a small legal jurisdiction and was closely linked to professional life in the Province. The Faculty of Theology had a very detached status. The University's statutes precluded the teaching of theology using public funds, but Queen's awarded degrees and diplomas in theology. The denominational colleges (the Presbyterian College and Edgehill College) were responsible for the teaching and most theology students were destined for the ministry. The Church of Ireland had its own theology hall in Dublin and the Roman Catholic Church trained its own priests, although many of them took arts degrees in Queen's and scholastic philosophy was taught for their needs.

The Faculty of Arts lacked fewer direct links with the professions, although the Department of Education was engaged in teacher training, in collaboration with the Ministry of Education. School-teaching was a common professional destination for arts graduates. Others entered the church or went into journalism. The higher ranks of the civil service absorbed a few arts graduates. Some

---

4 Moody and Beckett, *Queen's Belfast 1845–1949*, ii, 486–8.   5 This was a status granted by the University to staff in other institutions who taught university courses.   6 For a summary of developments see *Senate minutes 1952: Memorandum to the University Grants Committee*, para. 2.6; *Lockwood report*, 20–32; Moody and Beckett, *Queen's Belfast*, ii, 472–3.

also entered business, although local industry was not a larger recruiter of graduates.

The Faculty of Economics had a distinctive practical bent; until 1949 it had been known as the Faculty of Commerce. Its central activity was the teaching of economics, which equipped students for careers in administration, management and business. The Faculty also offered courses in accounting that helped graduates in obtaining professional qualifications. The BSc(Econ.) degree could also be obtained by part-time study in the evening. It attracted a considerable number of non-graduate school teachers. They were not necessarily deeply interested in economics but they wanted to become graduates in order to improve their career prospects.

ROBBINS AND LOCKWOOD

The pattern of studies in Queen's during the 1940s and 1950s, as in all British universities had evolved piecemeal over time. Government policy towards universities became more explicit following the publication of the Robbins report in 1963. It was a landmark in the history of universities in Britain, for it offered the first comprehensive survey of a system that had emerged piecemeal since the nineteenth century. The report recognized that universities relied heavily on money from the state and there was therefore a justifiable public interest in the work of universities, although this must not 'impair their legitimate rights of self-government'.[7] There was an echo of Newman, dressed up in the language of the economist, in its underlying philosophy:

> To devote resources to the training of young people may be, *au fond*, as much entitled to be considered a process of investment as devoting resources to directly productive capital goods. Judged solely by the test of future productivity, a community that neglects education is as imprudent as a community that neglects material accumulation. The classical economists, great supporters of education, had precisely this consideration in mind when they invented the phrase 'human capital'. And, provided we always remember that the goal is not productivity as such but the good life that productivity makes possible, this mode of approach is very helpful.[8]

At that time well under 10 per cent of the relevant age cohort entered higher education in Britain compared with 17 per cent in France and 48 per cent in the USA. The Robbins committee believed that there was a pool of untapped talent in Britain that could benefit from university education and recommended

7 *Report of the Committee on Higher Education* [*Robbins report*], 4. Robbins was himself an economist in the neo-classical tradition. 8 *Robbins report*, 204.

student numbers should be more than doubled from 216,000 to 560,000 by 1980/1. It rejected a 'manpower planning' argument for the expansion of universities because the labour requirements of any specific profession could be predicted only in the short run. What the nation required was a supply of men and women with trained intellects that could be turned in several directions.[9] The committee articulated a liberal philosophy of university education that had underpinned British universities for a hundred years and continued to do so for the next two decades. Its report laid the basis for the expansion of higher education by proposing the creation of new universities on green-field sites.

The Robbins committee dealt with universities in Great Britain. Two years later the Lockwood committee (chaired by Sir John Lockwood, Master of Birkbeck College, London) reported on the position in Northern Ireland. His committee accepted the philosophical principles expounded by Robbins with some reservations, quoting with approval Professor Max Beloff's criticisms: 'If the country requires more engineers, more doctors and dentists, more persons trained in the stiffer social sciences – economics in particular – why should it be wrong to spend public money on seeing that the country gets them, rather than more and not so good students of Chaucer or the Patent Rolls, or psephology?' Nevertheless, the Lockwood committee set out with a Robbins route map in its pocket. It reviewed the work of Queen's, Magee University College, which had had a long association both with Queen's and Trinity College, Dublin, the teacher training colleges in Belfast (St Mary's, St Joseph's, and Stranmillis College) the Belfast College of Technology, and Loughry Agricultural College. The committee briefly surveyed the history of Queen's and its relations with other institutions of higher education, and it debated the desirable size for the University.

The Lockwood report made seventy separate recommendations for the future of higher education in Northern Ireland. Four of them had major implications for the future of Queen's. The first was that there should be an extra 12,000 to 13,000 full-time places in higher education in the Province by 1980 (i.e. 4000 new entrants annually). Secondly, it recommended that a new university should be established to provide most of these places.[10] The third recommendation was for the creation of an 'Ulster College' by an amalgamation of the Belfast colleges of Technology, Domestic Science, and Art, and proposed colleges of commerce, catering, music and drama.[11] The Ulster College would offer 'technical education', conceived of as something between the skills of the craftsman and the operative and those of the scientist and technologist. The full import of this proposal was not fully felt for some years. It resulted in the establishment of the Ulster Polytechnic, a body that eventually swallowed up the new university. Finally, the committee recommended that the university sector should assume responsibility for teacher education.

9 *Robbins report*, 46, 268.   10 *Lockwood report*, summary of main recommendations, xi–xiv.
11 *Lockwood report*, xiii and 93–100.

Lockwood committee proposed the setting up of a new university because it concluded Queen's was unable or unwilling to expand sufficiently to cope with the predicted demand for university places. Lockwood agreed with the Robbins committee that economies of scale were best achieved in large institutions, but the committee doubted whether the argument applied to Queen's. Belfast was 'one of the most congested cities in the United Kingdom', and the University's departments were scattered and separated by busy roads. Queen's consequently suffered from 'some lack of cohesion and intimacy in many aspects' of its life. The committee thought it would be difficult for the University to expand its precinct to accommodate even 7000 students. An enlarged Queen's would add to the 'disproportionately ... centripetal attraction towards Belfast of the general life and economy of the country as a whole.'[12] The Lockwood committee toyed with the idea of a federal university, a 'Queen's University of Northern Ireland', made up of several colleges, but it concluded on the experience of London University that a federal structure was beset with too many difficulties.[13]

The Lockwood report therefore proposed only a limited growth of student numbers in Queen's. The University should continue to expand in applied science and technology, including architecture and town planning where it had already decided to increase student numbers by 25 per cent (from 732 to 915) between 1963/4 and 1969/70. Lockwood believed the latter figure could rise to between 2000 and 2500, although this would involve substantial changes in the current arrangements between the University and the College of Technology. The committee recommended that all degree work in applied science should be concentrated at Queen's and the College of Technology should in future confine itself to non-degree work. The Joint Authority for Higher Technological Studies should be discontinued. The Lockwood committee was worried whether Queen's could 'adapt [itself] to technological thought'.

> The only hesitation we have had in deciding to recommend that technological education in Northern Ireland should be catered for comprehensively within Queen's University rather than within a new technological university has arisen from our concern that Queen's University might approach this expanded and heavy responsibility with too little flexibility, and introduce reservations which in the event might make alternative provision elsewhere at a later date inevitable. We have noted, for example, the lack of progress in establishing effectively the sandwich degree course in engineering in sharp contrast with the development of sandwich degree courses in Great Britain. This provides an even stronger reason for a sense of urgency on the part of the University to establish and encourage further sandwich degree courses for engineers and technologist alongside traditional full-time courses. We are asking the

12 *Lockwood report*, 55–7.   13 *Lockwood report*, 53.

University to accept a very wide responsibility within the technological field and we are assuming that a second university will concentrate on subjects other than the technologies related to the industries of an urban environment.[14]

The idea of a technological university had been discussed widely. The Belfast Association of University Teachers suggested such an institution along the lines of Strathclyde in Glasgow or Herriot-Watt in Edinburgh, located perhaps in Lurgan or Portadown, then the site of the proposed new city of Craigavon.[15] In the event the Lockwood committee concluded that the new university should not be involved in engineering at all, but should focus its activities on agriculture and the biological sciences, studied not as 'isolated subjects' but as 'related parts' of a whole. For example, marine biology, subject already taught in Queen's, should be taught in a way that would permit a 'controlled harvesting of the sea'. However, the new university was not to be a 'biological' institution exclusively, but should offer courses in the behavioural and social sciences and also in the humanities including 'languages as a support for other subjects'.[16]

The argument for a broadly based education was elaborated further in the report's discussion of agriculture. The committee agreed with an earlier British committee that agriculture should form the basis of a 'general education'.[17] It regretted that in Northern Ireland students studied agriculture with 'a substantially vocational objective'. This was not surprising given the nature of the relationship between Queen's and the Ministry of Agriculture. The committee argued was what was needed were courses that would equip graduates to tackle problems of malnutrition and rural development in the under developed regions of the world: not so much muddy boots as shiny idealism. Queen's, it concluded, possessed more of the former than the latter. Furthermore, Lockwood believed agricultural education was 'no longer be appropriate in an urban university distinctly orientated towards technology and the applied physical sciences and hence would lack the necessary emphasis and priority'.[18]

The committee's ideas about teacher training were based on the belief that 'the function of preparing men and women for the teacher service [should be] teacher education rather than teacher training'. The former should be brought into the universities and 'we therefore favour the provision of the necessary facilities for teacher education within the framework of the new university'. There should be an education centre to educate students intending to work in primary schools and to offer courses in education and psychology. These subjects should be incorporated into 'ordinary' academic degrees. The committee

---

14 *Lockwood report*, 60–1.   15 AUT (Belfast), 'Evidence submitted the chairman and members of the Lockwood committee on university and higher technical education in Northern Ireland (March 1964), para. 13. QUB archive/E/7/9.   16 *Lockwood report*, 66–8.   17 *Report of an interdepartmental committee on the demand for agricultural graduates* [*The Bosanquet report*] (London, 1964).   18 *Lockwood report*, 73–5.

proposed the centre should eventually have about 1000 students. Lockwood rejected the idea of a Bachelor of Education degree as being merely an extension of the existing teachers' certificates; it smacked too much of training and not enough of education.

The committee was unclear how its recommendations would affect the relationship between Queen's and the teacher-training colleges. It hoped that 'after further examination the University will see its way to enter into full partnership with the training colleges and to give university acknowledgement to all who successfully complete training college courses by awarding them the University Diploma in Education'.[19] Queen's had suggested a number of possible ways of working with the colleges but there had been no formal discussions. The report ducked the thorny issue of the organization of teacher training along denominational lines.[20]

The committee wandered into territory that extended beyond higher education. It assumed that the urban and rural needs of Northern Ireland for higher education differed, and it engaged in social engineering in trying to counter the pull of Belfast by locating the second university in Coleraine. The town was a controversial choice. Armagh had a claim for a university going back almost two centuries, and Magee University College was already located in Derry. There were suspicions that local politics determined that 'unionist' Coleraine and not 'nationalist' Derry should be home to Ulster's new university. The determining issue, according to the public statements of the committee, was student residences. It believed neither Armagh nor Derry could immediately provide sufficient accommodation for students whereas Coleraine could draw on the boarding houses of Portrush and Portstewart.[21]

Queen's was alarmed its 'standing and usefulness' would be prejudiced by the proposals of the Lockwood committee. The University faced a future involving the loss of the Faculty of Agriculture and undefined arrangements for teacher education. Although the University was to retain a monopoly of medicine, 'at the present time', and to have an enlarged Faculty of Applied Science, many arts and science subjects it had taught for years were now to be offered at a rival 'modern university' able to 'take full advantage of recent ideas and developments in new universities on university organisation and government'. The new creation would not be 'limited by the projection of traditional values'.[22] By implication, Queen's was not in the vanguard of new thinking but was

19 *Lockwood report*, 82–5, 88. 20 *Lockwood report*, 37–45. 21 Interview with Dr R.B. Henderson, a member of the committee, October 2002. The case for Coleraine based on seaside boarding houses was challenged by the Belfast University Labour Club that pointed out the Robbins Report had recommended that two-thirds of students in the British new universities should housed in university accommodation. The Labour Club's choice was Derry, using Magee University as its core. QUB Labour group, 'Submission to the Lockwood committee on higher education in Northern Ireland' (1964), QUB archives E/7/11. 22 *Lockwood report*, 80.

hide-bound by tradition. The University was not comforted by the assurance from the Northern Ireland Minister of Education that it 'will continue to enjoy the same independence as other universities in the United Kingdom.'[23]

When the report was discussed in the University it was treated with considerable distain. Queen's was puzzled the committee had 'misgivings on the dichotomy between the academic and non-academic branches of the University's administration'. It believed Lockwood had not tried to understand the relationship.[24] But Queen's had deeper concerns. It did not understand how Sir John Lockwood and his colleagues could doubt the University's commitment to technological education when a previous Vice-Chancellor had been such an influential advocate. Why did the Committee think Queen's could not expand substantially? The answer was that the University had badly misjudged its response to the Lockwood committee. At one stage the Academic Council agreed the University should not make a submission to the committee, but would simply respond to any questions put to it.[25] But wiser counsels prevailed and a submission was prepared. When it came to the Senate in February 1964 it was barely two foolscap pages long; when printed it covered fewer than four quarto pages. By contrast, the SRC submitted a document that ran to fifty-four pages.[26] The University's submission had the virtue of brevity but it was almost dismissive about the idea of expansion.

Queen's reminded the Lockwood committee it had already announced its intention of growing by less than ten per cent by 1968 to 5170 students. It conceded it could go to 7000 by 1978 if pushed, but this would entail 'the maximum rate of expansion which is possible without introducing a serious danger of deterioration in the standards of teaching, research and amenities for students and staff.' Even the target of 7000 was hedged with qualifications. The Vice-Chancellor had remarked privately in 1962 that 7000 'is surely the maximum which would be suggested by even the most ardent expansionist.'[27] Student numbers had already increased by 51 per cent during the previous decade, and funding *per head* was only 62 per cent of that in Great Britain. There was 'the difficulty of persuading first-class staff to take up appointments in what is for many a peripheral area.' Existing buildings could not comfortably accommodate the present numbers of students; there was too little space for the erection of new buildings and an acute shortage of residential accommodation. The Library could not cope even with the present student population.

23 *Senate minutes, 1965*, 455.   24 *Senate minutes, 1965*, 89, 110. It did not seem to occur to the University that the nature of the relationship might indeed appear obscure to an outsider. 25 *Academic Council minutes*, 1963–4, 71.   26 QUB, *Submission to the Lockwood committee on university and higher technical education in Northern Ireland* (March 1964), QUB archives, E/7/9; National Union of Students, *Memorandum to the committee on higher education in Northern Ireland* (Belfast, 1964), QUB archives E/7/12; SRC, *Memoranda to the committee on higher education* (Belfast, June 1964), QUB archives E/7/14. According to Dr Henderson, 'Queen's was not at its best'.   27 *Standing Committee minutes*, 1962, 135–7.

The University raised a more fundamental objection by questioning whether there was a sufficient pool of untapped talent to benefit from university education. This challenged a central assumption of both the Robbins and Lockwood reports. Queen's also feared, not without reason, that a second university would duplicate its activities. It told the Lockwood committee, 'we naturally have no intention that Queen's should abandon the field of engineering' and argued that any teaching of technology in a new institution 'of university status' should be confined to the technical level, 'and so relieve our staff of all responsibility for non-degree education', adding 'Queen's reserved the right to make representations to the Committee about teacher-training at a later date. Possibly fearing that some people might break ranks, the University added that any submission from individual members of staff 'should not necessarily be regarded as reflecting University policies'.[28]

Most people within Queen's agreed the University was big enough already.[29] The SRC believed Queen's should be no larger than seven or eight thousand students. The Association of University Teachers argued 'that any increase in the present size of Queen's will seriously damage the whole quality of university life unless it is accompanied by the adoption of new plans and policies which must be both expensive and radical.' Nevertheless, one or two members of staff thought the University could grow substantially as long as the Belfast Corporation agreed to the compulsory purchase of property and that there was investment in new buildings. They also believed that the way Queen's was governed needed to be made more democratic.[30]

Following the publication of the Lockwood report, Queen's tried to argue it had not really meant what it said earlier about the difficulties of expanding and concluded sadly the Lockwood committee was wrong in several respects. 'While agreeing with many proposals made in the report, the University believes that the implementation of others affecting its own development would not constitute the best means of developing Higher Education in the Province.' Queen's welcomed proposals for an enhanced Faculty of Applied Science, but pleaded for the development of a 'balanced' Faculty of Science. It strongly deplored the proposed loss of the Faculty of Agriculture. The University defended its four-year honours course that had not found favour with the committee, but said it was willing to consider three-year degree courses 'for several subjects'. It

28 *Senate minutes*, 15 February 1964. 29 Many years later Professor Sir David Bates recalled that Queen's 'was frightened of growth. The majority of Academic Council (in Grant's time) wanted Queen's to stay the size it then was. My own view has always been that, as far as universities are concerned, size is desirable' (interview with Mr Alf McCreary, February 1992). Dr Grant's view, thirty years later, was that he persuaded a reluctant Academic Council to accept the NUU, but the evidence suggests that at the time he was himself unenthusiastic (M. Grant, *My first eighty years* (Henley-on-Thames, 1994), 144). 30 National Union of Students, *Memorandum to the Committee on Higher Education*, p. 25; QUB, Submission to the Lockwood committee, paras. 16–18, appendix II.

justified its record on graduate studies and agreed to establish a working party on teacher education.[31]

The Lockwood report was sent to the faculties for comment. The Faculty of Arts mounted a prancing high horse, outraged by the proposal 'to reduce artificially the size of the Arts Faculty, and considers the proposal of the committee an improper means of directing potential University entrants in Arts subjects to seek admission to other institutions of higher education in the Province.' The Faculty of Law, on the other hand, agreed that law enrolments in Queen's should be kept to a ceiling of 250 and believed that a 'full' LLB should be instituted in the new university. The remaining faculties seem not to have responded.[32]

Queen's duly appointed a working party on teacher education. After two years of unhurried reflection it recommended the formation of a Faculty of Education and an Institute of Education. The three colleges, St Mary's, St Joseph's, and Stranmillis were to offer four-year BEd degrees (not a route suggested by Lockwood) and a three-year certificate of the University. It also proposed a one-year postgraduate certificate that could be taken either at Queen's or in the colleges.[33] There was no reference to an education centre as recommended in the report.

As for the Lockwood committee's other recommendations, the Faculty of Applied Science expanded much as the University had planned and Lockwood intended. Queen's did not lose agriculture; the Faculty of Arts continued to grow notwithstanding it now had competition from a near neighbour. The Faculty of Law continued its traditional role of educating lawyers to become barristers and solicitors; and medicine retained its monopoly of the training of doctors. The Faculty of Economics led the way to three-year honours degrees.

Was the New University inevitable? The Province needed more higher education places and Queen's was reluctant to provide them. But by the end of the century Queen's contained close to 20,000 students, which was 5000 more than the Lockwood report had set as a target for the whole Province in 1978. They were taught in new, existing, or refurbished buildings; indeed in the early 1990s the University concluded it had too much teaching space and sold buildings thought to be surplus to requirements. Many students now lived in halls of residence or university houses within walking distance. Lecturers had been recruited from Britain and elsewhere, although the Troubles had made this difficult in the 1970s.

With hindsight, Queen's could have accommodated the growth envisaged by the Lockwood committee, but only with a major investment in staff, buildings, and equipment. At the end of the twentieth century the two Northern Ireland universities together contained 40,000 students. It is highly unlikely that

31 *Senate minutes, 1965*, 87–90. The working party reported two years later.   32 *Academic Council minutes, 1964–5*, 4 June 1965.   33 *Academic Council minutes, 1966–7*, 107 and 200–5.

Queen's alone could have coped with so many unless it had become a multi-campus university of a federal kind, a development explicitly rejected by the Lockwood committee, but which eventually came about when the Northern Ireland Department of Education merged the New University of Ulster and the Ulster Polytechnic. One point is clear. Queen's played its hand badly in the early 1960s and had to live with the consequence for the rest of the century.

LIFE AFTER LOCKWOOD: CHILVER, BUTLER, AND BEYOND

The New University of Ulster began teaching in October 1968 with 400 students and 95 full-time teaching and research staff. It aimed to have more than 6000 students on its campuses at Coleraine and Magee (which had been absorbed into the New University) by 1980. A decade later, eighteen months before the target date, the Northern Ireland Department of Education (DENI) set up a review group chaired by Sir Henry Chilver, Vice-Chancellor of Cranfield University, 'to consider the present provision of higher education in Northern Ireland, to review both the general and the particular needs of the Northern Ireland community in the 1980's and 1990's for higher education (including advanced further education) and to make recommendations.'[34]

DENI had become worried that the New University had not grown as expected. It was teaching fewer than 2000 students instead of the projected 6000. There was a related problem with teacher education. Queen's, the NUU, the Polytechnic, Stranmillis College, St Joseph's College and St Mary's College between them had places for almost 2000 trainee teachers, which was nearly 30 per cent more than the estimated demand for teachers in the Province.

The Chilver committee reviewed the likely level of demand for full-time higher education and concluded that in the early 1980s there would be 13,600 students in the Province. There would then be ten years of decline, followed by an increase 'to something like its present level by the end of the century'. Financial constraints would make satisfying the demand difficult, but the review group hoped that access to higher education, particularly for mature students, would be widened. The guiding principle of the group was that higher education should be 'as flexible and cost-effective as possible'.[35]

The review group quickly produced an interim report dealing with teacher education. It recommended this should continue at Magee College, and the Polytechnic should concentrate on specialist areas such as physical education,

34 DENI, *Report of the Higher Education Review Group for Northern Ireland* [*The Chilver report*] (Belfast, 1982), iv. Unless otherwise indicated the statistics in this section are taken from the report.   35 Sir Peter Froggatt, Vice-Chancellor at the time, described the report of the review group as 'unclear, contradictory in places; has no feel for H.E. ... [a] mausoleum of jargon much of the worst type' (Hand-written file note 1982. Uncatalogued QUB papers).

home economics, communication studies, and retardation.[36] In Belfast 'purely academic and economic arguments tend to lead to the conclusion that all three colleges and the QUB teacher education provision should be amalgamated'. There was, however, the 'insuperable problem', of how to retain a 'voluntary and denominational element'. The group proposed a compromise. The various Belfast institutions should be brought together as a Belfast Centre for Teacher Education. The St Mary's and St Joseph's colleges should amalgamate, and there should be a physical concentration of teacher training at Stranmillis.[37] Chilver was soon to learn that compromises were not accepted readily in Northern Ireland when denominational issues were involved.

The review group published its main report in March 1982. This tackled the failure of the New University to develop. The group considered closing it down, but concluded 'on balance' that it should continue in existence, although with an 'emphasis on activities relevant to the needs of the Northern Ireland community'. Queen's, it decided, should not expand further but should shift towards 'inter-disciplinary studies', part-time courses, and three-year honours' programmes. The Polytechnic should confine itself to sub-degree and vocational courses and reduce its teaching in general arts. There should be an independent 'Co-ordinating Body' to advise the minister responsible on the requirements of Northern Ireland for higher education.

No sooner had the Chilver review group published its findings than DENI issued a statement of its own rejecting most of it.[38] Instead of continuing as an independent institution, the New University of Ulster was to be merged with the Ulster Polytechnic into a body enjoying university status. The report had been a disappointment to DENI, which was worried by the costs of maintaining three institutions: Queen's, the New University, and the Polytechnic. DENI explained its decision in tortuous but diplomatic language 'The Government has given careful consideration to the particular recommendations which the Report makes in respect of NUU, but has concluded that more radical measures are necessary if it is to have a worthwhile and durable role.' It continued:

> The Government believes that a consolidation of Northern Ireland's higher education system is necessary, and that can be achieved by pooling the resources of NUU and the Ulster Polytechnic ... These two institutions have complementary characteristics. Together they would form the basis for a new split-site university which could provide the geographical and academic spread of provision which Northern Ireland requires. This new institution, which would replace both the NUU and the Polytechnic,

36 DENI, *The future structure of teacher education in Northern Ireland: an interim report of the Higher Education Review Group for Northern Ireland* (Belfast, 1980). 37 *Interim report*, paras. 8.8–8.38. 38 *DENI, Higher education in Northern Ireland: the future structure* (Belfast, 1982).

would be expected to maintain the practical and vocational emphasis of the Polytechnic, and to incorporate into this the strongest aspects of the NUU. This combination would produce a strong and efficient institution with a distinctive role which would complement the traditional academic emphasis of the Queen's University of Belfast (QUB).[39]

For Queen's the implications were serious. DENI was proposing to create a federal university with a range of sub-degree and degree courses calculated to be 'relevant' to the needs of Northern Ireland. Many people in the University concluded, correctly, that the new infant would be the pampered child of DENI. Ever since the Lockwood report, Queen's, according to its own lights, had done more than had been required of it in educating the young people of the Province. It had continued to teach agriculture. Neither the faculties of science nor arts had withered on the vine. The Faculty of Applied Science had grown. Law had flourished, diversifying into joint degrees with languages and business courses. The Faculty of Economics and Social Sciences now taught management and accounting, to say nothing of sociology, social work, and politics. Medicine had followed its lordly way as though the NUU – and, indeed, the rest of Queen's – never existed. The University had established a Faculty of Education. It had a respectable record in research, far better than either the New University or the Polytechnic. What more could it have done?

That was not how the review group and DENI read the evidence. The Chilver report concluded, the 'overall picture' of Queen's was of a university with a high proportion of full-time students straight from school; one that was 'fairly competitive' in attracting well-qualified school leavers; one that recruited most of its students locally; and one that concentrated on undergraduate studies.[40] Queen's had not lived up to the mark.

The University reacted sharply to the findings of the Chilver review group.[41] It criticised the 'rather facile distinction' between 'pure' and 'applied' research it made and complained that 'the recognition given to research of any kind is sparse and is rather grudging in relation to this University, while being surprisingly fulsome in relation to the Polytechnic.' Even on Chilver's own figures Queen's had consistently attracted annually at least sixteen times more grant income for research than the Polytechnic. The University noted 'with surprise the resurrection of a proposal to remove the Faculty of Agriculture & Food Science from Queen's'. This subject had been 'specifically excluded' when the review group was appointed.

The University mounted a strong justification of its three-year, four-year degree structures. If, as had been proposed by some educational reformers in

---

39 *DENI, Higher education in Northern Ireland*, para. 1.9. **40** *Chilver report*, 116. **41** Statement of the University's views on the Chilver report, uncatalogued papers. QUB archives.

Britain, there were to be any broadening of the sixth form curriculum in schools, the need for a four-year degree would be all the greater. The University rejected the charge that it lacked commitment to 'broadly based and vocational' courses and part-time studies. One-third of all employment vacancies for non-medical graduates did not require specific entry requirements. Honours degrees in Queen's were not 'narrow', and there were many courses that were inter-disciplinary. It was caustic about modular courses ('it is not clear what is meant') without dismissing them entirely. As for part-time studies, Queen's pointed out that they existed at the graduate level and that economics had been available as an evening course for half a century. Any further expansion of part-time educa-tion would depend on adequate funding for both the University and students. The University concluded by reiterating 'our continuing readiness to consider change and development', while seeking 'to avoid the pursuit of merely fash-ionable trends'.

The University was outraged by DENI's rejection of the Chilver report without consultation. It did not object to a second university in the Province – it had lived with the NUU for almost two decades – but deplored the merger of the NUU with the Polytechnic, which would create a monster and deprive Ulster of a polytechnic. The merger left unresolved the nature of the relation-ship between Queen's and the new institution. DENI established a steering group to oversee the amalgamation that did not include any representatives from Queen's, even though the two universities were to be 'distinctive', yet 'complementary'. The Queen's Vice-Chancellor was appointed to the group as a nominee of the NUU, but he was 'invited' to resign by Mr Nicholas Scott, the Northern Ireland minister with responsibility for higher education. He had read the Queen's response to the Department's proposals and 'found it difficult to see how Dr Froggatt's membership of the Steering Group ... could be reconciled with his own university's critical views both of the concept of the new institu-tion and of the way in which the planning has been handled'.[42]

In his report to the Senate in 1982 the Vice-Chancellor painted an apocalyp-tic picture of the future. An over-mighty polytechnic would swallow the NUU and Magee, and DENI would be overwhelmed by the expense of feeding the creature it had created. The University Grants Committee would not know how to cope with a polytechnic-cum-university. Worst of all, Queen's would be 'pushed as it so obviously is to the periphery of government's current think-ing'.[43]

Some parts of the nightmare came to pass. For the next decade and a half Queen's had to take account of the University of Ulster (the name of the merged NUU and Polytechnic) at every turn. Even the names carried connota-

---

42 *Vice-Chancellor's report, 1982–3*, v. Copy of a letter from Mr Nicholas Scott to Sir Robert Kidd, Chairman of the steering group, 16 August 1982. QUB archives. See also letter from Mr Scott to Sir Peter Froggatt, 16 August 1982.   43 *Vice-Chancellor's report, 1981–81*, 11.

tions: the Queen's University of Belfast, traditional, stuffy, introverted, metropolitan; the University of Ulster, modern, up-to-date, in touch with the needs of town and countryside. Queen's and the University of Ulster were to be distinct, but they were also supposed to be complementary. How was this to be? In practice, 'complementary' too often meant 'competitive' as the University of Ulster introduced degrees that replicated courses that had for decades been the territory of Queen's.

The worries felt by Queen's came to a head when the UGC decided to fund research in universities on a selective basis. In 1986 DENI set up a working party under the chairmanship of Sir Clifford Butler, formerly Vice-Chancellor of Loughborough University, 'to consider how research effort can currently be concentrated in the two universities in the light of resources currently available, and in prospect, and to make recommendations'.[44] The working party was supposed to deal with research, yet its conclusions were more significant for undergraduate teaching. It produced an interim report at the end of 1986. This recommended that the teaching of single honours physics and chemistry should be concentrated at Queen's and staff and student places in these subjects be shifted from the University of Ulster. There was an important caveat: 'the provision of funding consequent on this recommendation would depend on the University's ability to recruit suitable qualified students'. Research and teaching in the biological sciences should continue in both universities. But the most important proposal was that 'research and development and consultancy in business studies should be concentrated in UU', with students and staff transferred from Queen's. The working party made another (half-hearted) attempt to reduce the duplication of teacher training. It also proposed 'a mechanism' to encourage collaboration in health and community care, and an examination of the possibility of automated library system for the two universities.[45] Its final report a year later added little. It repeated the interim findings and described how they were being implemented. The new sections, dealing with the remaining aspects of the work of the two universities, urged collaboration. In ten brief paragraphs it used the words 'collaboration' or 'collaborate' nine times, and 'complementary' on three occasions.[46]

At first sight Queen's seemed to do well by creaming off single honours teaching in physics and chemistry, but the arrangement left joint courses in these subjects at the UU, which proposed establishing a Department of Applied Physical Sciences to organize them. This seemed to Queen's to be a door back into full-scale physics and chemistry degrees. More importantly, there was a only limited number of qualified students coming from the schools to read the natural sciences. Therefore the student places moving from the University of

---

44 Working Party on Research Selectivity, *Final report to the Department of Education for Northern Ireland, the Queen's University of Belfast and the University of Ulster [Butler report]* (Belfast, 1987), vi. 45 *Butler report*, vii. 46 *Butler report*, viii.

Ulster to Queen's were 'empty boxes'. With no students to fill them there would be no funding. Conversely, the demand for courses in business studies was increasing throughout the whole university sector and it was not difficult for the University of Ulster to recruit students. Indeed, there were enough left over to follow joint courses, such as business studies and a foreign language, at Queen's. The University had been allowed to keep joint courses, but without single honours courses to provide the core and the staff to teach them, it became very difficult to mount them. To complicate matters, Queen's retained degrees in accounting. These might have moved to the UU along with business studies, but Queen's enjoyed strong links with the Institute of Chartered Accountants in Ireland and the Institute was reluctant to sever them.

To strengthen research in the Province, the minister responsible for higher education (Dr Brian Mawhinney) made an additional £0.8m in 1987–8 to both universities (with a promise of perhaps more in the future) to be shared equally. Queen's argued it should get the larger share because of its greater research activity, but DENI was determined that its new baby should not founder. The minister also supplied an additional twenty postgraduate awards a year (enhanced in value to attract students to the Province) and seven awards in science and technology to be allocated (not equally) between Queen's and the University of Ulster.

It is difficult to know whether Queen's might have done better had it argued its case more forcefully to the Butler working party where it had two members. There was no university-wide discussion of the proposals, as there had been in the case with Chilver (and before that with Lockwood). Business studies in Queen's had not developed in a satisfactory fashion in the years before the Butler report, and it was vulnerable to a take-over.[47] Even so, the loss was damaging. Business courses were potentially money-earning activities in a way that physics and chemistry were not. Their transfer to the University of Ulster strengthened a popular belief that Queen's was not really interested in serving the local community. Perhaps Queen's should not have been too worried by perceptions, but they added to the defensive position that the University adopted in its dealings with DENI over the next decade.

The years following the Butler working party were difficult ones for Queen's as a new Vice-Chancellor (Sir Gordon Beveridge) struggled to keep it afloat financially while forever looking over his shoulder at the expansion taking place on the shores of Belfast Lough. He succeeded in maintaining the balance sheet in the black, but the cost was high as academic developments were delayed and posts frozen with glacial intensity. As he lamented, 'planning within the University during the last few years has of necessity been financially led'.[48]

---

47 Sir Peter Froggatt told the present writer several months before Butler produced its interim report that it was inevitable that Queen's would lose Business Studies. **48** *Vice-Chancellor's report, 1988–9*, 2, 10.

At the beginning of the 1990s the University found itself facing new funding arrangements. The government had become concerned about the rising costs of higher education and wished to regulate the expenditure more tightly. It transformed the UGC, whose functions had been advisory, into the University Funding Council (the UFC) with strong powers of direction. The UFC in turn was quickly transmogrified to the Higher Education Funding Council for England (HEFCE). Scotland and Wales had their own councils, but the Westminster government (this was the time of direct rule) decided that Northern Ireland's two universities should nestle under the (benign?) wing of the English council, suitably tweaked by DENI towards local requirements. To aid its task DENI created the Northern Ireland Higher Education Council (NIHEC). Queen's had arrived at the end of the twentieth century swathed in acronyms.

In a characteristic passage, Sir Gordon Beveridge wrote in his annual report in September 1990, 'I am glad to be able to tell you that Queen's is not one of those allegedly "bankrupt" universities mentioned in a somewhat strident Press recently. We are financial healthy, and although we would not wish to give the impression of carefree affluence, we have achieved, through prudent housekeeping and strict financial controls, a level of reserves which is the envy of our sister institutions.'[49] The affectation of carefree affluence was the last thing that Sir Gordon could ever be accused of. Financial rectitude set the tone throughout much of the 1990s. The Vice-Chancellor wrote gloomily in his tenth and penultimate report in September 1996, 'the financial situation for all Universities [last year] took a turn for the worse'. Queen's was faced with an immediate reduction of seven per cent in its annual income and a possible reduction of 30 per cent in capital funding.[50] In his farewell report to Senate in September 1997 Sir Gordon foretold of further gloom ahead and warned, 'Dearing will not be a panacea for all our ills, and in the short-term the proposed cut-backs in our research funding give considerable cause for concern.'[51]

THE DEARING REPORT

The 'Dearing' to which the Vice-Chancellor referred was Sir Ron Dearing who was appointed by the Secretary of State for Education and Employment in May 1996 to chair a committee 'to make recommendations on how the purposes, shape, structure, size and funding of higher education, including support for students, should develop to meet the needs of the United Kingdom over the next 20 years, recognising that higher education embraces teaching, learning, scholarship and research.' The chairman was a former chairman of the Post

49 *Vice-Chancellor's report, 1989–90*, 1. **50** *Vice-Chancellor's report, 1995–6*, introduction and p. 2. **51** *Vice-Chancellor's report, 1996–7*, introduction.

Office and membership was drawn from universities and other institutions of higher education, from schools, industry and commerce. There were also members from the regions of the United Kingdom; the Northern Ireland representative was Sir George Quigley, Chairman of the Ulster Bank. The mammoth report was the first comprehensive survey of higher education since Robbins, and it included Northern Ireland in its work.[52]

The background to the committee's work was the expansion of higher and further education during previous decades. Between the Robbins and the Dearing reports the full-time student population in the United Kingdom had increased nearly six-fold, the age participation index (API) five-fold, and the percentage of GDP devoted to higher education by 64 per cent. The costs of higher education were rising at a speed that alarmed the government. In Northern Ireland there were nearly 40,000 full-time and part-time students in higher and further education in 1994–5 and the API was substantially higher (42 per cent) than elsewhere in the United Kingdom. There was an acute shortage of higher education places (between 5000 and 12,000 depending on how they were calculated).[53]

Much of the Dearing report was concerned with the ways by which higher education should be funded. It proposed that universities should rely more on fee income, research grants, and contracts, and less on block grants from the government. For Queen's the recommendations signalled a severe tightening of the belt unless the research profile of the University could be raised substantially and income from non-governmental sources increased. Raising money became a major preoccupation of the new Vice-Chancellor (Sir George Bain) in 1998. His predecessors had all had reason to be anxious about the financial well being of the University, but none had had the need to run Queen's in quite so businesslike a fashion. The trick was to keep in mind that the business in question was that of learning.

CONCLUSION

Both the Robbins and Lockwood reports took a liberal view of higher education and accepted there was untapped talent that would benefit from higher education. The Chilver and Butler committees were more concerned with structures and financial considerations and less with principles; their recommendations led to a greater interference by politicians and civil servants in the affairs of the University. The Dearing committee articulated a philosophy of 'the learning

52 The National Committee of Inquiry into Higher Education, *Higher education in the learning society* [*the Dearing report*] (London, 1997). The section on Northern Ireland is in the main report, pp. 363–5. In addition to the main report there were four volumes of appendices and fourteen reports covering various aspects of higher education.   53 *Dearing report*, 445–58.

society'. It believed there was a reservoir of mature and part-time students with the ability to benefit from higher and further education. In this way it had links with Robbins, but there was also a strong element of utilitarianism in the report.

> Experience suggests that the long-term demand from industry and commerce will be for higher levels of education and training for their present and future workforce. The UK cannot afford to lag behind its competitors in investing in the intellect and skills of its people. While the United States of America is a strong investor in higher education, and has high rates of participation, the Far East is increasingly setting the pace. In Japan, participation in higher education is already more than ten percentage points higher than in the UK and, with demographic changes, participation by young people there will exceed 50 per cent in 2000–2010 without an increase in total expenditure on higher education. A significant proportion of such participation is at levels below first degree.[54]

Queen's was treated by the Dearing report as part of the United Kingdom's system of higher education (this had not be the case with previous reports) and it could not stand aloof from the requirement of government and society that universities should educate large numbers of students. At the end of the twentieth century the University was faced with two twin challenges. One was to widen access to higher education and at the same time seek alternative sources of income. The other was to the regional economy and at the same time stand tall in the international world of scholarship.

There was a fundamental question hanging over all universities. Was mass higher education compatible with high scholarly standards? The reduction in per capita funding had set alarm bells ringing. Universities claimed that rising student-staff ratios imperilled the quality of teaching and research. The government responded by questioning whether society was getting value for money from its universities, perhaps forgetting the Robbins dictum that the 'goal [of universities] is not productivity as such but the good life that productivity makes possible'. The outcome of the concerns was the introduction of two quasi-independent forms of scrutiny of the work of universities, the Research Assessment Exercise (RAE) and the assessment of teaching quality (the TQA). Good RAE and TQA results gave Vice-Chancellors something to boast about at graduations. But their imposition circumscribed the independence that universities, Queen's included, had treasured for more than a century.

54 *Dearing report*, para. 1.14.

4

Who pays?

In the previous chapter we examined the relationship between Queen's and the state. An important dimension of that relationship was finance. A university, like a teenager turning twenty, is legally independent but in need of money from his or her parents. The parent for Queen's – a single parent for much of the time – has been the state. The ancient universities have their endowments, but even they cannot survive without money from the public purse. Queen's is not an ancient foundation but had been set up by an act of parliament and paid for by the government. There were a few other sources of funds available to the University, including student fees (significant until the early 1960s and again in the 1990s), income from commercial activities, contracts and gifts. But these were of minor importance until late into the twentieth century. A major change in the history of Queen's during the 1980s and 1990s was the gradual reduction in its reliance on annual government grants.

Over the course of the second half of the twentieth century the cost of running Queen's increased almost thirty-fold in real terms (from under a quarter of a million pounds to over £6 million) and many times more at current prices. Until the early 1980s real income grew more quickly than the numbers of students, but it then failed to keep pace with the growth of the student population. By 1999 real income *per capita* had fallen to its lowest point for more than a quarter of a century. The reason was simple. The Westminster government was no longer prepared to finance the work of universities from taxation at the levels it had done in the past. All universities were in the same predicament, but some possessed private income and many raised more research income than did Queen's. The University desperately needed to find sources of income to supplement government grants.

GOVERNMENT GRANTS

Grants from central and local government were important throughout the second half of the twentieth century. As table 4.1 shows, their contribution to total rose from the end of the Second World War to 80 per cent in the early 1970s and then fell to less than half by the end of the century.

Table 4.1: Sources of income, 1945–99[1]

Year	Government grants %	Academic fees, etc. %	Research grants and contracts %	Other operating income %	Endowments, interest, etc. etc. %	Income at current prices (£s)
1945–9	65.3	24.7	0.0	6.6	3.4	227,300
1950–4	71.1	18.8	0.0	5.9	6.2	404,700
1955–9	75.9	15.0	0.0	6.2	2.9	694,200
1960–4	78.9	14.2	0.0	4.7	2.2	1,335,500
1965–9	79.6	10.5	5.2	2.9	1.8	3,107,000
1970–4	80.4	6.8	9.0	2.6	1.2	6,156,300
1975–9	76.3	11.9	6.6	3.2	1.9	15,592,000
1980–4	70.8	14.5	8.0	4.1	2.6	34,536,700
1985–9	67.7	11.1	9.6	9.1	2.5	53,004,400
1990–4	43.5	20.6	12.6	19.9	3.5	98,177,200
1995–9	46.5	18.2	14.9	18.3	2.2	126,400,200

The government grant was made up of several elements. There was a historical component consisting of an annual statutory grant of £50,000 to which had been added £12,500, which was income accruing from the Irish church temporalities fund and other minor sources. The origins of these payments lay in the nineteenth century and after 1920 Stormont inherited the responsibility for paying them. During the 1920s the county and city councils in Northern Ireland began to contribute a few thousand pounds a year between them, and rebates of rates were a further source of support. The combined sums fell far short of what was required. Every year, therefore, the statutory grant was supplemented by an extra-statutory payment that swamped the statutory grant.

The size of the extra-statutory income was determined after discussions between the University, the Ministry of Finance, and the University Grants Committee, a body created in 1919 to advise the Westminster government on the financial needs of British universities. After Partition its authority did not extend to Ulster but after the Second World War the Northern Ireland Ministry of Finance was happy to accept its guidance. The UGC operated with the lightest of touches. It occasionally offered advice about how money might be spent, but that was all.[2] Government scrutiny of the use of payments made to Queen's was closer than that experienced by universities elsewhere in the United Kingdom. Under the terms of the Irish Universities act in 1908 Queen's had to submit its accounts annually to the comptroller and auditor-general.[3] His British counterpart did not have full access to the accounts of universities there until 1968.[4]

1 The figures are based on the annual financial statements. For details see appendices 3.1 and 3.2. 2 G. Lockwood and J. Davies, *Universities: the management challenge* (Windsor, 1985), 12–14. 3 *Vice-Chancellor's report, 1953–4*, 168. 4 *Review of the University Grants Committee* [*the Croham report*] (London, 1987), 10.

The Westminster/Stormont grant was technically a deficit grant. That is, the UGC calculated the cost of educating a student in the arts, sciences, etc. and set this against any fee income received by the universities; the balance (the 'deficit') was covered by the grant. The UGC developed a system of quinquennial funding that for three decades after the war gave universities a financial stability necessary for long-term planning. The system was simple to administer and worked well as long as inflation was low; rapid inflation during the 1970s eventually brought its death knell. The quinquennium in Northern Ireland ran a year later than that in Britain, a delay that caused difficulties in the cash-strapped years of the 1970s and 1980s.

A recurring complaint of the University after 1945, and indeed earlier, was it was under-funded compared with British universities. This was a weakness inherited from the 1920s and 1930s when the income available to the Stormont government was limited. After the war the Northern Ireland government and the UGC did what they could to close the gap. A member of the UGC told Mr George Cowie in 1947, when he was contemplating moving from the University of Aberdeen to take up the post of Secretary to the University, that 'for the first time in its existence Queen's was about to get a real blood transfusion of finance'.[5] It was badly needed.

There was a gradual improvement in the financial position of Queen's during the 1950s and 1960s. Inflation was low and the Bursar rarely needed to bother the Senate with financial business except when the quinquennial plans were being prepared. Indeed, in 1962 the Vice-Chancellor, Dr Grant, came close to telling the Senate that the University was having difficulty in spending money:

> If all our requests [for the quinquennium 1963–8] are granted we shall by 1968 be spending about 50% more on these items of salaries etc. than we are spending now. Hitherto our expansion of staff has been severely limited by shortages of land, space, premises and accommodation. This implies no lack of generosity in the past by the Government (on the contrary): it was no use for us to ask for more staff until we had somewhere to put them, and that is why our Government grant fell below those of universities in Great Britain of comparable size.[6]

The passage is a puzzle. Under-funding had been a chronic condition of the University, and Dr Grant's predecessors had worked with some success to remedy the problem. But most of all, the Vice-Chancellor's judgment did not fit the facts. During the 1950s Queen's had spent a great deal on new buildings and equipment: teaching space and the numbers of academic staff had almost doubled. Sir Arthur Vick, Dr Grant's successor, continued to be worried about

5 Interview with Mr Alf McCreary, 1991. 6 *Vice-Chancellor's report, 1961–2*, 298.

under-funding a decade later. The problem still existed 'though not perhaps to the degree stated by colleagues'.[7]

During the 1970s rapidly rising prices all but obliterated the landmarks that had once guided financial planning in universities. In an attempt to control its own expenditure the government at first reduced and then stopped giving supplementary grants to universities to compensate for increases in non-academic salaries. Queen's was faced by a large loss of income that was kept within limits only by freezing vacant academic posts.[8] The financial position became chronically precarious, and Sir Peter Froggatt, Vice-Chancellor from 1976, penned many elegant (and occasionally inscrutable) paragraphs bewailing the near impossibility of academic planning. The government consigned the quinquennial system to the scrap heap and replaced it by annual allocations of shrinking real value. For Queen's the interjection of Stormont between the University and the UGC added to the difficulties by delaying the announcement of the grant. In 1978, for example, the grant for 1978–9 was agreed only ten days before the beginning of the new financial year. The next year it was announced a month early (and was bigger than expected), but hardly early enough to aid sensible planning. In 1980 the grant letter arrived two weeks after the new financial year had begun. As Sir Peter Froggatt put it, the government's game by now was 'waiting for Chilver' and the waiting paralyzed all financial projections. 'Or are we', asked the Vice-Chancellor in one of his more dramatic moments, 'waiting for Godot, expected but never arriving?'[9]

Godot, *alias* the Chilver report, arrived in March 1982 and excited a Vice-Chancellorial disquisition on its financial implications long even by Sir Peter's own generous standards. The annual grant was declining by 5 or 6 per cent a year and the University was forced to restrict student entry to preserve the 'integrity of the unit of resource'. Before the Chilver report and DENI's statement rejecting most of its recommendations, the New University of Ulster and the polytechnic had been there to take the students unable to gain admission to Queen's. But now there was only the embryonic University of Ulster. The future of higher education in Northern Ireland was very uncertain.[10]

Following the creation of the University of Ulster the UGC established a Northern Ireland Working Party (NIWP) to advise DENI on the funding requirements of its two universities. In August 1983 there was a change in the formal position of the UGC. It ceased to be merely an adviser to DENI and became responsible for the financial needs of the two Northern Ireland universities in line with British universities, although it continued to work through the NIWP. In June the following year the NIWP recommended a period of level funding for Queen's (i.e. maintaining the real value of income per head of

7 *Vice-Chancellor's report, 1971–2*, 4–5. 8 *Vice-Chancellor's report, 1973–4*, 5–7; *1974–5*, 5–6. 9 *Vice-Chancellor's report, 1977–8*, 5–6; *1978–9*, 5–6; *1980–1*, 6–8 and 9. 10 *Vice-Chancellor's report, 1981–2*, 4–12.

student) for two years, with vague assurances about the future.[11] If it had been sustained, level funding would have resulted in a further financial catching up with British universities. But within a year or two level funding had 'sunk without trace'. The Westminster government had now embarked on a policy of 'selectivity' by funding some universities more unequally than others on the basis of the perceived quality of their research.[12] Selectivity was not helpful to Queen's.

Continuing high rates of inflation made the system of funding for universities through block grants unattractive to the government. An alternative method was to make *per capita* payments to universities based on student numbers and their distribution across subjects, plus a judgment about research. In this way the treasury was able to keep a tighter grip on expenditure. Early in 1981 the UGC introduced a technique of 'formula funding'. The Vice-Chancellor explained the method to a patient and possibly puzzled Senate. Three elements determined the size of the annual grant: student numbers, research achievements, and 'special factors'. For Queen's, the largest part of its grant was decided by student numbers and their subject distribution (a medical student was worth more than an arts student). The University did well on student numbers as long as it had the freedom to determine the size of its student population (it soon lost this freedom), but it did not fare well on the research count. 'Special factors' took into account circumstances specific to individual institutions (location, fuel costs, etc.). The formula was elaborated over the years and the research element became increasingly important.[13] Research – or the relative lack of it – was becoming a millstone around the neck of Queen's. Had the University's research earnings been higher, the whittling away of the student-based grant would have mattered less. So, over the last two decades of the twentieth century, there was growing pressure on academics to carry out research, particularly of a kind that attracted funds from the research councils. The scholar who spent the bulk of his or her time teaching and running the University with only an occasional foray into print became an endangered species.

Inflation did more than sweep away quinquennial funding; it raised questions about the workings of the UGC itself. In 1982 the Secretary of State for Education and Science invited the committee to ponder its own future and functions. It published the result of its deliberations two years later.[14] Unsurprisingly, the UGC believed that it should continue in existence and to arbitrate on the financial requirements of universities. It recommended that the total student intake in Britain should be increased to about 600,000 over the next three years and then be held steady until the end of the decade. The future beyond 1990 was too impenetrable for predictions about the optimum size of the

11 UGC, Northern Ireland working party, *First report* (Belfast, 1984), 5–6. 12 *Vice-Chancellor's report, 1983–4*, no pagination. 13 *Vice-Chancellor's report, 1985–6*, 5–7; *Croham report*, 29. 14 UGC, *A strategy for higher education into the 1990s* (London, 1984).

student population to be made. The UGC recommended that increases in student numbers should be matched by a corresponding growth in staff numbers and that the government should compensate universities for at least part of the costs of premature retirement schemes introduced in the 1980s. It should also ensure level funding for universities until at least 1990. Finally, the UGC suggested that its remit should be extended to cover the capital plans of universities and not merely their recurrent costs.

The growth of higher education was gathering momentum, which added to the government's worries about the cost of funding of universities. It appointed a committee under the chairmanship of Lord Croham to review the work of the UGC. The committee recommended the UGC should be changed into a council to supervise the expenditure of universities as well to advise on income. The new body would remain independent of government and be composed of no more than fifteen members drawn more or less equally from academic and non-academic life. The chairman was to be a person with 'substantial non-academic experience' but possessing a 'strong interest' in higher education. There would also be a full-time director-general who would be the accounting officer. The council would operate a system of triennial funding, the level of which would be decided after consideration of the government's guidelines on the objectives of higher education. It would distribute the research element of grants selectively, 'balanced by measures designed to promote quality in teaching.' The quality indicators for teaching and research currently being developed by the UGC and the Committee of Vice-Chancellors and Principals (CVCP) were to be employed to judge the performance of institutions. The new body would have 'unambiguous powers' to attach conditions to grants, including 'positive or negative earmarking of funds'. It should, further, adopt a 'varying approach' to the financial management of universities and require the submission of annually audited financial statements.[15]

Thus was born the Universities' Funding Council (UFC), which established *dirigisme* as an unabashed feature of university financing; the autonomy of universities was being severely compromised. Unlike the UGC, whose role was advisory, the UFC interfered in the affairs of institutions of higher education. It did not have a long existence. It was soon replaced by higher education funding councils for England, Scotland, and Wales. There was no funding council for Northern Ireland; instead for the purposes of higher education the Province became a colony of the English council (HEFCE). In the 1940s and 1950s the Queen's principal source of income had been no more than a local phone call away and perhaps morning coffee with the appropriate minister. Now it was a trek through a trail of bureaucracy with no assurance of a pot of gold at the end.

The changes in funding arrangements of universities that began in 1981 were described by Sir Peter Froggatt as 'seminal or apocalyptic'. The UGC 'bent or

15 *Croham report*, passim.

perhaps even broke ... a principle, whereby a student would attract to the pub-
lic-purse income ... of the university of his choice an amount of money
determined solely by his category of enrolment and the subject ... studied'.
Instead the government was proposing to vary the amount of funding from one
university to another according to a formula.[16] Worse was to come the following
year when the 'free market' in undergraduate admissions came to an end. No
longer could universities decide how many students they could take, confident
that the 'unit of resource would follow'. The Northern Ireland Working Party
now set target numbers for the University, which risked penalties if it either
overshot or undershot.[17]

The changes in funding methods had been financially driven, but their
impact was as great as though as they had been introduced for purely educational reasons. They did not quite nationalize the universities but they imposed
constraints on them that compromised their freedom. They resulted in the reg-
ulation of student intake and altered the emphasis between teaching and
research within universities. Queen's had always been a busy teaching university.
That is not to say that research had been unimportant. The University expected
lecturers and professors to carry out research, but the subjects they chose to
pursue and how they divided their time between teaching and research was a
matter of personal choice. But this could no longer be the case because formula
funding put a premium on research The scholar who chose to nurse his or her
students through the complexities of existing knowledge rather than adding to
its stock was a drag on the research assessment exercise and hence on income.
The style of doing research also changed. Collaborative research that attracted
large grants from the research councils became more prized than the work of an
individual achieved by the investment of time and thought but with only a little
expenditure of somebody else's money.

By the 1980s the financial climate facing all universities was chilly. For
Queen's it was arctic. Formula funding worked to its disadvantage. The main
component in the formula, the number of undergraduates, was no longer fully
in its control. Another part of the grant was determined by the University's
research performance, one indicator of which was income gained from research
councils and contracts. Queen's research earnings were well below the national
average.[18] The University's total income from government sources, therefore,
was smaller than it would have been had it been more successful in winning
research money.

The consequences of a reduced level of income because of indifferent
research were not confined to research. Lecturers and professors were paid to
carry out both activities. A reduction in the government grant for whatever reason, or the failure of income to grow in line with student numbers, depressed

16 *Vice-Chancellor's report, 1982–83*, i.   17 *Vice-Chancellor's report, 1983–4*, no pagination.
18 *Senate minutes, 1988*, 279.

student-staff ratios and resulted in more hours devoted to teaching. The more time lecturers spent teaching (including preparation and marking), the less time they had for research and publication. Queen's was in a trap. Its grant was not big enough, because of its research performance was not strong enough. Therefore the student-staff ratio was high, and because of this it was not easy to raise the research profile.

Throughout the 1980s and 1990s Queen's suffered a continual downward pressures on its *per capita* income derived from the government. It was not alone. The Dearing committee reckoned that between 1997–8 and 1999–2000 there would be a decline of between six and seven per cent across the university system. Such a process of attrition was unsustainable 'without significant damage to the quality of the student experience and the research base.'[19] By now a growing proportion of the income of Queen's was coming from student fees and other sources.

STUDENT FEES

It is sometimes forgotten that before the recommendations of the Anderson committee were implemented students were responsible for their own fees and maintenance costs. There was a small number of scholarships and bursaries available from schools, the local authorities, and from Queen's itself. Nevertheless, at the beginning of the 1950s more than 60 per cent of students had no financial support beyond what their families gave them. Fees covered only a fraction of the costs of the University. When Queen's increased fees in 1950 it acknowledged that it 'would add to the burdens of those who are trying to give their children the best education possible'. But the Vice-Chancellor pointed out that fees were lower than elsewhere, 'and it may be some consolation to those who pay fees to know that for every £1 which is paid in fees the student is being subsidised to the extent of £5 from other sources.'[20] In 1962 mandatory grants were introduced for undergraduates. Northern Ireland was in two minds about mandatory grants, but it could hardly stand out against what was happening elsewhere.[21] From that date until the end of the 1970s close to 90 per cent of the income of the University's income was obtained from central and local government through a combination of the block grant and student fees.

19 The National Committee of Inquiry into Higher Education, *Higher education in the learning society* [*Dearing Report*] (London, 1997), main report, 266–7. There are other calculations that put the decline even greater. For example, the AUT predicted that the cumulative decline in the funding of higher education in the United Kingdom between 1995/6 and 1998/9 would be 11.4 per cent: AUT, *Efficiency gains or quality losses?* (London, 1996), 6.   **20** *Vice-Chancellor's report 1949–50*, 206.   **21** The University was worried that its ability to choose students would be compromised and that the quality of the intake would fall.

The balance between the grant and the fee income altered as the level of fees was raised. Between 1976 and 1979 undergraduate fees were increased nearly three-fold and postgraduate fees four-fold. Full-time undergraduates continued to have their fees paid by their local education authorities and so were not affected. All that was happening was that some of the costs of higher education were switched from the treasury to local rates. But postgraduates, most of who paid their own fees, and part-time students, were faced with sharply rising bills at a time when Queen's was trying to increase their numbers.[22] The move to a larger fee element of income posed a dilemma for Queen's. It could try to defend student-staff ratios in the face of a reduction in the block grant by restricting student intake, but only at the risk of losing fee income. The advantages of fees over the block grants were not lost on the government that progressively shifted funding to the former.

The proportion of the University's income derived from student fees more than doubled during the 1980s and 1990s as the value of the block grant fell by £2 million. The rise in fee income was the product of an increase in *per capita* fees paid by or on behalf of students and a rise in the number of students.[23] In 1997 the Dearing committee recommended a further move 'towards a system in which funding follows the student' so that by the year 2003 sixty per cent of public funding would be determined by student choice.[24] Soon after the Dearing report was published the government decided that undergraduates should pay their own fees up to a limit of £1000 (later raised to £1125).

The growing importance of fees encouraged a scramble for overseas students who paid full fees and who could usually be accepted beyond quotas set by the government. At the end of the twentieth century foreign students contributed almost £3 million a year to Queen's. Their money was greatly needed and they added an international flavour to the student population. The overseas market was highly competitive and the University had to work hard to recruit them.

The end of the century marked the end of forty years of free education for home-based undergraduates. Most students were now responsible for paying their own fees (albeit capped). Maintenance grants had also been phased out and replaced by loans. Nobody could be sure what effect these changes would have on the demand for university places in Northern Ireland where earnings were only 80 per cent of the UK average. There was understandable apprehension that the demand would be curtailed as a result. The continuing growth in student numbers suggests that this did not happen, but many students had to spend a lot of time on part-time jobs in order to finance their studies.

The new funding arrangements made local school leavers think hard about the benefits of going to Queen's rather than going to universities in other parts the United Kingdom or in Ireland. Queen's had been the first choice for the

22 *Vice-Chancellor's report, 1977–8,* 7–8.   23 *Financial statement, 1990–1991,* 2.   24 *Dearing report,* 297.

majority of pupils from the local grammar schools for generations. During the 1970s and 80s the post-Robbins universities in England and Scotland attracted a growing number of students. But the ending of grants, their replacement by loans, and the introduction of fees, made Queen's a cheaper option. There remained, nevertheless, a competitive edge among universities. As league tables began to rank universities according to the quality of their teaching and research, prospective students and their teachers scrutinized them with some interest. Universities needed to demonstrate to students and employers of graduates that they provided good teaching. One way of doing this was to achieve good degree results. The 2(i) became the standard degree during the 1990s; previously it had been the 2(ii).[25] Was this grade inflation, the result of better teaching, better examining, or more highly motivated students? All universities protested vigorously that their teaching was getting better. Nevertheless, the suspicion continued to hang in the corridors of learning that the shift to student fees as a significant source of university income was having consequences on the standards of learning.

RESEARCH GRANTS AND CONTRACT INCOME

Research grants and contracts were a third source of income. The annual accounts did not distinguish income from research grants until 1967. Thereafter research grant income grew considerably in absolute terms and eventually as a percentage of total income from the late 1970s (see table 4.1). Success in winning grants became the touchstone of scholarly virility. Until the 1960s most of the research carried out in the University was financed from the block grant, and only a small proportion of the research costs came from the research councils or industrial contracts. This was a consequence of the so-called 'dual-support system'.[26] An unspecified proportion of the block grant to all universities was spent on research, most of it in the form of academic salaries. In 1982–3 the UGC estimated that 30 per cent of the block grant supported research, but nobody really knew because research and teaching were both parts of a lecturer's duties and there was no formal division of time between one and another. One or two government ministers in the 1980s began to mutter that university research was a black hole into which unaccountable sums of money poured.

The dual support system survived as long as the rate of inflation was low, but rapidly rising prices in the 1980s undermined its foundations. The Advisory Board on Research Councils, which was responsible for advising the government of the financial needs of all the research councils, complained, 'the dual

---

25 For a discussion see chapter nine. 26 For an account of the dual support system see, Advisory Board of the Research Councils, *Report of a joint working party on the support of university scientific research* (London, 1982). 27 Quoted in Lockwood and Davies, *Universities,*

support system is currently under severe strain and is not working properly.'[27] The government was intent on squeezing the research element out of the block grant, thus forcing universities to look elsewhere for money to finance research. Research grants thus became doubly important for universities. Grants to individuals were additions to the total income of their universities. But they also served as indicators of the success of institutions. Following the biblical injunction, 'to him that hath shall be given', the more successful a university in the research council stakes the larger was its block grant. The hunt for grants and contracts became almost as time-consuming as the pursuit of scholarship itself and successful academics treated them as trophies to be offered to the committee gods that ruled on promotions.

Although the number and value of research grants gained by Queen's academics were increasing, the share of research income to total income during the 1970s was less than 8 per cent, well below the national average of 13 per cent.[28] In the humanities and social sciences there was little pressure on academics before the 1970s to look for grants. A pen and paper, some trips (subsidised by the University) to the archives or research libraries, plus a good deal of thinking time, did not require a grant from an outside body. In the sciences things were different; equipment was expensive and the specialised research laboratories were far away. But from the 1970s scholars in all faculties were impelled to look for grants. By the end of the century the share of research income to total income almost doubled to 15 per cent. This still left Queen's somewhat down the research-earning league.

The principal research councils were the Agricultural Research Council (ARC, later the Agricultural and Food Research Council), the Medical Research Council (MRC), the Natural Environment Research Council (NERC), the Science and Engineering Research Council (SERC), and the Economic and Social Research Council (the ESRC, originally known as the Social Science Research Council). The British Museum and the Royal Society were also involved in dispensing research grants. The humanities had no research council until late in the century, but the British Academy had limited funds at its disposal. The research councils received their funds from the science budget distributed by the Secretary of State for Education. Research council money, therefore, was, like the block grant, government money, but it was money that was competed for by all universities.

The Universities Funding Council conducted the first reasonably reliable research assessment exercise in 1992 (an earlier exercise in 1988 was fairly crude). It demonstrated that neither of Northern Ireland's two universities stood high among the UK research rankings. DENI therefore set up a fund (known inscrutably as 'DevR', standing for development research funding) of

222. 28 Lockwood and Davies, _Universities_, 220–4; M. Shattock and G. Rigby (eds), _Resource allocation in British universities_ (Guildford, 1983), 103–4; _Lockwood report_, 165.

£9 million a year for three years to strengthen the research of Queen's and the University of Ulster. The amount was then reduced to £5 million, and over time it disappeared. The consequence of the phasing out of DevR was that in Northern Ireland research funding from the government between 1993 and 1999 fell by more than 10 per cent in real terms. At the same time there was a rise of 7 per cent in Great Britain.[29]

In 1999 Queen's earned £20.5 million from research grants and contracts. Of this £8.3 million came from the research councils, and £12.2 million from contracts awarded by industry or public utilities.[30] These were extremely welcome even though in the research assessment exercises they were regarded as 'soft money' because, unlike grants from the research councils, they were not usually gained in a peer reviewed competition. Queen's had for many years received a grant from the Ministry (later Department) of Agriculture and from local authorities as payments for services, but substantial industrial contracts were difficult to obtain because the local industrial base was small.

Queen's worked hard to strengthen its links with industry. In 1984 the University set up a joint venture company called QUBIS Ltd (Queen's University Business and Information Service), the purpose of which was to explore avenues of 'mutual gain.' By the mid-1990s QUBIS employed a graduate staff of 200 and had a turnover of over £10 million in companies developing processes based on research conducted in the University.[31] The Northern Ireland Technology Centre was established to facilitate technology transfer between the University and industry. Ninety-five per cent of its income came from industrial earnings. The QUESTOR Centre was created in 1989 as a co-operative venture involving five University departments and nine industrial members. Its purpose was to carry out basic research into ways of minimising environmental damage caused by industrial processes.

Teaching companies were another way of raising money. Several companies were established during the 1980s to assist in technology transfer between the University and industry. They were mainly based in Northern Ireland, and were spread over a wide spectrum including chemical analysis, packaging, computer software, textile printing, concrete manufacture, quarrying, pharmaceuticals, veterinary products, baking, cleaning materials, meat processing, and many others.

OTHER INCOME

Queen's possessed only a modest portfolio of endowments, which were never enough to make life comfortable. It managed to earn a useful sum from invest-

---

29 *Dearing report*, 454–5.   **30** *Financial statement 1998–9*, 14.   **31** *Vice-Chancellor's report, 1983–4*, no pagination; *Lockwood report*, 447.

ments during the 1980s and '90s when interest rates were high, but this was a precarious source of revenue. The University was late into the game of asking its *alumni* for money in a focused fashion. In 1949 the centenary appeal raised nearly £200,000, some of it contributed by the government. During Sir Peter Froggatt's time in office the Canada Room and the Council Chamber were refurbished by money raised by public subscription, including donations from the Canadian government and the Canadian provinces. An appeal planned to mark the 150th anniversary of Queen's in 1995 did not take place because it became tangled up in the controversies aroused by charges of discrimination and the decision no longer to play the National Anthem at graduations. At the end of the decade Queen's established a development office and money was sought from private sources for specific purposes. The grandest example was the refurbishment of the Great Hall at a cost of £2.5 million. The *alumni* of Queen's were beginning to receive requests for money in a manner that graduates of other universities had been used to for years. At last gifts and endowments were making a contribution to income, although they still amounted to only a few per cent of the total.

In one way and another Queen's was searching for methods of financing itself that freed it from the umbilical cord of government. But, like Alice, it had to run faster and faster to stand still. All universities were in the hunt for non-government money and it was not easy to catch up with the pack. Nevertheless, the effort had to be made, for faced with an inexorable decline in income per head from the government (whether in the form of a block grant or fees paid by local authorities) the only alternative facing the University was a slow decline into academic penury.

SPENDING THE MONEY

Table 4.2 summarizes the ways in which Queen's spent its money during the second half of the twentieth century, employing the heads of expenditure adopted at the end of the century. The categories are by no means watertight. The second column includes only the salaries of academics (professors, lecturers, etc.), the academically related staff (the Librarian, etc.), and the senior administrators. The salaries and wages of clerical, manual and other staff are included within the various other categories of expenditure. Taking all staff together, from the Vice-Chancellor to part-time cleaners, the University spent roughly two-thirds of its income on labour, with some tendency for the proportion to fall over time. Academic salaries normally accounted for 70 to 75 per cent of the combined salary costs of academics and administrators. Universities were labour-intensive enterprises. Any squeeze on income, therefore, bore down heavily on staff and especially on non-academic staff whose conditions of employment were less secure than those of professors and lecturers.

Table 4.2: Breakdown of expenditure, 1945–1999 (percentages)

	Academic and administrative salaries	Academic support	Student support	Premises, equipment, furniture	Library, computing services	Adminis- tration	Other, restructuring, unallocated
1945–9	59.5	6.7	5.0	21.6	3.2	3.6	0.5
1950–4	67.9	7.4	5.5	11.0	3.8	2.8	1.7
1955–9	69.2	7.0	4.5	10.4	3.9	2.0	2.9
1960–4	66.9	9.3	3.7	10.0	3.7	1.9	4.5
1965–9	60.2	17.6	2.8	8.8	5.6	2.3	2.8
1970–4	55.0	18.6	3.0	12.5	6.7	2.4	1.9
1975–9	50.0	15.1	3.0	19.9	8.3	2.1	1.6
1980–4	51.2	15.7	2.6	18.2	8.3	1.0	2.9
1985–9	47.1	19.2	2.5	19.2	7.0	1.1	4.0
1990–4	42.8	17.6	3.1	18.5	5.7	1.4	10.8
1995–9	41.9	25.9	3.9	14.6	1.9	5.8	5.9

As a proportion of the total, spending on academic and administrative staff was highest in the 1940s and 1950s, but declined from about 1960. There were several reasons for this. The costs of equipment were rising. Academic work in the natural and applied sciences was always an omnivorous user, and with the increasing emphasis on research the demand for hardware and consumables grew ever greater. By the 1980s, the use of equipment had spread also into the humanities. Personal computers, replete with word-processing packages, spreadsheets, databases, statistical and graphing packages, and links with the world-wide-web, had colonized the desks of all but the most die-hard of academics. At the end of the century there were not many scholars remaining who wrote their articles with pen and paper and who relied on a long-suffering secretary to turn their handwriting into something legible.

In teaching, too, machines were beginning, if not to replace lecturers, at least to assist them to cope with deteriorating student-staff ratios. In economic terms there was a replacement of labour by capital. The photocopying of articles and book chapters by students became – almost – a substitute for buying books. The University installed workstations in order that students could roam the internet in search of information for their essays. The Library itself became automated, with electronic catalogues replacing index cards. The increasing use of equipment to assist in teaching raised pedagogical issues. If students could get their information from the worldwide web what was the use of lectures and lecturers? What future was there for the Socratic method of teaching now that so much learning was taking place in front of a screen?

During the second half of the twentieth century there was a large increase of expenditure on what the accounts described as 'academic support'. This category included everyday housekeeping expenses such as laboratory equipment, departmental grants, travel and conference grants, payments to tutors and demonstrators, funds to assist in the publication of research papers, and the expenses of external examiners. But academic support included also a substantial chunk of the salaries paid to research staff employed on research contracts. The employment of research staff accounted for most of the increase in spending on academic support from 7 per cent of the total in the 1940s to more than a quarter by the end of the century.

Throughout the 1940s and 1950s the Library stood alone as the repository of knowledge, absorbing around three or four per cent of annual income. In good years books and periodicals made up a little under half of Library expenditure (the rest went on staff and incidental costs), but it was often considerably lower. During the 1950s the University began to develop its computer services and in 1958 a sum £1000 for computers appeared in the accounts for the first time. The allocation was repeated in each of the following two years but then ceased for several years. In 1966 nearly £20,000 was set aside for computers, and during each of the next four years expenditure averaged over £46,000. Then came another pause, but during the 1970s computer expenditure grew rapidly from £190,000 in 1972 to £1.2 million in 1981. Ten years later the figure was £3.7 million. Centralised and distributed computer facilities had become as necessary to the academic life of the University as the Library. In 1991 expenditure on computing services for the first time exceeded spending on the library. At the end of the century the Library and the Computer Centre were merged into a single body under the title of 'information services'.

Another expanding category of expenditure was on 'student support'. This included money spent to assist students with their social, sporting and academic lives, as well as transfers to the Students' Union (part of the student fees paid by local authorities was for the support of student unions). More costly still for the University, was the growing expense of maintaining halls of residences, catering services (they were meant to be self-financing), and paying for the University Health Service. In the late 1940s student support averaged around £6.5 a year per head. In the 1990s the comparable figure was £310, say roughly £65 in 1940s prices.

What had students gained from this ten-fold increase in real spending? In the 1940s their union building was a cramped structure at the lower end of University Square. From the mid-1960s students had spacious premises in University Road (they became less spacious as numbers increased). The successors of the students of the 1940s and 1950s had the option of living in halls of residence or self-catering Queen's houses. Their predecessors had the choice of home or lodgings except for the fortunate few who found places at Riddel Hall, Aquinas Hall, or Queen's Chambers. There were spacious playing fields at Upper Malone in place of the muddy pitches at Cherryvale, and a physical education centre in the Botanic Gardens. There were counselling services, a health service, and a careers' advisory service.

It is difficult to know whether the undergraduates of the 1990s felt themselves better provided for than their parents and grandparents. A university of 18,000 students was a less friendly place than one of 2000, and it was easy to become lonely in a crowd. Students in the 1990s were treated as adults and their expectations were shaped by the attitudes of society at large. They would not have tolerated the conditions of those eighteen-year-olds whose childhoods had been spent in years of wartime austerity, or whose adolescent lives during the 1950s and 1960s were bounded by formal parental control.

Queen's spent heavily on maintaining its premises. Expenditure averaged about 15 per cent of the total, but it varied a good deal from year to year. Building expenses were normally spread over several years and were met by special allocations tucked away in the reserves. Regular costs included routine maintenance, cleaning, heat, light and fuel expenses, minor works, telephones, and portering. There was a big jump in spending in the 1970s, caused by rapidly rising prices and the costs of repairing premises that were showing their age. These included venerable structures such as the Lanyon Building that had defied the Belfast climate for generations, as well as 1960s buildings wilting after scarcely a decade in the wet. The Troubles impinged, too, and for many years during the 1970s and 1980s there were high security charges to be met.

The final column of table 4.2 includes expenditure on a range of miscellaneous item. 'Restructuring' referred not to buildings but principally to staff costs including during the 1980s and 1990s the costs of premature retirement schemes introduced by the University to reduce the salary bill. The costs of implementing legislation relating to employment and safety in the work place also became a drag on the budget.

CONCLUSION

The financial history of the second half of the twentieth century mirrored the expansion of higher education and changes in attitudes towards universities and their funding. The huge increase in the amount of public money that poured into university education during the 1960s and 1970s did so as the result of recommendations contained in the reports of the Robbins and Lockwood committees. The government accepted that higher education enhanced the wealth of the nation. But its attitude became more questioning as the costs of maintaining universities and their students increased. It was not so much that the benefits of a university education were being queried – although there were doubts on that score – but whether they could be achieved more cheaply. Perhaps more important, since the immediate beneficiaries were the students themselves, the question emerged whether they should not bear some of the costs.

How Queen's was financed was not a question that greatly interested academics as long as their salaries rose in line with the earnings of comparable professions and their research and teaching were adequately funded. Neither of these conditions was met in the late twentieth century. There was a golden period in the 1960s when the concern of heads of departments was how to spend money rather than how to make economies, but for the final thirty years of the twentieth century the problem was the other way round. Money, how to get it rather than how to spend it was a problem that would not go away.

5

Managerial and bureaucratic devices

When in 1949 Sir Eric Ashby was wondering whether to come to Queen's as its Vice-Chancellor he was advised by the outgoing incumbent, Sir David Keir, to preside over the University as he would an Oxford college and 'abstain from managerial or bureaucratic devices'.[1] The professors and lecturers were fiercely jealous of their independence and they were few enough in number to decide matters among themselves. There was a Secretary and a Bursar and one or two senior administrators to attend to necessary housekeeping but the academics ran the University. The Senate was responsible for the general management of the University but it did not interfere in academic matters

Even before Sir David Keir offered his advice, the separation of administration from matters academic was difficult to sustain. In 1946 he told the Senate:

> Up to the present the administrative system of the University has not expanded *pari passu* with the expansion of its academic work. New buildings, an increased academic staff, a very large rise in the number of students enrolled, additional courses of study, and similar fresh responsibilities have of themselves imposed multifarious new duties on our administrative offices. Apart, however, from the multiplication of purely internal functions the University, like other bodies, has come to be involved in external relations as were quite unknown or at the most quite rudimentary a score of years ago. Negotiations and correspondence with public authorities both in the Province and elsewhere, the maintenance of necessary contact with other seats of learning at home and abroad and with professional organisations of many kinds have become a day to day part of our administrative work.[2]

The twin pressures of a growing University and proliferating external pressures reached unimagined heights by the end of the century. It was now impossible for academics to run the University with the support of just a handful of administrators. Managerial and bureaucratic devices could not be avoided. With the passing of the years these devices had not been embraced with fervour, but they had become unloved features of university life.

1 Taped interview with Mr Alf McCreary, 1990. 2 *Vice-Chancellor's report, 1945–46*, 161.

FOUNDATIONS: CHARTERS, STATUTES, STRUCTURES,
MEMBERS, AND OFFICERS

The charter and statutes of 1849 established the academic and administrative framework of the University. They also defined the roles of the principal officers (the President, Vice President, the Registrar, the Bursar, the Librarian). Teaching was arranged in three faculties: Arts (with two divisions, literary and scientific) Medicine, and Law.[3] In 1908 the newly independent Queen's University was granted a charter modelled on that of 1849. The members of the University were now the Chancellor, the Pro-Chancellors, the President and Vice-Chancellor, the members of the Senate, the Academic Council, the General Board of Studies, the lecturers, members of Convocation, and the matriculated students. There were minor amendments during the years that followed and major changes in 1982. Thereafter there was a continual process of adjustment, made possible by more flexible wording in the 1982 statutes.

According to the statutes, the Chancellor of the University is the 'head and chief officer' of the University elected by Convocation. In practice he is a figurehead who sometimes presides at graduations and occasionally chairs the Senate. But he or she has other roles to play, fund raising, for example, or exerting influence in the mysterious corridors of power. Sir Eric Ashby (a former Vice-Chancellor) became a member of the House of Lords. Members of the royal family, ceremonial figures *par excellence*, are in demand in Britain, but are too contentious for Northern Ireland, as are retired politicians. Queen's has traditionally looked for people who have an Ulster connection. The Earl of Shaftesbury, Lord Londonderry and Field Marshal Alanbrooke were scions of Ulster families. Sir Tyrone Guthrie's Ulster roots were geographical (County Monaghan) and he had a talent for upsetting the *status quo*. Not only did he become the Chancellor as a result of the first (and only) contested election in the history of the University, in 1964 he made a speech in Belfast City Hall, then a bastion of unionism, declaring the border to be 'wildly artificial and detrimental to the interests of this country as a whole.' The following weeks were filled with the sounds of the University distancing itself from its head and chief officer.[4] Given his background, one might have thought that theatre studies would have developed during his reign, but it was not to be. More recently Queen's has turned to academics (the election of Professor F.S.L. Lyons as Chancellor was cruelly frustrated by his premature death), to businessmen (Sir Rowland

3 For details see Moody and Beckett, *Queen's Belfast, 1845–1949*, ii, 734–46. 4 *Belfast Telegraph*, 10 October 1964. A 'senior member' of the University commented, 'I assume that the Chancellor must have been speaking on his personal behalf', and indeed a statement to that effect was later issued. According to the widow of a professor at the time, Sir Tyrone Guthrie had been irritated by being delayed at the border by the B Specials while driving from County Monaghan for the event and was merely expressing a view on traffic delays, not on politics.

Wright, Sir David Orr), and to international figures (Senator George Mitchell) to serve as the ceremonial face of the University.

The effective head of Queen's is the President and Vice-Chancellor, described in the 1908 charter as 'the principal academic officer' responsible for the academic management of the University. The Senate appoints the Vice-Chancellor and he presides over Senate in the absence of the Chancellor or Pro-Chancellors. He also chairs meetings of the Academic Council. In 1950 a retired professor greeted the newly arrived Sir Eric Ashby by telling him that his office was as superfluous as the fifth wheel on a carriage, but he was welcome nevertheless. The sentiment has been repeated – less elegantly – many times since. But Vice-Chancellors, together with their senior colleagues, set the academic course of the University. He or she is constrained by the strength of the balance sheet and the objectives of government policy, but within those parameters Vice-Chancellors have a central role to play in the performance of the University. It is a nice question, to take just one example, whether Queen's would have been so unenthusiastic about expansion at the time of the Lockwood report, had the then Vice-Chancellor been determined that the University should grow.

The Vice-Chancellor is responsible to the Senate for the performance of the University. The members of the Senate in 1908 were the principal officers of the University, the Secretary of the Academic Council, and the President of the Students' Representative Council, if a graduate, four nominees of the crown, 'of whom one at least shall be a woman', and eight elected members of Convocation, together with elected representatives of the professoriate, the local authorities, the Belfast Chamber of Commerce and the Royal Victoria Hospital, plus up to four co-opted members.[5] There was thus a mix of University and community interests, reflecting the intention of its founders that Queen's should be a university for the region.

The 'internal academic affairs of the university' is the responsibility of the Academic Council. In 1908 it was composed of the Vice-Chancellor, the professors, and a small number of co-opted lecturers. There were four faculties (Arts, Science, Law, and Medicine), to which were added Commerce in 1910, Applied Science and Technology (1921), Agriculture (1924), and Theology (1926). The Secretary of the Academic Council until 1966 was a professor and a powerful person in the affairs of Queen's.

Another body dating from 1908 was the General Board of Studies consisting of all the lecturers of the University. All changes in regulations affecting academic matters were referred to the Board for comment and potentially it possessed considerable power. But over the years attendance at the Board dwindled and by the 1980s it had become a poorly attended chamber for debating general issues. Occasionally more active was Convocation, a body composed of graduates, together with the professors, the lecturers, and members of the

5 Moody and Beckett, *Queen's Belfast*, ii, 820.

Senate. Its three functions were to elect a Chancellor, to elect representatives to Senate, and to comment on any business relating to the University. Convocation was deeply attached to its Senate membership and it fought hard during the 1980s and 1990s to prevent it being reduced. Convocation usually slumbered peacefully, but it could be stirred from its sleep, most notably during the National Anthem debate in 1995

THE 1982 CHARTER AND STATUTES

The 1908 statutes survived with minor amendments until 1982; they were then substantially revised. The Vice-Chancellor, Sir Peter Froggatt, told Senate that they 'will raise their hats to those who framed our foundation Charter which has proved, over seventy years, to be robust and as suited to today's as it was to yesterday's circumstances.'[6] In fact, Queen's had been bursting out of her Edwardian corset for many years and the statutes had long been in need of restyling.

The first steps were taken, unintentionally perhaps, in 1964 when some members of Senate complained that agenda and committee papers were arriving later than the statutes specified and their consideration was therefore technically illegal.[7] The University responded by appointing a committee, which moved at a measured pace, until more than a decade later, when no original members were still serving and several were dead, it produced a report proposing changes far exceeding the procedural. The University petitioned the Privy Council for a new charter and statutes. Their drafting took another five years but they finally arrived in 1982. Then came the task of translating statutes into detailed regulations. Two decades to produce a new academic framework was a long time, even by University standards.

The general thrust of the revised arrangements was to create a more flexible administration that could be adapted to changing circumstances within Queen's, and respond quickly to developments outside. The Senate now included representatives of the education and library boards, but industry and commerce no longer had a direct voice in the government of Queen's. The largest single group remained Convocation with ten members (two more than earlier) who ensured that the opinion of middle-class Ulster was loudly heard. Their presence added to the sense that Queen's was a pillar of the Province. The academic representation on Senate continued; and membership was extended to the non-academic staff. A consequence of the new statutes was to increase the size of the Senate to over fifty and to skew the composition towards the public sector.

The Academic Council was also enlarged. The Council had been established when professorial authority was strong, but since the 1940s the ratio of non-

6 *Vice-Chancellor's report, 1980–1*, 5.   7 *Senate minutes, 1964*, 3, 60, 121–2.

professorial staff to the professoriate had grown greatly. After 1986 professors were no longer members of the Council by virtue of their status, although many remained members because they were deans or heads of departments. The number of elected non-professorial representatives was increased. Five students were nominated annually by the Students' Union; they had agitated for membership for many years and at last they achieved more or less what they wanted. The changes resulted in an unwieldy body with a membership close to 200; if everybody turned up there were not enough chairs for all of them to sit down. The Academic Council continued to have its own Secretary, and since 1966 the post had been full-time. The Secretary of the Academic Council was, in effect, the deputy Vice-Chancellor. The non-academic business of the University was in the hands of an Administrative Secretary and the Bursar.

An important change in the working of the Academic Council had already occurred in 1972 with the creation of an Academic Board consisting of representatives of the Academic Council and the Students' Union in approximately equal numbers. The intention was to give students a greater voice in the affairs of the University. The Academic Council delegated to the Board matters concerning discipline, degree regulations, prizes and scholarships, and staff-student relationships at the departmental level. The Board had the power to make recommendations to the Academic Council, but not to set policy. In many ways the Academic Board took over the functions of the General Board of Studies.

The statutes relating to faculties and departments were amended to make it easier for the University to institute changes to academic units. Deans remained, as they always had been, the chairs of faculties elected annually from among the professors, readers, and senior lecturers of the faculty. The formal existence of departments was acknowledged for the first time. They had not been referred to in the 1908 statutes and in the early 1930s the Vice-Chancellor had strongly opposed 'departmentalism' because it was contrary to his concept of a university.[8] But departments had come into being *de facto*. When in 1958 the University created a chair of political science in place of a lectureship, the Faculty of Economics sought an assurance from the Academic Council that the subject should continue as a department of the faculty (there had been a suggestion it might go to arts). The Academic Council replied, 'the subject of political science should continue to form a department in the Faculty of Economics, though it is not sure if the word 'department' has any statutory meaning'. Under the new statutes heads of departments, unlike deans, were appointed by the Boards of Curators, thus leading to an anomaly of a departmental head who was part of the management structure, and deans who were more akin to shop stewards.[9] Deans had no authority, other than that of persuasion, over the heads of department, whose responsibility was to the Vice-Chancellor.[10]

8 Moody and Beckett, *Queen's Belfast*, ii, 502–5. 9 *Academic Council minutes, 1958–9*, 19.
10 The uncertain power of deans was illustrated in 1954 when a lecturer, who was also a head

The new statutes defined the Vice-Chancellor as the chief academic and administrative officer (previously he had been the principal academic officer). The office of Pro-Vice-Chancellors was recognized for the first time. Before 1966 a Pro-Vice-Chancellor had been appointed only to cover the period between the departure of one Vice-Chancellor and the arrival of the next. Dr Grant had created vice presidents to help him in the running of the university. Sir Arthur Vick then appointed two Pro-Vice-Chancellors for periods of four years. The new statutes allowed for three Pro-Vice-Chancellors chosen from among the professors by the Senate on the recommendation of the Vice-Chancellor. For many years the Vice-Chancellor chose his own Pro-Vice-Chancellors, but in 1998 the new Vice-Chancellor introduced a system of application and interview. Until the 1990s Pro-Vice-Chancellors combined their managerial duties with their departmental activities (teaching and research). But as Queen's became larger, Pro-Vice-Chancellors became practically full-time managers with specific responsibilities. In the eyes of many academics this was not a change for the better since, so it was claimed, Pro-Vice-Chancellors lost touch with the day-to-day practicalities of dealing with students.

The 1982 statutes allowed for the existence of an Academic Assessor, a Registrar, a Bursar, a Librarian, a Secretary to the Academic Council, an Administrative Secretary, 'and such other holders of posts as the Senate may from time to time determine'. The Academic Assessor was a retired professor whose task was to sit on the Boards of Curators to ensure comparability of standards in academic appointments across the disciplines. The functions of the other posts are clear from their titles. The crucial post, in view of what happened later, was that of the Registrar. Queen's had never had a full-time Registrar. When the post had been filled it was held by a professor on a part-time basis. For many years it was not filled at all. The Secretary of the Academic Council carried out many of the duties that in an English university were the responsibility of a Registrar. After 1982 whether or not Queen's needed a Registrar became an issue that excited much debate since it touched on the raw nerve of what many academics considered to be their independence.

---

of department, was discovered 'conducting a sort of correspondence course' instead of coming to the University to give lectures. The dean informed the Vice-Chancellor that since he had 'no status in respect of the head of an independent department, I therefore leave this somewhat difficult baby in your lap.' The Vice-Chancellor bounced the baby back to the faculty to deal with, but eventually he wrote to the lecturer, telling him he needed faculty permission for his 'unusual but perhaps quite effective way of conducting university courses' (Uncatalogued letters, QUB archives, 1954). The baby was temporarily put to bed when the Academic Council agreed that lectures in the subject be held at the lecturer's house in Orlock, County Down on Saturday afternoons, the students not objecting. The final solution was that the lecturer resigned.

A REGISTRAR: TO HAVE OR NOT TO HAVE?

Since 1908 the day-to-day running of the University had resided with the Vice-Chancellor and the Secretary of the Academic Council, plus the professors collectively in Academic Council. These arrangements had certain advantages, although speed was not one of them. Professor Waterhouse, Professor of German between 1932 and 1953 later recalled the process of making even minor changes in regulations or course structures:

> In Queen's ... administration observed the leisurely decencies of democ-racy. The Head of the Department addressed himself to the Faculty, the Faculty addressed itself to the Academic Council and the General Board of Studies, and these in turn addressed themselves to the University Senate, which in the fullness of time, say six months, instructed the University secretary to inform the Head of Department of the result of his application. It took a little time for the newcomer to learn the drill, but, like Leacock's rule for growing asparagus, the drill worked. To obtain a crop next year all one had to do was to go out into the garden last year but one and trench the ground thoroughly to a depth of three feet. This is the essence of all 'planning'.[11]

It was becoming plain that the asparagus mode of management was no longer adequate. Sir Peter Froggatt set out the problems in a paper before the Academic Council in December 1983.[12] Because of the increasing demands placed on the University by external bodies such as the UGC, and the additional administration caused by competition from the University of Ulster, it was nec-essary to reduce the cycle of business meeting, so cutting down the burden of committee work. This would result in decisions being taken by the Vice-Chancellor and his senior colleagues, thus undermining the authority of the Academic Council. There was a related problem caused by the breakdown of the quinquennial system. Long-term planning had become nearly impossible and the finance committee had been pushed into a quasi-planning role as it allocated grants year-by-year. In 1980 the University had formed a scrutiny committee (also known as a moratorium committee) to decide whether vacant posts could be filled and this too was taking over the functions of planning. The Vice-Chancellor suggested the establishment of a policy planning committee to establish the 'right' relationship between policy and funding. The committee would form the 'hub' of a ring of sub-committees. It would also be the first step in the reorganization of whole committee structure; otherwise the changes

11 *Belfast News Letter: Queen's University Jubilee Supplement*, April 9 1959. Stephen Leacock was a well-known Canadian economist and humorist. 12 *Academic Council minutes, 1983–4*, 65–74.

would be self-defeating. He hoped the Academic Council would accept his suggestions, but he 'expressed his disappointment at Council's seeming lack of
adventure and reluctance to experiment' whenever changes in the system of
University management were suggested.[13]

A second and crucial step in the reorganization of the management was to
establish the post of a full-time Registrar to co-ordinate the administration.
Prompted by the Vice-Chancellor, the Senate set up a working party in April
1984 'to examine the senior administrative structure and posts of the
University'. The time was propitious since several senior administrators were
about to retire and the Vice-Chancellor himself intended to follow them within
two years. He explained the need for a Registrar:

> In Northern Ireland Queen's has had to face the same challenges [as faced
> universities elsewhere] and in addition cope with the implications of the
> Chilver Report, the emergence of the new University to be established by
> the merger of the New University of Ulster and the Ulster Polytechnic,
> the N.I. Working Party recently set up by the UGC. etc.–all against
> the background of an unstable political situation and in the shadow of
> terrorism.[14]

The working party quickly concluded Queen's needed a unified system of
administration from October 1984, 'and that the head of this system should
have the designation of Registrar.' This would bring Queen's in line with most
British universities. The working party suggested there should be three administrative divisions, headed respectively by the Secretary to the Academic
Council, the Administrative Secretary, and the Bursar, all reporting to the
Registrar. It also recommended the creation of other posts, notably a personnel
officer, and administrators responsible for data processing, and public relations.

The Senate readily accepted the proposals but the Academic Council was
deeply suspicious. Its Secretary would become subordinate to the Registrar and
academics would become burdened by those managerial and bureaucratic
devices that Sir Eric Ashby had been warned against. Professor Kirk, a Pro-
Vice-Chancellor and a member of the working party, did his best to assure the
Council this would not happen. He was eloquent, but unconvincing. A motion
in Academic Council urging the Senate to think again was rejected only after a
long debate and by a very narrow margin (twenty-three votes for and twenty-
five against, with five abstentions).[15] The Academic Council found it hard to
accept that the University needed a more efficient administrative structure. But
the case for a Registrar was irrefutable, or so it seemed at the time.

13 *Academic Council minutes, 1983–4*, 61.   14 *Senate minutes, 1984*, 250–1.   15 *Senate minutes, 1984*, 250–1; *Academic Council minutes, 1984*, 305–9. An attendance of 53 at a Council
meeting held in late June when many members were examining in the University and elsewhere indicates a high level of interest.

The University spent a good deal of 1984 and early 1985 searching for a suitable candidate. The post proved difficult to fill for these were not auspicious years in which to attract people to Northern Ireland. Eventually, in July 1985, Mr Fred Smyth, a Queen's law graduate, currently deputy registrar at Stirling University, was appointed and by October he was in post.[16] In June of the following year he became ill and was absent for three months. He returned to work in September, but was ill again in May 1987 and resigned in September (he died in December that year). The Secretary of the Academic Council, the Administrative Secretary, and the Bursar then shared the duties of the Registrar. The experiment with a full-time Registrar had lasted for less than two years and it was not continued. In October the new Vice-Chancellor, Sir Gordon Beveridge, told the Senate he had considered the future of the post.

> Additionally, he had had informal advice from a leading Registrar from Great Britain. Arising from these deliberations, it was his view that the office of Registrar should be left vacant for the time being. During the present period of rapid change and at a time when the University's structure, including its committee structure, was being changed radically, it would be unfair to involve a newcomer in such a degree of complexity. Accordingly, he proposed to continue to call upon the Registrar's group of senior officers, i.e. the Secretary to the Academic Council, the Bursar and the Administrative Secretary, for assistance in running the University, as he had done for the greater part of the past year.[17]

Fourteen months later, the Vice-Chancellor announced that the Registrar's Group was working well and would be formalized as the Administrative Management Group. There was no need for a Registrar. One member of Senate asked about the additional burden of work falling on the senior officers. The Vice-Chancellor assured him that 'the three officers would be responsible corporately, for the conduct and supervision of the administration of the University'. Nobody inquired how this would work in practice and the Senate accepted the assurance almost without demure, being reluctant to go against the wishes of the Vice-Chancellor.[18] The Academic Council was more than happy to agree with the Vice-Chancellor because it had never really wanted a Registrar in the first place.

How was it that in the space of less than three years Queen's had changed its mind? There had been no easing of the bureaucratic deluge pouring down on the Vice-Chancellor. On the contrary it had intensified and one might have thought that he would have welcomed an umbrella. But there was a new Vice-Chancellor

---

16 *Senate minutes, 1984*, 306, 324–6, 369, 374; *Senate minutes, 1985*, 249, 251 and 329.
17 *Senate minutes, 1986*, 131 and 288; *Senate minutes, 1987*, 601, 659 and 768–9.   18 *Senate minutes, 1988*, 491–2.

who declared his management style to be 'hands on'. He wished to be directly involved in administration as well as in management and setting policy.[19]

In the years that followed there was a widespread feeling within Queen's that the ship was drifting. It was difficult to identify any policy other than that of reducing costs.[20] It is a moot point whether the drift resulted from the lack of a compass or whether the seas were so stormy that no pilot could have steered a clear course. The Vice-Chancellor and his team struggled valiantly to avoid one financial rock after another. They succeeded in keeping the vessel afloat but only at the price of turning some of the crew into the lifeboat of premature retirement. Most academic subjects survived, but resources were stretched thinly and staff morale became seriously jaded. In the interests of the health of the University it might have been better had weak academic areas been abandoned. The Academic Council would have been extremely hostile since it had a sentimental attachment to all that had gone before.

The need for a Registrar was raised again from an unexpected direction. In 1992, following an unfortunate case before the Fair Employment Tribunal the University commissioned outside experts to examine its employment practices. Among the points raised in their report was whether the University required a Registrar. The report conceded that the post was not directly relevant to the question of whether employment practices were fair or unfair. But it suggested that the absence of a Registrar meant that there was nobody with specific responsibility for fair employment issues. Queen's should look at the matter again.[21]

The Senate found time in 1993 to debate the *pros* and *cons* of re-establishing the Registrar's post. The advantages were identified as a unified administrative system that 'would lead to more effective use of resources' and provide better support for the Vice-Chancellor, who could then concentrate on strategic issues. A Registrar would bring 'new blood' into the management team and he or she could be given the specific responsibility for equality of opportunity issues. On the other side of the argument, it was claimed that a Registrar would simply add another layer of administration and the University would lose the collective wisdom of the academic management group. An old spectre was raised. The Academic Council feared the post would undermine its authority and 'inhibit the increasing integration between academic and non-academic areas'. With some misgivings, the Senate continued to accept the Vice-Chancellor's preference for a 'hands on' style of management and the University continued to manage (or rather not to manage) without a Registrar.[22]

19 The phrase is quoted in Employment Equality Services, 'Review of the structure, procedure and practices of the Queen's University of Belfast as they relate to the provision for and application of equality of opportunity and fair participation in employment' (The Queen's University, Belfast, 1993), para. 2.39. The Vice-Chancellor used the phrase on many occasions in the University.   20 A good deal of this section draws on the author's memory of events.   21 See chapter ten for a discussion of the fair employment issues.   22 *Senate minutes, 1993,* 152–6 and 168–9.

CREATING A CAMEL

Whether or not to have a Registrar was not the only issue Queen's had on its managerial mind. In April 1984 the Committee of Vice-Chancellors and Principals (the CVCP) set up a committee to inquire into the efficiency of universities. The chairman was Sir Alex Jarratt, a businessman and Chancellor of the University of Birmingham. The committee commissioned studies into the management of six universities representing a range of institutions with different origins and histories and it took into account the objectives of universities. It examined the prospects for universities from '1981 and beyond'.[23]

The committee's report focused on the separation that existed in most universities between the lay bodies of universities responsible for financial and employment matters and the bodies in control of academic affairs (the Senate and the Academic Council in the case of Queen's). It doubted whether this was a sensible division of powers when the government was determined to see that it was getting value for the money it gave to universities. The committee produced five sets of recommendations. The first directed the government to set out broad financial guidelines in place of the former system of quinquennial planning. Secondly, the UGC was told to consult with Vice-Chancellors (was this not happening already?) and to encourage collaboration between universities. For Northern Ireland this meant Queen's getting together with the University of Ulster, which was not an easy task considering the suspicion Queen's had harboured of the upstart since the Chilver report. The Jarratt committee also instructed the CVCP to encourage universities to adopt best practices in management and to extend its role in the training of Vice-Chancellors and other senior officers. The UGC and CVCP were advised to strengthen the relationships between their secretariats.

Of immediate relevance to universities, the committee urged them to ensure that their lay and academic bodies asserted 'their responsibilities in governing their institutions notably in respect of strategic plans to underpin academic decisions and structures which bring planning, resource allocation and accountability together into one corporate process linking, academic, financial and physical aspects.' Vice-Chancellors should be clearly identified as the chief executive of their universities; they might even be re-designated as chief executives. There should be clear budgetary delegation to faculties and departments, consistent performance indicators, fewer committees, and more delegation of responsibility.[24] Put simply, universities should have clearly defined management structures.

Queen's established a working group of its own to consider the implications of the Jarratt report. The Senate had only recently accepted a new set of

23 CVCP, *Report of the steering committee for efficiency studies in universities* [*the Jarratt report*] (London, 1985), para. 2.2. 24 *Jarratt report*, chapter 5.

statutes and the prospect of having to start all over again was not appealing. When the working group presented its report to Senate in June 1986 it was divided into three parts. The first outlined the management structure of Queen's up to the present; the second proposed necessary short-term changes; and the third outlined medium and long-term re-organization the group thought necessary. The working group claimed that Queen's had anticipated the Jarratt committee in several respects. For example, a policy planning committee had been established in 1981 as a joint committee of the Senate and Academic Council. Queen's had set up a management information system, and there was a new administrative structure headed by a Registrar. A development appeal had been started in 1981 to augment government money, with a target of £1.5 million. There was a new information office and the University's public image was improving as a result. Some of these claims were rosy-eyed. The development appeal did not quite reach its target, the public image of Queen's became dented over the years, and a management triumvirate had replaced the Registrar.

When the working group turned its attention to short-term changes, it concluded, surprisingly, that the influence of the Senate in University affairs had not diminished over the years; it thought, nevertheless, there should be a 'streamlining' of business. It saw no virtue in changing the title of the Vice-Chancellor to that of chief executive. Neither did it favour full-time Pro-Vice-Chancellors, although it recognized they might become necessary in the future. The group could not make up its mind what to do about deans. For the moment it recommended they should continue to be elected by their faculties, but if they were to become part of a management structure they would have to be appointed by the University. The working group was also undecided about the role of heads of departments, but it thought their appointments should be limited to three to five years at a time.

The working group had hit a problem that frustrated every attempt to streamline the management of the University. The Academic Council did not want academic affairs to fall into the hands of managers and it regarded deans as academics, not managers. The Academic Council told the working group:

> With regard to Deans, careful thought should be given to the duality of their role where, in consort, they were expected to act in an overall University capacity whilst at the same time being structurally responsible and accountable to those who elected them. Thus there was a conflict where central policies may be at odds with the ambitions of individual faculties. It was important that the traditional authority and positions of Deans should not be eroded. Heads of Departments on the other hand were contractual appointments and responsible to Senate through the Vice-Chancellor.[25]

25 *Academic Council minutes, 1985–6*, 235.

The working group was critical of the University's procedures for long-term planning. Most planning decisions assumed the University would be expanding, whereas the reality for the future was that income was contracting in real terms. Queen's allocated resources according to what had happened in the past rather than what was needed for the future. Although there was a policy planning committee, there was no corporate plan charting the future.

A brief paragraph in the report proposed that staff performance should be appraised periodically. The working group agreed with the Jarratt Committee that there had been a 'somewhat intermittent approach' to the training of university lecturers. The prospect of appraisal caused loud squawking in the nest, but it became a fact of academic life. The working group also suggested there should be management training for senior academics, (Pro-Vice-Chancellors, deans, and departmental heads), as well as for administrators.

When it turned to long-term changes needed to the management system, the working group identified the revision of the committee structure of the University as the Holy Grail. A reduction in the number of committees had been an ambition of every Vice-Chancellor since 1950. It never happened. Committees were like dragons' teeth: cut one down and a dozen sprouted in their place. When Sir George Bain assumed office in 1998 he could hardly get through the door for committees.

The working group's report was sent to the faculties and the Academic Council for comment. It came back to the Senate in May 1987. The position of deans and heads of departments remained unchanged for the moment. The group now proposed a four-tier committee structure. At the top were the Senate and the Academic Council. The second tier had the Policy Planning Committee sitting spider-like in the centre of a web, the threads of which ran upwards to the Academic Council and the Senate, horizontally to the Finance Committee and the Committee of Deans, and downwards to five committees responsible for the estate, staffing, external relations, computing and information technology, and the Library. These five made up the third tier. In the basement of this committee world was a tangle of petty committees and sub-committees, each with specific responsibilities.[26]

Before the year was up, Queen's created a new Jarrett working group. The old one was disbanded because it was thought to be no longer appropriate to deal with outstanding business, which was mainly of an academic nature. The priorities of the new group were to review the committee structure of the University yet again and to consider further the place of deans and heads of departments in the managerial structure of the University. The new group contained more academic representatives than had its predecessor.[27]

In June 1988 the new working group presented fresh proposals to the Senate; they had previously done the faculty rounds and been debated by the Academic

26 *Senate minutes, 1987,* 624–7. 27 *Senate minutes, 1987,* appendix G.

Council. The proposals addressed the issues of faculties, schools, departments, and the position of deans. There was general support for a rationalization of departments. The traditional structure was made up of a large number of small departments headed by a professor and grouped into nine faculties. The faculty members elected their dean who was therefore 'their' man – or occasionally their woman. The working group concluded that many small departments responsible to the Vice-Chancellor was an inefficient way of conducting business and recommended their consolidation into larger groupings to be known as schools. This would, so it was believed, lead to a more rational use of teaching and research resources, protect small subjects, and reduce overhead costs. One or two schools had been formed during the early 1980s but these had been 'informal and haphazard'. The working group suggested that schools should become the basic units for the allocation of resources. They should be managed by a director appointed by the Board of Curators for a period of five years. The schools should be further divided into departments (or divisions) with heads appointed by the curators for a fixed term of three years. Finally, there should be a school board, advisory to the director.

The logical implication of this plan was to treat schools as big departments (with subdivisions) and group them into faculties headed by an appointed dean responsible to the Vice-Chancellor. This was, indeed, one proposal from the working group, with the added suggestion that the number of faculties be reduced to five or six. But the working group also made an alternative proposal. This was to retain the existing departments and the nine faculties, which would now contain both schools *and* departments; the deans would continue to be elected by their fellows. In this model the director of the schools would have a direct line of communication to the Vice-Chancellor, but not the deans. The latter would be members of various planning bodies, but would lack managerial authority.

The result was a muddle, the product of a struggle between traditionalists and reformers. The former were wedded to the historic nine faculties with their elected deans. Many academics believed that small was beautiful and so regarded small departments as a good thing and large schools as a bad thing. The traditional nine faculties (they were, in fact, not quite so traditional as some of their defenders believed) had some functional justification. The Faculty of Theology was composed mainly of recognised teachers working in the denominational colleges. The Northern Ireland Department of Agriculture financed the Faculty of Agriculture. Much of the work of the Faculty of Education was conducted in Stranmillis and St Mary's colleges. The defenders of the *status quo* pointed out, with some justification, that schools were an additional layer of administration, intermediate between departments and faculties. The reformers, on the other hand, argued that a managerial chain of command was necessary and elected deans did not make sense in such a structure.

The new Jarrett working group endorsed the proposals of it predecessor that retained the Policy and Planning Committee as the hub of the University's planning processes. It suggested renaming the committee the Planning and Resources Committee (the PRC), a change meant to emphasise its role matching financial resources to academic developments. The Committee of Deans should also be renamed (it might become the academic affairs committee) and a new committee should be set up to look after external affairs. There should also be a new body integrating the work of the Library and information technology.

The group's work was not yet completed. In October 1988 it presented yet another report, which was intended to be the University's final word, or rather many words, on new management structures.[28] It boasted that ten schools were already up and running, and 'around' twenty-five were promised in the near future. The report contained a mass of detail on budgetary delegation, accountability, purchasing, space management, and space charging.[29] It turned out, though, to be not the last word. There was unfinished business, the most important of which was the future of faculties and the role of deans. At the same time changes to the Senate and Academic Council remained to be decided.

Like an old soldier refusing to die, the proposals to implement the Jarratt reforms returned to haunt the Senate in April 1989. Now it was faced with proposals to reduce its own size and that of the Academic Council, but there was nothing fresh about faculties and deans.[30] An anguished debate was taking place behind the scenes. More than three years later, in May 1992, the Senate was told that 'a number of consultative meetings' with directors and the Committee of Deans had 'considered the matter on a number of occasions'. This was committee-speak for 'we can't make up our minds'. The Senate was assured that there was 'general acceptance' that more than twenty directors of schools reporting directly to the Vice-Chancellor was not practical. The solution might be 'an additional tier' of managers between the directors and the Vice-Chancellor.[31] The Senate was promised more definite news later. It had to wait another year for the glad tidings.

This is not to say that nothing was happening. The Vice-Chancellor nominated five of the nine deans to be 'selected deans' (a phrase quickly translated into 'super deans') to head the new faculties. He explained his motives to the deans early in 1993. 'My major concern now is to involve the academic side of the University to the fullest possible extent in determining University policy and participating in the decision-making processes.' He needed a simple system of line management via deans and directors. He recognized faculties were the structures through which academics were able to share in the running of the University, but nine faculties and nine deans were too many. Hence his arrangement whereby five of the nine became line managers. At the same time he wished that deans and directors should keep up with their academic work.[32]

---

28 *Senate minutes, 1988,* 444–53.   29 These were schemes for charging departments at least notional rents for their premises.   30 *Senate minutes, 1989,* 156–61.   31 *Senate minutes, 1992,* 198.   32 *Academic Council minutes, 1993,* appendix A, after p. 144.

The deans of Law, Agriculture, Education, and Theology, who did not become super-deans, resented their relegation to a lower division. Nobody was happy, not even the super deans. It was hardly surprising, therefore, that when new proposals for faculty re-structuring again came before the Senate in 1993, they did 'not fit the particular options originally suggested ... but rather represent a development arising from the discussions which have taken place and which are considered generally acceptable'.[33] The nine faculties remained in being but the five academic groupings created by the Vice-Chancellor were confirmed, although there were some changes in nomenclature. They were to be headed by a 'manager' called a provost who would be appointed by the Board of Curators. But there was no agreement on what the new structures should be called. The Senate was told that:

> The Committee of Deans considered whether the groupings should be given a particular name (e.g. 'College' was considered) but agreed this was undesirable and that the only designation needed was to specify that the constituent parts of the groups using a wording of the form 'Schools in the Faculty of ...'. The present Faculties will continue, with Deans elected in the same manner as at present. In particular, Faculties will still meet to consider academic matters and report to Academic Council.

The Senate could be forgiven for feeling confused. It was being asked to confirm the existence of five bodies lacking names responsible for financial and related matters, which would exist alongside (or on top of) the nine existing faculties (all with deans) to deal with academic affairs. Even at the level of names, the arrangements did not work. The word 'college' soon came to be used for the groupings in lieu of any thing else. The provosts were given not titles but were labelled, A, B, C, etc. like so many coat pegs. Provost A was in charge of [the college of] Arts and Theology, and the Institute of Irish studies. Provost B reigned over Education, Economics and Social Sciences, and Law, and the Institute of Professional Legal Studies, the Institute of European Studies, the Institute of Continuing Education, and the Institute of Computer Based Learning (it became known as the college of bits and pieces). Provost C had the easier task of managing Agriculture, Food Science and the Natural Sciences. Provost D looked after Engineering and the Northern Ireland Technology Centre. Provost E presided over the Faculty of Medicine and the Health and Health Care Unit. To simplify matters (or was it to confuse them?) a provost could be a dean but he or she could not be a director of a school (except in the case of medicine). It had taken several years and many committees to invent a camel. The Senate was now asked to let the beast loose 'as quickly as is practicable'. And so it was, and it humped its way around Queen's for the next five years.

33 *Senate minutes, 1993*, 301.

There was work still to be done. The statutes had to be modified to accommodate the roles of managerial provosts. In 1995 the Vice-Chancellor replaced his informal Vice-Chancellor's committee (consisting of the Vice-Chancellor, the Pro-Vice-Chancellors, the Secretary of the Academic Council and the Bursar) by an executive board with an enlarged membership including also the five provosts, the Administrative Secretary, the Director of Human Resources, and the Estates Officer. One member of the Academic Council was worried about its large size. The Vice-Chancellor explained, 'the committee was less an executive committee than a committee of executives.[34] It was also necessary to tidy up institutes and centres that had grown Topsy-like in recent years. One or two, such as the Institute of Irish Studies and the Institute of Professional Legal Studies had high profiles. But others were hardly known beyond (and occasionally by) their members. The Senate eventually decided that an institute was a body of scholars engaged in interdisciplinary studies that crossed faculty boundaries, and should possess the full panoply of a director, a board of management, and a budget. A centre was contained within a faculty (a kind of embryonic institute) sharing the budget of the school and with an appointed head.[35]

During the protracted discussions about faculties (or colleges) and deans (or provosts), changes to the Senate and Academic Council had been left on one side. The 1982 statutes had increased the size of both in a laudable attempt to broaden representation. But they had become too large to be effective. In October 1988 the new Jarratt working group announced that it intended shortly to pronounce on the size of both bodies.[36] True to its word, in April 1989 it suggested a halving in the size of the Academic Council. The cull was to be at the expense of heads of departments (replaced by directors of schools) and the professors. The Senate was similarly in line for slimming. Since 1982 Convocation had elected ten members, but the working group recommended that the number should be reduced to six. There should be fewer nominated persons, a reduction in staff representation, and the elimination of representatives of the Better Equipment Fund (a relic of the past). In the other direction, the working group proposed there should be 'up to five persons, drawn from professional, commercial and industrial circles, as may be co-opted by the Senate.' The object was to reduce the size of the Senate from 55 members to 46.[37] The Convocation would have none of it. It tried to get its numbers increased to eight. One member argued passionately that universities had been bastions of academic independence since the Middle Ages. By implication, the Queen's Convocation was a stalwart defender of Queen's independence. The Senate, like the Academic Council, was reluctant to recognize the need for change when its own membership was threatened; it was still awaiting its reformation a decade later.

34 *Academic Council minutes, 1995*, 300. 35 *Senate minutes, 1991*, 246–7 and 486–7.
36 *Senate minutes, 1988*, 446. 37 *Senate minutes, 1989*, Appendix I. For the Better Equipment Fund see Moody and Beckett, *Queen's Belfast*, i, 349–51.

Sensible persons outside the University, had they followed the tortured discussions in the Senate and Academic Council, might have wondered how a
group of intelligent people could have produced such a cumbersome structure.
The University was not unaware of the problem. In 1997 the Senate established
a strategic review group to recommend structures that would assist Queen's in
carrying out its teaching and research responsibilities effectively.[38] It quickly
concluded that the administration was 'over-complicated with confusion over
reporting arrangements and management attention focused very widely in a
number of areas.' The Senate commissioned a report for the incoming Vice-
Chancellor, written by the registrars of two English universities, Warwick and
Cambridge. 'The first thing that strikes any outsider to Queen's is the extreme
complexity of the academic chain of command. Bearing in mind the size of the
University we can say with some confidence that there is nothing quite like it
within the UK.'[39] The report continued:

> There are too many committees, too much paper and too frequent meet-
> ings. Business is passed from one committee to the next with virtually the
> same cast of committee members nodding it through, refining it or further
> slowing it down with little evidence that the various stages add anything to
> the quality of decision-making. Moreover, instead of committees consid-
> ering clear proposals brought forward for their comment and approval,
> they are for the most part presented with undigested problems which
> somehow they are expected to discuss and recommend solutions to. This
> represents a simple failure of management.[40]

There was more in similar vein. The Policy and Resources Committee had
become 'a rubber-stamping body', and over the years Queen's had added to the
layers of management (the report identified at least five), which was the opposite of what the Jarratt committee had recommended. The Senate still did not
see its role as being concerned with questions of finance and strategy, and the
Academic Council had become poorly attended, its members believing that its
business appeared to have been appropriated by other bodies.[41]
How did the University get itself into such a tangle? The unwillingness of
the Vice-Chancellor in 1986 to continue with a Registrar did not help. But the
academic staff must share the responsibility by resisting changes or pretending
they were not needed. The continuation of the faculties and their elected deans
alongside the colleges with their appointed provosts was a misguided attempt by
the University to appease everybody. Some of the fault lay with the Senate.

38 The Queen's University of Belfast, *Report of the Strategic Review Group* (Belfast, 1997),
69–70. The group was established at the instigation of Mr Noel Stewart, the honorary treasurer.   39 M. Shattock and D. Holmes, *The governance, management and administration of the
University* (January 1998), para. 4.1.   40 Shattock and Holmes, para. 3.1.   41 *Report of the
Strategic Review Group*, 69; Shattock and Holmes, paras 3.1, 3.2 and 4.1.

During the months that should have been devoted towards putting Queen's into good shape the Senate had other things on its mind. It spent many hours debating discrimination in employment, ceremonial at graduation, entertainment at garden parties and the display of Irish language signs in the Students' Union.[42] These were important matters given the turbulence of the times and they generated some fine impassioned speeches, but they deflected attention from other important issues. The honorary treasurer for much of the period (Sir Ewart Bell) complained repeatedly that his financial reports were squeezed between long debates on community issues and the desire of senators to get to lunch.

There was an additional explanation, an attitude of mind that has existed as long as universities have existed and which is one of their most endearing and infuriating features. It had been identified early in the century by F.J. Cornford and stated in the form of a question: 'has it occurred to you that nothing is ever done until everyone is convinced that it ought to be done, and has been convinced for so long that it is now time to do something else?'[43] Queen's adopted new arrangements reluctantly, bit by bit, whilst leaving in place the former structures. The Jarratt committee had been established to encourage universities to become more efficient. Queen's had tried to do so, but it had not succeeded. Sir Ewart Bell's successor as honorary treasurer (Mr Noel Stewart), an accountant appointed after a long career in business, remarked that if the University were a commercial enterprise it would soon go out of business. This did not happen, but it became encumbered by the lumber of an old bureaucratic structure that had long since ceased to function efficiently and burdened by a new one that hardly seemed to work at all.

CAGING THE CAMEL

The report commissioned for the new Vice-Chancellor was painfully frank. The academic work of the University had become 'subordinated to an over-dominant administrative and bureaucratic culture which is unresponsive to academic concerns'.

> The most important question that Queen's has to ask is whether its ambitions are entirely local and regional or whether it wishes to play in a larger league. There are many purely domestic and political reasons which help to explain why it no longer occupies the role it once had within UK higher education, but these are not the only reasons. The prospect which is now available is to combine a larger UK and international focus with an equally significant regional role, but if the University is to achieve this it must take

42 See chapter ten.   43 F.M. Cornford, *Microcosmographia, being a guide for the young academic politician* (Cambridge, 1908), 2.

the kind of modernising steps which other universities have done. It needs to be recognised that Queen's has fallen significantly behind many of its obvious comparator institutions in the UK and that even they are being overtaken in the UK and in Europe by universities which have more dynamism, strategies better adapted to new agendas, and more effective decision-making processes.

The report recommended 'the re-establishment of the post of Registrar ... who should be formally and legally the secretary of all University committees and responsible for the efficient conduct of their business'. Other recommendations included stripping out unnecessary structures and simplifying the chains of responsibility.[44] Matters moved quickly following the arrival of Sir George Bain at the beginning of 1998. He announced that he and the Pro-Vice-Chancellors needed to be free to concentrate on long-term strategic and policy issues. 'That is why I believe we need what a company would call a Chief Operating Officer and what most universities call a Registrar to give coherence to the administrative structure and to ensure that operational matters are dealt with efficiently.'[45] Vacancies among the senior officers resulting from retirement, resignation, or death, made a re-organization easier. The post of Registrar and Secretary of Academic Council (the two functions were combined) was created. The duties formerly exercised by the Secretary to the Academic Council became the responsibility of an Academic Registrar who reported to the Registrar. What many members of the Academic Council had feared had come to pass. The post of Administrative Secretary ended on the retirement of the current incumbent, his duties largely subsumed by the Registrar. By the beginning of the new century the University had a unified system of administration and a Registrar's Office impressively housed in the south wing of the Lanyon building (close to the new and even more impressive Vice-Chancellor's suite). For the optimistically minded the move of part of the administration from the architecturally undistinguished building that had housed it for almost thirty years to the splendour of the refurbished Lanyon was a symbol of resurgence. The cynics (there were many of them) simply regarded it as the administration running off with the cream.

For a decade the reform of the Senate had hung in the air. In the first year of the new century it was finally forced to contemplate its future.[46] Its role was now defined as 'the executive governing body of the university'. Thought was given briefly to the advantages of dividing the Senate into two, consisting of a Senate of 15 to 20 members with decision-making powers, and much bigger court of up to 100 members representing all strands of Northern Ireland society which would act as a 'sounding board', but the idea was not pursued. Earlier

44 Shattock and Holmes, paras 2.1, 3.1, 3.6, 4.1, 4.2, 4.8, 5.4 and 8.1.   45 *Senate minutes, 1998*, 24 February, 1–2.   46 *Senate minutes, 2000*, 43–69.

proposals for reform had set the size of Senate at around 45. Now the Senate was being invited to consider a reduction to 32, principally by cutting the representation of Convocation from ten to two or three, abolishing the crown nominees, and removing the right of the education and library boards and the Eastern Health and Social Services Board to have members. To replace them, the Senate could nominate at least four people to represent business, commerce and the professions and four from education, the city and community and other bodies. The effect of these changes, consciously or otherwise, was to bring the composition of the Senate closer to that of the foundation body in 1908. Convocation protested against the reduction of its representation, this time in vain.

The academic structures also needed to be revamped. The Academic Council became composed of heads of academic units and not of professors by right of rank. Its secretary became the Academic Registrar. The number of faculties remained at five, headed by deans appointed by the University; but the unloved names of colleges and provosts were abandoned at the beginning of 1998. The schools were broken down into their component subjects (for example, the school of social sciences was divided into schools of management and economics, sociology, politics, etc.); in effect they became departments under a new name. Heads of schools were responsible to deans, and deans were responsible the Vice-Chancellor. Queen's had become managerial.

CONCLUSION

In 1959 Sir Eric Ashby described the relationship between the academic and administrative parts of the University:

> Even what are commonly thought to be the highest flights of [university] policy cannot be originated by some isolated administrator sitting at a desk: they have to originate among the men who are actually doing the teaching ... In general, the more the teaching staff share in originating policy in the University, the better the policy is likely to be. The translation of policy into action is another matter: in general professional administrators are better at it than academics. This distinction needs to be explained to eager academics who want to play a greater part in running the university.[47]

In the 1940s and 1950s the managerial structures of Queen's had been minimal. The Bursar and a small group of administrators looked after the finances, kept the grounds and buildings in order, attended to personnel matters, and

47 *Vice-Chancellor's report, 1958–9*, 2–3.

dealt with miscellaneous housekeeping. There were committees attending to this and that (too many of them even in 1950) which gave academics with a taste for committee work the opportunity to be involved actively in the affairs of a small college. Beyond that, 'administration in Queen's was separate from teaching, except for such officers as Deans and Advisors of Studies'.[48] Such cosy arrangements crumbled as the University grew bigger and under the weight of government scrutiny.

The process of adapting the University to the new world proved painful. Eventually, by the end of the twentieth century Queen's had in place an academic management system intended to cope with the pressures of changing times. Its most distinctive feature arrangements was a chain of command running from the Vice-Chancellor and Pro-Vice-Chancellors, to the deans, and hence to heads of schools. In the jargon of the time, Queen's had become 'top down'. None of this, of course, guaranteed that the University would be a better place academically. That would depend, as Sir Eric Ashby recognized much earlier, on appointing good scholars. But efficient bureaucratic and managerial devices were also necessary.

48 Professor Waterhouse, in *Belfast News Letter: Jubilee Supplement*, 9 April 1959.

6

Bricks, mortar and some concrete

Universities require buildings, the nature of which is conditioned by function, fashion, technology and cost. 'It would be wrong', wrote the architect responsible for the refurbishment of the Great Hall at the end of the twentieth century, 'to assume that physical characteristics are unimportant. A fine hall in a beautiful building will make a worthy statement about the quality and accessibility of the institution.'[1] Charles Lanyon included a Great Hall in his design for the University, echoing the traditions of learning inherited from medieval places of learning. The Roman Catholic churches built in nineteenth-century Ireland, with steeples soaring above their Anglican neighbours, were statements in stone about the liberation of a once suppressed faith. The Belfast City Hall, newly constructed in 1906, two years before Queen's gained its independence, 'stood mathematically centred in neat rectangular plots, guarded by City Fathers frock-coated in stone, large feet firmly planted on Irish soil – theirs by divine right of conquest – from which sprang carefully tended beds of red geraniums and blue lobelia and white alyssum, floral proof of civic loyalty to Union Jack and British crown'.[2] The Parliament building at Stormont, opened in 1934, looked back to the great days of Empire as well as looking forward to the panorama of Belfast below.

Buildings rarely please everyone. The Belfast architectural historian, Charles Brett, condemned the Keir Building as an 'ugly mass' that dominated the nearby Friar's Bush graveyard.[3] The University's intention had not been to dominate but to provide adequate facilities for the study of the sciences. (When the building was completed, the University threw a party for the local residents.) Whatever their virtues or failings, buildings are pledges to the future. Charles Lanyon planned the college that bears his name at the very time that the Great Famine ravished the land in confident affirmation of the eventual prosperity of Ireland. The architects a century and a half later were working in different circumstances, but, like Lanyon, they were building not merely for the present, but also for posterity.

---

1 Introduction to a programme for a concert held in 2001 to raise funds for the restoration of the Great Hall. *The Queen's University of Belfast Foundation, honorary graduation ceremony and gala concert, Thursday 24th May 2001: programme* (2001), 13.   2 D. Felicitas Corrigan, *Helen Waddell: a biography* (London, 1986), 49.   3 C.E.B. Brett, *The buildings of Belfast, 1700–1914* (Belfast, revised edn 1985), 9.

PRE-WAR LEGACIES AND POST-WAR DIFFICULTIES

Queen's emerged from the Second World War severely short of space. The Lanyon building was shared between academics and administrators who metaphorically jostled one another for offices. There had been a limited amount of new building during the 1930s, including the agriculture building in Elmwood Avenue and the Whitla Hall, commenced before 1939 but not completed for another decade. When the University Grants Committee visited the University in January 1945 it had 'no hesitation in saying that the accommodation now available is totally inadequate in size, character and equipment to the existing or future needs of the University'. It praised 'the ingenuity with which use has been made of every inch of the available space [but] it is a matter for regret that such ingenuity should ever have become necessary'.[4]

Nowhere was it easy to find space even for a desk for an additional clerk. A serious problem was looming in the Library that was running out of shelves and seats.[5] There were thoughts of extending the Library westwards to face the Whitla Hall, but the best that could be done was to insert a floor for readers in the catalogue room and fit bookcases into the alcoves.[6] Of even greater concern to students in search of food as well as of learning, there were few places to eat. The Great Hall was therefore turned into a dining room.[7] This was made easier by the removal of the Mitchell organ to the Whitla Hall, leading to a claim that 'the Great Hall [has been] restored to something like its original appearance and proportions by the removal of the organ'. The claim has an odd ring in light of the restoration work half a century later.[8]

The scarcity of accommodation threatened the quality of teaching and research, especially in chemistry, zoology, botany, and civil engineering. Because of post-war shortages of building materials little could be done other than to make plans, erect temporary buildings, and engage in palliative tinkering: some re-decoration, extensive electrical rewiring, and tidying up the lawns and shrubbery. The University did, however, buy land for future buildings and put money aside for when materials were available. Resources were found to complete the Whitla Hall, which had been in use in a semi-finished state since 1942.

BUILDING IN THE 1950S AND 1960S

The ceremonial opening of the Whitla Hall in February 1949 marked the beginning of two decades during which the University was engaged in 'a large scale [building] programme, comparable to that which had marked the early years of

4 *Vice-Chancellor's report, 1944–5*, 146.   5 *Vice-Chancellor's report, 1944–5*, 148 and 151–3. 6 *Building Committee minutes December 1949–November 1950*, 38 and 41–2.   7 *Building Committee minutes February 1948–November 1949*, 141, 304; *February 1951–December 1952*, 7.   8 *Vice-Chancellor's report, 1946–7*, 192–3; Moody and Beckett, *Queen's, Belfast 1845–1949*, ii, 531 and 535.

the University.'[9] The list of achievements was impressive: the completion of the Whitla Hall; the conversion of the Great Hall into a dining hall; the Stranmillis (later the Keir) building; the geology building in Elmwood Avenue; the clinical block and an additional floor on the Institute of Pathology at the Royal Victoria Hospital; a new floor on the agriculture building; the New Physics Building; modifications to the Library. Work was also started on the rehabilitation of the old chemistry building on the north side of the quadrangle for biochemistry and physiology, and plans were afoot to convert the Ulster School for the Deaf and Blind (popularly known as the Deaf and Dumb Institution) on the Lisburn Road into a students' centre. Both these projects were ultimately abandoned. During the 1950s the designs were being drawn for the Ashby building to house electrical and mechanical engineering, and the Faculty of Economics was waiting the go-ahead for a new building on the site of Elmwood House (it was never built). In the early 1960s a start was made on the Library tower and on the students' halls of residence at Holyrood (later known as Queen's Elms). The microbiology building was constructed at the Royal Victoria Hospital. There were minor but valuable developments: a new boat house; a cricket pavilion; a hut for the dramatic society; and a continual process of buying and adapting houses in University Square and elsewhere for academic use.

In 1951 the Vice-Chancellor was able to make only re-assuring noises about building progress, but he had news of substantial advances the following year. Two new medical blocks and the geology building were well on their way, reconstruction in the quadrangle and the Library was finished, and work was about to begin on the Stranmillis site. Many new staff were being recruited, and although 'a lively department would rather be overcrowded than over-worked ... there is a limit to overcrowding beyond which the conditions for good work deteriorate.'[10] When the University made its submission for future funding to the UGC in 1952, it catalogued £750,000 worth of building completed, or in progress during the previous quinquennium. During the same period the University had purchased fourteen houses, most of them in University Square, for academic purposes or for student and staff accommodation. Queen's requested £2.5 million for new building and maintenance. This did not include £900,000 required for the building at Stranmillis.[11]

The quinquennial grant yielded £1.9 million for premises. The Stranmillis building was already well under way and the University hoped to start other projects shortly. There was even better news to tell the Senate in 1954 when the Institute of Pathology was formally opened and extensions to the agriculture building were completed. The 'formidable steel skeleton' at Stranmillis was arousing 'considerable public interest.' This was code for community criticism of the University's building programme, but the Vice-Chancellor assured the

9 Moody and Beckett, ii, 531.   10 *Vice-Chancellor's report, 1951–2*, 161.   11 *Memorandum to the UGC*, 1952, 5–6 and 17–18.

Senate that Queen's had less space per student in 1953 than it had in 1914. The buildings opened in 1953–4 were the first major developments since 1939.[12]

Work at the Stranmillis site to house chemistry, botany and biology and civil engineering commenced in earnest in June 1950. It was described later as 'the greatest addition to the University property in its history.'[13] The details of its construction kept the buildings committee busy throughout the decade. In the early stages, post-war restrictions on the supply of materials impeded progress. The site was difficult to work on and the special needs of the various departments had to be taken into account. The right sorts of bricks to withstand the rigours of the Ulster climate absorbed a lot of time and enabled the professor of engineering to demonstrate his knowledge of the more esoteric aspects of their manufacture. Ulster pride (and employment) had to be satisfied by using local materials and workmen where possible. There were seemingly trivial matters to attend to, such as a request from the senior boiler men to wear white overalls instead of blue since white was more appropriate to their status. The building was finally ready for opening in May 1959 by the Duke of Edinburgh and was named after the Vice-Chancellor during whose tenure of office it had been planned. Not everybody was pleased with the result. A local architect (it had been designed by a London architect) denounced it as 'bad taste, bad planning, trashy design, occupying a huge site.' He favoured, instead, something like the Elmwood Hall, with a campanile, set in a pleasant garden.[14] Whatever the force of the other adjectives, 'trashy' does not quite fit as a description of the solid bulk of the building.

The Keir Building was the key to other developments. In 1954 the University decided it could not accommodate physics as well as chemistry and civil engineering. An additional building was therefore required. This was erected on the site of the former UVF hospital at the south side of the University campus. Queen's had owned the wooden huts since 1918 and they had long outlived their usefulness. The plan was for a physics building costing roughly £500,000, although there was considerable debate about the estimates.[15] The new physics building made agonisingly slow progress (the physics lecturers were continually changing their minds) under the guidance of a local architect. The Queen Mother, suitably attired in the doctor's robes she had received as Duchess of York, eventually opened the building in 1962.

With the needs of chemistry, physics, and the biological sciences attended to thoughts turned to the rehabilitation of the old chemistry building on the north side of the quadrangle for the use of physiology and biochemistry. In February 1958 the architect concluded gloomily that the building was 'far from ideal'. The University Grants Committee, which was paying the bill, wondered if a new building might be cheaper, but the buildings committee was set on pushing

12 *Vice-Chancellor's report, 1953–4*, 164. 13 *Building Committee minutes, 1957*, 4. 14 *Northern Whig*, 21 February 1962. 15 *Building Committee minutes, 1957*, 284–7.

ahead with rehabilitation.[16] Worries about the costs nevertheless persisted and in early 1960 the buildings committee agreed to the alternative scheme of demolition and starting afresh.[17]

An enterprise with an unhappy outcome was the proposed conversion of the former Deaf and Dumb Institution in the Lisburn Road into a students' centre. The University had purchased the school (another Lanyon construction) in 1954 and planned to adapt it into a students' centre, including a cafeteria capable of feeding 2600 students a day, with a theatre, a library, and a Physical Education Centre. A catering expert hired by Queen's reported that the project was not economically viable within the confines of the existing building. There were also practical worries about the dangers to life and limb of ravenous students swarming across the University and Lisburn Roads. These were not assuaged by some ingenious calculations from the Vice-Chancellor showing that traffic flows in London were greater than anything that the Lisburn Road could produce.[18] The architect was also concerned about the difficulties of converting a crumbling Victorian building – the soft sandstone was decaying – intended for quite a different purpose. A radical idea was beginning to emerge, that the building should be demolished, but there were many voices within the University and in the City urging its preservation on aesthetic and historical grounds. A suggested compromise was to retain the façade for university purposes but to demolish the structure at the rear. The result, the University's architect advised, would not be practical either architecturally or aesthetically. Another suggestion, supported among others by the London architect, Sir Hugh Casson, was to keep the façade as a 'folly' and to erect a new building behind it. In this way it was claimed the vista at both ends of the Elmwood Avenue would be filled by a Victorian structure. (This is not in fact the case. By looking eastwards along Elmwood Avenue the view is of the Whitla Hall, not the Lanyon Building.) Eventually the buildings committee agreed reluctantly that because of its poor condition and the high costs of conversion the entire building should be demolished.[19] This was not done for another three years.

At the end of 1960 the University reviewed its building plans and shuffled the pieces around. The Deaf and Blind School site was no longer to be used for the students' centre. Queen's decided more practical solution was to build a new union close to the main site, at the corner of Elmwood Avenue and University Road where the old Queen's Elms already provided accommodation for a small number of male students and staff. The University had acquired land in Botanic Gardens for a physical education centre incorporating a swimming pool. The Faculty of Economics, which had hoped for a new building at the Elmwood site, was now to be housed in a building on the north side of the quadrangle where

16 *Building Committee minutes, 1958*, 69–70 and 245.   17 *Building Committee minutes 1959*, 49–51; 1960, 18.   18 *Building Committee minutes 1955*, 199; 1959, 44–8, 247–8 and 287–8.   19 *Building Committee minutes, 1960*, 180–3, 260–5 and 493–8.

the old chemistry building had stood. Physiology and biochemistry, together with anatomy, were to have a new pre-clinical building on the site of the Deaf and Dumb Institution – with or without a façade. The planning committee recommended that Sir Hugh Casson should be appointed to orchestrate the entire building programme.[20]

There were problems with the new arrangements. The demolition of Queen's Elms, together with the destruction of the Deaf and Dumb Institution, added to University's a growing reputation for architectural vandalism. The economists would have to vacate Elmwood House before their new building was ready. It was suggested the façade of the Deaf and Dumb Institution (the folly) might provide a temporary home, but the medical professors were against the idea, not out of respect for the reputation of economics, but because they thought it would delay the construction of their pre-clinical building. Students needed a refectory until the new union was ready. They were temporarily accommodated in a pre-fabricated structure (the south dining room) beside the Whitla. Although some residences would be lost from the Queen's Elms, new halls were planned on the Malone Road. By October 1961 the plans were well in hand.[21] Building commenced soon afterwards and the halls were largely complete by 1968.

Two major projects launched in the late 1950s progressed to satisfactory conclusions. One was the construction of what became known as the Ashby Building for the departments of electrical and mechanical engineering. This was the University's first venture into high-rise concrete architecture and it caused some concern to local residents worried about ancient lights, and to the City corporation whose architectural sights were traditionally set rather lower. But the confines of the site made vertical building necessary.

The Ashby Building had its origins in 1954 in the agreement between the University and the College of Technology jointly to supply higher technological education. The University proposed to the UGC a building of 100,000 square feet costing £800,000 (it eventually cost over £1 million). The architects designed an eleven-storey concrete tower with two double storey blocks linked at ground level. Building commenced in 1960 and was completed in 1965, much more speedily than the Keir Building and the new physics building.[22]

The second project was the Library tower. In 1959 the Library had seating for fewer than 400 readers and its bookshelves were expected to be full within five to six years. The University therefore planned a tower to the east of the Library (the idea to build westward onto the lawns had been abandoned), together with a catalogue hall, a periodicals room, and study carrels, capable of meeting the University's needs for the next thirty or forty years. The tower

20 *Building Committee minutes, 1961*, 8. 21 *Building Committee minutes, 1961*, 615–16.
22 *Building Committee minutes, 1960*, 327–30; D. Evans and P. Larmour, *Queen's: an architectural legacy* (Belfast, 1995), 46–7.

would be linked to the old building by a bridge. With the accommodation available in the Medical Library and the library in the Keir Building, Queen's could provide seating for almost one-third of its student population, which was similar to that in many British universities.

The Library tower was finished in 1967. It left uncertain the fate of the original building, but there were thoughts – nothing more – about knocking it down and replacing it with something new. Its salvation was the agreement of the UGC for the construction of the Science Library in Chlorine Gardens, thus absorbing the funds that might otherwise have been spent at the old Library site. The building was used temporarily as an exhibition centre and office space. The Science library was finished in 1969 and brought to an end library expansion for the time being. But the tower was never a success. Architecturally it jarred with its surroundings, and growing student numbers were outstripping its capacity even as it opened.[23] To compound the problem, stringent fire regulations limited the number of readers to 600. By the 1970s the need for more library space was again acute.

If the thought of demolishing the old Library, built in 1866 and extended thirty years later, sent shivers down the spines of conservationists, what would they have made of Sir Hugh Casson's suggestion to erect a twenty-storey tower on the front lawn? In 1964, when the Lockwood committee was cogitating but had not yet reported, the University reviewed its estate in the unwelcome expectation that would have to cope with more students. Sir Hugh cast his eye over the wide expanse of lawn facing University road and concluded that Queen's could not afford to leave it all under grass. The choice seemed to be either to construct a low-level building over most of the grass, or leave more green space and build a tower. Since a building of six floors would require lifts why not go the whole way, and soar to twenty storeys? The building might also be linked by a subway to the union building on the other side of University Road. The result would be a tower (of Babel?) of 150,000 square feet for the Faculty of Arts, or possibly to be shared with administration. But Sir Hugh concluded that arts and administration would not be happy bedfellows, so he suggested a separate building for the latter on the eastern side of the campus. The Senate was not taken with the idea of a skyscraper on the front lawn. Instead the arts departments were gradually tucked away in houses along University Square.

As Queen's became larger so it accumulated more administrators and they needed a home of their own. An Administration Building therefore was planned. Its building history made erratic progress as aesthetic and practical interests collided. In July 1968 the University considered suitable locations and eventually settled on the site of the former anatomy building at the east end of the quadrangle. Anatomy was moving into the pre-clinical building near the City

23 *Building Committee minutes 1959*, 131–4; 1966, 118–24 and 148; Evans and Larmour, *Queen's: an architectural legacy*, 28, 49.

Hospital and the old premises were being demolished. The Professor of Architecture asked whether his students could carry out a design study for a new building. The University agreed, although it also appointed a professional architect. Meanwhile the Professor of Business Studies wrote a report on the advantages and disadvantages of 'Burolandshaft', otherwise known as 'office landscaping' or POP (Panoramic Office Planning). This gem of jargon had been brought back to Queen's by a working party that toured Britain in the spring of 1969 inspecting various administration buildings.[24] Although in the nature of things a large proportion of the staff working in the new building was likely to be women, there were no women on the working party.

The issue that roused the greatest interest among academics was not whether administrators wanted potted plants in their offices, but what the building would do to the look of the campus. The architect produced a design for a five-storey building protruding westward into the quadrangle. However, the removal of the old building had opened up the possibility of an enlarged quadrangle. A campaign to 'save the quad' was commenced by the unlikely figure of Howard Warrender, Professor of Political Science.[25] He urged the University to 'give high priority to ensuring that the green area in the main quadrangle is extended as much as possible'.

> Sometimes it is important to plan buildings; sometimes it is more important to plan the spaces between them. A case in point is the main quadrangle, where there are strong reasons for extending the green area. These reasons may be summarized as follows: (i) it is important to be clear about the essential function of the main quadrangle. Thinking in terms of the Oxford and Cambridge Colleges, for example, it may be thought of as the College Quadrangle. This would I think be a considerable mistake. Colleges also have gardens and the main quadrangle at Queen's is essentially the college garden. It is the place where people sit in fine weather, where garden parties are held, etc. It is clearly a social and recreational centre of considerable importance. In fact, it may be said that Queen's is unique in this respect. The function of the main quadrangle could easily be destroyed and there would be no substitute, nor any prospect of one developing. (ii) The University has expanded considerably since the main quadrangle was designed. Over the last few years alone numbers of students and staff have nearly trebled. It is therefore appropriate that the central area which is the focus of the University should be extended. A University of some six or seven thousand students would amply justify it.

Professor Warrender offered four alternative proposals for consideration. In the first, the eastern boundary of the quadrangle would be made level with the

---

24 *Buildings committee minutes, 1968*, 336–7; 1969, 192, 209–13, 259 and 495–516.
25 Professor Howard Warrender was an engagingly unconventional man and an erratic

existing stone balustrades. The new Administration Building would therefore have to be swung onto a north-south axis and extend back into the car park. A bolder suggestion still was to align the boundary of the quadrangle level with the eastern end of the social science building, that is beyond the balustrades. The administration building would then sit squarely on the car park and extend to the drill hall, where the Heaney Library now stands. An even more adventurous suggestion was to move the building onto a large site in College Park intended for applied mathematics and physics. Finally Professor Warrender envisaged a quadrangle extending all the way back to College Park East. 'This plan is well worth considering and would allow for new buildings of considerable height and (one hopes) of some significance.'[26]

Professor Warrender did not doubt the needs of administrators. But his case was not totally devoid of self-interest; an east-west Administration Building would block the view from several of the rooms in the new social science building where he had his office. Nevertheless, the issues he raised were important. The builders in 1845–9 had not allowed for a quadrangle to complement the Great Hall although one had evolved over time. The Great Hall had been debased into a cafeteria and the quadrangle was in danger of being hemmed in by towers of brick and concrete. The Warrender plan asked for a balance between space and buildings where creative imaginations and pleasurable dalliance could have full reign.

The 'save the quad' campaign was not immediately successful. In April 1970 the buildings committee judged the existing east-west design 'an excellent one'. Subsequently the architect submitted two plans, the original one on an east-west axis and an alternative on a north-south axis. A majority of the committee still preferred the original. But the Academic Council was rumbling in the background and eventually the building was aligned north to south. This raised worries about additional costs, and some trimming was needed. Building work was scheduled to commence in September 1971, more than three years after the first plans had been drawn up.[27] It was eventually finished in the spring of 1975 and the administrators were able to work among their potted plants. With its completion, construction on the central site was completed for the time being.

There was another project demonstrating what one generation regarded as sensible was seen in a different light by another. The Great Hall had been adapted to serve lunches, but it remained a vast space soaring to the rafters. In June 1953 the building committee considered inserting an upper floor, thus creating a two-level dining room. The architect for the Stranmillis building ('bad

attender of meetings of the Faculty of Economics, usually arriving late, if at all, and leaving early. He startled his colleagues one afternoon by attending and declaring himself to be a 'save the quader'. **26** *Building Committee minutes, 1970, 199–221*; *Academic Council minutes, 1969–70, 124.* **27** *Building Committee minutes, 1970, 264–9, 283–5, 330, 363–5, 387, 509–10, 558–60, 599–601 and 602–5; 1971, 37–42; Academic Council minutes, 1969–70, 235–7 and 272–3.*

taste, bad planning, trashy design') was consulted and redeemed himself by advising against the modification because it would destroy the proportions of an historic building.[28] Three years later the Great Hall was in a dilapidated condition and the University considered taking expert advice on what to do. At Easter there were 'two nasty falls' during a conference as delegates tumbled off a dais nearly eight inches deep that stretched a considerable length into the body of the hall. The solution suggested was to remove the dais at a cost of £350.[29] The offending platform survived, nevertheless, until 1960 when the University decided to convert the hall into a full-blown dining room. Once more the question of an extra floor was discussed. The buildings committee looked back into the past and concluded:

> Over the years the views of prominent architects have been sought as to the desirability of forming an additional floor in the Great Hall. Their unanimous opinion has been against such a floor as it would spoil the proportions of the hall, but if the hall is now to become a dining hall, and possibly later a cafeteria, and is unlikely ever to revert to its present status, it might be considered opportune to examine the suggestion afresh as a more attractive refectory and additional formal dining room and/or examination hall will result.[30]

The idea of the second floor was eventually abandoned because the kitchen would not be able to cope with 700 lunches a day that two floor would make possible. Otherwise the Great Hall continued its descent into dinginess. The kitchen was enlarged and a revolving door was cut into the cloisters. The hall was painted a shade redolent of a Belfast November (later it was repainted in what one visitor described a 'germaline pink') and assumed the drab appearance that it wore for the next forty years, until a new generation decided that Sir Charles Lanyon was right after all and that a great university needed a Great Hall.

There was a wistful note in the Vice-Chancellor's report for 1954–5. 'One thinks nostalgically of the medieval universities which owned so little property that they could, if provoked, pack their belongings and migrate to another city.'[31] Perhaps he had spent too many weary hours attending the buildings committee debating the virtues of local bricks. But he was too much of a realist not to appreciate that a growing university required new buildings. Not all the buildings erected during the 1950s and '60s stood the test of time, but the building programme during those decades enabled a much-expanded Queen's to continue its tasks of teaching and learning in relative comfort.

---

28 *Building Committee minutes, 1953*, 17–18. 29 *Building Committee minutes, 1956*, 111. It cost a great deal more to restore the dais in 2000. Unfortunately there were then some more falls. 30 *Building Committee minutes, 1960*, 8, 20–1, 92, 508 and 513. 31 *Vice-Chancellor's report, 1954–5*, 158.

CONSOLIDATION AND RETRENCHMENT: THE 1970S AND 1980S

The pace of construction slackened at the end of the 1960s. The University was materially equipped for a population of 7000 to 10,000 students and there was a general perception that Queen's had reached its maximum size. The Troubles put a damper on expansion and they inflicted heavy security costs for the University, thus straining the resources available for building. Rampant inflation eroded the University's income and at the end of the 1970s the financial freeze imposed by the government made new building extremely difficult.

In 1971 the University, in agreement with the Belfast Corporation, defined its precinct. During the 1950s and 1960s Queen's had erected new buildings and converted others as the opportunity arose. Often pressing requirements had determined what had to be done, although Sir Hugh Casson had been appointed to give coherence to developments. But inevitably the needs of the University and the interests of private residents clashed from time to time. The idea of the precinct was to define a zone within which University development would be confined. Future building would occur within the precinct (there were some defined exceptions). As private property became available within the precinct Queen's would have the option of buying it. Owners of property within the zone should not change it use without the University's agreement.

The northern boundary of the precinct was drawn at Lower Crescent (at the time the city planners had the idea of cutting a ring road on the line of the crescent). The eastern boundary was marked by University end of Rugby Road, and the western boundary was defined by the pre-clinical building on the Lisburn Road, together with the University's space in the City Hospital. The southern limit was less clear-cut. College Gardens formed one part of the boundary between the Lisburn Road and the Malone Road. The Botanic Gardens restricted expansion of the main site. But the junction of the Malone and Stranmillis roads embraced a triangular area that extended southwards to Beechlands.

Within the precinct there was a rough functional distribution. The humanities, social sciences and administration were clustered around the Lanyon building. The natural and applied sciences were located on the south side of the main site and in the Malone-Stranmillis triangle; and medicine was at the City and Royal Victoria hospitals (well outside the precinct). The University's hope was that the precinct would contain its building needs until at least 1978. It would allow buildings to be constructed with the minimum of disruption to the work of the University and its neighbours, it would group buildings together in a rational way, it would use land sensibly, and it would promote good architectural and civic design.[32]

32 The draft precinct plan was prepared in February 1971 and presented to the Academic Council. It was submitted to the UGC for the quinquennium 1973–8 and agreed by the Belfast Corporation. *Academic Council minutes, 1970–1*, Appendix, not paginated; *Academic Council minutes, 1971–2*, draft submission to the UGC, para. 3.1.3.

The precinct plan included ambitions that were not fulfilled, such as an arts centre close to the Students' Union and a multi-storey car park on a place to be determined. There were to be footbridges at the junction of the Malone and Stranmillis roads so that students could walk from the residences at Queen's Elms to the Lanyon and the Union without being mown down by the traffic. There were other developments already in hand or planned, such as a common room in a building shared with the Ulster bank, the book shop and a post office on the corner of College Gardens and University Road, and a building for the bio-sciences to the north of the Keir Building. The common room project involved the demolition of a much admired Victorian building.

With the definition of the precinct came a greater attention to landscaping. The University tried to arrange grassy areas and bushes around new buildings such as the Keir and the Ashby; and the student residences at Queen's Elms had been particularly well landscaped. But the Lanyon Building, the Students' Union, and University Square posed special problems, not least because of the traffic flows and the need for car parking. In 1977 the University commissioned a report that included a proposal to close University Square to traffic. The entrances to the Lanyon building and the roadways within the main site were to be realigned. Shrubs, sculptures, and outdoor seating would adorn the areas in front of the Students' Union and along Elmwood Avenue. The plan foundered on the thorny issue of traffic.[33] University Square remains open to cars and buses to this day, although the main entrance to Queen's has been shifted and front of the Lanyon building has been improved. Even the stark face of the Students' Union has been given a softer aspect.

Three issues dominated the 1970s and 1980s: the refurbishment of existing buildings; security costs arising from the political unrest; and the high costs of energy fuelled by the increases in the price of oil in the early 1970s. At the forefront of the rehabilitation programme was the Lanyon Building. The University appointed a local architect, Robert McKinstry, to advise on its future. He reported it to be in generally good condition except for the loss of many diamond window panes on the west front. He recommended the entrance hall should be left as it was apart from the addition of swing doors into the quadrangle. He suggested that the staircase on the south side should be shifted to the north and opened out in line with Lanyon's original plan for a grand staircase. This staircase would lead to a new council chamber and reception suite. The Great Hall was suffering from 'starkly unrelieved walls', a cramped entrance, dismal lighting, and dreary curtains. The architect recommended the erection of balconies at both the northern and southern ends and an upper gallery at the eastern side to be used for exhibitions. He also proposed improving the kitchen, enlarging the Vice-Chancellor's suite, and refurbishing the accommodation used by pure mathematics at the southern end of the Lanyon Building and extra-mural studies at the northern end.[34]

33 *Building Committee minutes, 1977,* 29, 168–9, 209–13 and 313.   34 *Building Committee*

The buildings committee was happy with most of these suggestions, except for the northern gallery. The problem, as ever, was money. The estimated costs of upgrading the accommodation for pure mathematics and extra-mural studies were £113,060, and the diamond windows at the front between £17,000 and £18,000. Who knows what the rehabilitation of the Great Hall and a council chamber would cost? In February 1976 the chairman of the buildings committee wondered whether the project should be pursued since the UGC was unlikely to provide the money and the University's own funds could not stand the strain. The best hope was that the UGC would pay for the refurbishment of the north and south wings for academic use, the Historic Buildings Committee might fund the re-glazing, and DENI might give a contribution because of the historic importance of the building. When DENI was approached it was sympathetic but could not offer anything more substantial than sympathy for about five years. The buildings committee concluded reluctantly that the Lanyon project could not be given a high priority.[35] But the building was too important to be left quietly decaying.

In October 1981 Queen's launched a development appeal with the intention of raising £1.5 million by the end of 1983. This would finance various projects, including the Lanyon rehabilitation.[36] In the spring of 1983 the University decided to go ahead with part of the rehabilitation plan: the council chamber and reception room (to become the Canada Room), the Vice-Chancellor's suite, and accommodation for extra-mural studies. The cost was estimated at £350,000. There was £160,000 available from the development appeal, the Department of the Environment was expected to give £33,000, and the Vice-Chancellor allocated £140,000 from the sale of surplus land at New Forge.[37] Finally, the Canadian provinces made substantial contributions to the completion of the Canada Room. The University hoped, vainly, that the work would be finished by the summer of 1985. Eventually in 1986, ten years after the first plans had been drawn, the Lanyon Building, except for the Great Hall, had been refurbished.[38]

The old Library had a swifter passage towards rehabilitation. The completion of the tower in 1967 had left the future of the original building uncertain. For several years it had been threatened with demolition until in 1974 it became a listed building. The tower had been intended to serve as a book store with only a small number of readers' spaces. An additional building, probably on the site of the old Library, had been envisaged to accommodate the staff and most of the readers. In fact the tower was used as the Library proper with a heating system designed to keep books but not readers at an optimum temperature. In 1976 it

minutes, *1975*, 210–13.   35 *Building Committee minutes, 1976*, 34, 53–462–8 and 307.   36 *Vice-Chancellor's report, 1981–2*, 16.   37 This was made possible under a so-called 'interchangeability' scheme whereby universities could sell redundant property purchased with government funds and devote the proceeds to other purposes. Senate minutes 1982, 185.   38 *Building Committee minutes, 1983*, 161–74 and 200–1; 1984, 215; 1985, 88, 169 and 236.

housed 465,000 volumes (107,000 more than had been planned), 56 staff, and had 560 reader places. The capacity available was only 84 per cent of UGC norms. In May 1975 the University appointed the Cambridge architects, Twist and Whitley, to produce a range of proposals for additions to the Library. One was a minimal adaptation of the Library into a store for 87,000 books and 152 spaces for readers, as well as a catalogue area and an issue desk. The second plan was to link the old Library to the tower by a bridge at the first floor level. The ground floor would contain a catalogue hall, an issue desk and a bibliography suite holding 9,000 volumes. On the first floor there would be space for 65,200 volumes and 176 readers and also accommodation for the University's special collections and archives. Above the special collections there was to be an under-graduate collection. The scheme would cost £281,000 and result in a net gain of space for 38,000 volumes. The third proposal was more radical still; it was to demolish the music department (the old students' union) and extend the Library eastwards.[39] In the event the UGC approved the second scheme (minus the undergraduate collection). The money would not be available until 1980–1, but Queen's decided to press on with the preliminary work.[40] The building was eventually handed over to the University in July 1983.[41] Even so, the Library remained cramped and at peak times there were queues at the door. The open-ing of the Heaney Library in the mid-1990s containing the undergraduate reading collection alleviated the congestion for the time being.

The 1970s brought with them two unwelcome problems. The first was the oil crisis of 1973 that afflicted all universities, although it had a peculiar Northern Ireland twist. The University was an omnivorous consumer of fuel because its buildings had been constructed when it was cheap. In the academic year 1968–9 Queen's spent £127,000 on heat, light and water, the equivalent of 3.2 per cent of total expenditure. By 1975–6 the sum was £830,000 or 5.5 per cent of the total. Thereafter the growth in expenditure was checked as a proportion of the total. Nevertheless, by 1980–1 fuel costs broached £1 million and they rose steadily throughout the decade. Queen's was paying 57 per cent more than a British university would have to pay for a similar consumption. All universities received some help from the UGC for their fuel bills, but Queen's had no com-pensation for the exceptionally high local charges. The University formed a committee to monitor and measure consumption; it attended to the mending of window frames, fixed draughty doors, dimmed corridor lighting, confiscated electric fires from offices (a time-honoured activity), and issued posters exhort-ing economies.[42] By the end of the 1980s the University had learned how to cope with an age of high fuel costs.

The second problem was the Troubles. Any university located in a city is

39 *Building Committee minutes, 1976*, 108–47.   40 *Building Committee minutes, 1976*, 274 and 447; *1978*, 91–2.   41 *Building Committee minutes, 1983*, 250.   42 *Building Committee min-utes, 1976*, 484–6; *1977*, 45, 80–3.

exposed to what might be called peaceful vandalism: graffiti, broken windows, burglaries, and the like. But the community disturbances that erupted at the end of the 1960s elevated such past-times to dangerous levels. Bullets and bombs forced Queen's to spend more money than it could afford on protecting and repairing its premises and ensuring the safety of staff and students. The list of building damaged was long. Foremost was the Great Hall, fire-bombed in 1981 but saved from destruction by the prompt action of the security guards. The Malone club house was destroyed by a bomb and there were attacks on the computer centre, the Department of Celtic, and the book shop.[43] On a single night in May 1972, fifty-three windows in the Students' Union were smashed by a mob trying to break in. Over the months explosions damaged properties on the Malone Road, Stranmillis Road, Botanic Avenue, Rugby Avenue and College Gardens. Even the risk of attack on vulnerable buildings or those containing valuable equipment compelled the University to spend money strengthening its defences.

The University established a security service in February 1970 consisting of a security officer, an assistant, and twelve security guards. As the Troubles intensified so the security force grew to thirty by June 1972 and by September five more men were required for the Ashby-Keir complex and two for the Queen's Elms.[44] Numbers were increased again in 1975 on the advice of the police, even though there was a 'cease fire' in operation. By April 1978 the security force had been enlarged to fifty-six.[45]

Security costs were a heavy drain on the accounts. Until 1980 DENI met the full costs, but in that year DENI reduced its share to 75 per cent. This left the University with a bill of £105,000 for the year 1980–1. Throughout the 1980s the net cost to the University averaged £135,000 a year. Similar charges were incurred in the early 1990s. Since the UGC did not make grants for security, money destined for general academic purposes had to be used.[46] The sum of £135,000 might have paid for a modest building or four rather less modest professors.

New building did not come to a halt during the 1970s and 1980s. In 1980 the buildings committee reported a respectable list of achievements over the previous years including a pharmacy building, animal houses for psychology, and premises for the medical research unit. Money had been found for the old Library, for the renovation of the field centre at Murlough, near Newcastle, and there were plans for the rehabilitation of the Mulhouse building at the Royal

---

43 Republicans attacked the Computer Centre, claiming that it was working for the army. Loyalists attacked the Celtic Department because of its assumed connections with Gaelic culture. Had they been better educated they might have attacked the Department of Scholastic Philosophy next door. The rationale for targeting the bookshop is not clear. **44** *Building Committee minutes, 1970*, 88, 1971, 33–6 and 452–69; *1972*, 352–5, 417, 455–7, 492–6 and 538–40. **45** *Building Committee minutes, 1972*, 352–5; *1975*, 263–71; *1978*, 181–2. **46** *Senate minutes, 1980*, 385.

Victoria Hospital for conversion into a Medical Library, and for a palaeoecology laboratory.[47] There was more progress to report in 1985. The Department of Architecture had a new building in Chlorine Gardens, additional student residences had been built, the palaeoecology laboratory was nearing completion, and the restoration of the Lanyon Building was nearly finished. By the end of the decade the technology centre had been built, more student accommodation had been planned, and a restoration project was underway on residences in Mount Charles.[48]

Some projects were made possible as the government allowed the University to sell building purchased earlier with government money and use the proceeds for other projects. Queen's owned approximately 300 buildings and it compiled a list of property that might be sold immediately or over the next five years. If all these sales were realised (not all were), the income would exceed £6.6 million. At the same time the University listed projects worth more than £7.7 million ranging from work already underway, such as the refurbishment of University Square, to additional student accommodation. Some of these plans came to pass in the 1990s.[49]

Nevertheless, compared with earlier decades the 1970s and 1980s were years of consolidation. The main brake on expansion was inflation. One positive development was that Queen's became more sensitive to its physical environment. Its own plans for renovating the Lanyon Building and the old Library, for landscaping, and the definition of the precinct, chimed in with the Department of Environment's creation of an urban conservation area. But conservation came with a price tag. There was a nice balance to be kept between maintaining buildings of historical or architectural interest and teaching and research.

QUEEN'S AND CONSERVATION

In 1960, when the University was considering building the Library tower, the architect received a letter from an official (possibly an architect) at the UGC:

> In my opinion your design is completely logical and good in itself. I think, also, that it will not be out of harmony with the existing 'Gothic' buildings, unless harmony is regarded as meaning identical in style. In any case the existing buildings, while having a certain interest as being typical of a certain school of Victorian Gothic, do not constitute a masterpiece. I think it would be absurd to subordinate all future building to these existing buildings – antiquarianism run mad. Clearly Queen's must gradually change as generations pass; the existing buildings may also remain as a

---

47 *Senate minutes, 1980*, 139 and 352.   48 *Senate minutes, 1985*, 253–4, 420–2, 1988, 423.
49 *Senate minutes, 1987*, 924–31.

curious nucleus of future extension, but *not* as governing the form or style of such extensions.[50]

The correspondence neatly summed up the University's dilemma. The brick monster which was the Keir Building had upset residents of the Stranmillis Road; and neither had the white concrete of the Ashby Building found favour. The demolition of the Deaf and Dumb Institution had been a painful episode as Queen's struggled to reconcile nostalgia with financial realities. The University had to match its needs for libraries, laboratories, lecture theatres and student residences to its income. It also had to work within the restrictions imposed by the UGC and local planning authorities. There was also the issue of what was and what was not good architecture. The Lanyon Building, the finest Gothic building in Belfast, was one model, but so was the 1930s Whitla Hall. The Ashby Building demonstrated the possibilities of new materials and techniques.

With so many masters to satisfy it is unsurprising that Queen's succeeded in annoying all of them. In March 1972 the magazine *Fortnight* published an article entitled 'Victoriana Vandalised: Queen's University and the art of destruction'. It was a robust and partly unfounded attack on the 'haphazard development-planning' of the University and the 'Philistine attitude' of its buildings committee that, according to the author, had no architects among its members. The list of the University's sins was long. It included the demolition of the Deaf and Dumb Institution, Queen's Elms, the gate lodge to Botanic Gardens, and the Royal Terrace on the Lisburn Road. An ugly brick box containing the common room, the Ulster Bank and the post office had replaced College Green Terrace. The old Library survived for the moment, but its future was threatened. Queen's, the article conceded, was not the only villain. Terrorist bombs and an 'anti-Victorian attitude' aided and abetted the University in its destructive intent.

The vandalism did not stop at demolition. In place of vanished Victoriana, Queen's had erected the 'gargantuan grey Goliath' of the Physical Education Centre, the 'glaring white boxes, like sophisticated Portakabins' housing applied mathematics and the Computer Centre, the new Administration Building ('a few marks for red brick but why not try to get a matching sort'?), the common room, squatting 'squarely beside Methody', and 'worst of all is the Students' Union'. To compound the sins, these monstrosities were the work of 'foreign', that is, English architects. Admittedly Queen's had become more 'sensitive' to the virtues of Victorian buildings than it once had been, thanks to the work of the Ulster Architectural Heritage Society established in 1967.[51]

The chairman of the buildings committee, Mr Charles Kinahan, had no difficulty in refuting some of these charges.[52] Queen's had never owned the

---

50 *Building Committee minutes, 1960*, 433. 51 M. McDowell, 'Victoriana vandalised: Queen's University and the art of destruction', *Fortnight*, 21 March 1975, 10–11. 52 C. Kinahan, 'Queen's University and the art of development', *Fortnight*, 11 April 1975, 17–18.

Botanic Gardens gatelodge or the Royal Terrace, so it could hardly be blamed for their destruction. The buildings committee included two architects. As for engaging foreign architects, he pointed out Northern Ireland and England were both parts of the United Kingdom. In any case, Belfast architects had designed the Library tower, the physical education centre, the social science building, and the Students' Union. Matching bricks for the administration building had been unobtainable. The Deaf and Blind School had been demolished only after much soul-searching. The old Library was not under threat. This was not quite true; for years Queen's had thought about knocking it down. Sensibly, the chairman did not refer to Queen's Elms or College Gardens Terrace. The University, he continued, was not an institution founded to preserve historic buildings but a working university with a duty to educate students within cost limits fixed by the UGC. It had bought very few buildings in order to demolish them; it had spent money on restoring houses in Mount Charles and University Square when it would have been cheaper to flatten them. New building had not been 'haphazard'. The University had had a development plan since 1960, overseen by Sir Hugh Casson (he did not mention the proposed twenty-storey tower on the front lawn), and it had recently defined its precinct with the approval of the local planning authorities.

The University had a strong case, but it was hard-pressed to defend the aesthetic qualities of the buildings at its eastern boundary, such as the sophisticated portakabins, that were the products of industrial building techniques. The best the most recent historians of the University's architecture have been able to say about the students' union building was that it does 'not quite rise to the occasion, facing the Lanyon Building'.[53]

Alistair Rowan, the architectural historian, took a more sympathetic view of the University's problems in 1982. He noted, 'the University area is one of the city's greatest environmental assets'. It was the centre of an urban conservation area. The Elmwood Hall, owned by Queen's, illustrated the difficulties this caused. The spire had been encased in scaffolding for three years. How could the University justify spending £70,000 on it restoration when money was so tight for teaching? The Elmwood difficulty was eventually solved by a grant from the Historic Buildings Council, but the general problem remained.[54]

Some of the criticisms of the University's attitudes struck home. Not all of its architectural adventures had been successful. But the establishment of the Ulster Architectural Heritage Society and the creation of the urban conservation zone both fostered a growing awareness of the value of the nineteenth century heritage. From the 1970s all the University's plans for its estate contained an explicit commitment to the environment. The commitment was not

---

53 Evans and Larmour, *Queen's: an architectural legacy*, 47, 48.   54 A. Rowan, 'A perfect university suburb: The Queen's University district, Belfast', *Country Life*, 23 June 1982, 1688–90.

always easy to fulfil, not only because of financial and practical constraints but also because opinions differed about was aesthetically good.

RATIONALIZATION AND RENEWAL IN THE 1990S

The 1990s fall into two distinct parts. In 1993 the University set out its strategy for capital development over the following five years. It was 'primarily a major rationalisation of its existing purpose-built buildings, together with certain other buildings'. Effort was to be concentrated on making a more efficient use of existing properties. There was a major problem with maintenance. In 1989 the backlog of maintenance had been priced at £60 million and it was increasing by the year. There were not enough student residences. Queen's had built 400 study bedrooms between 1989 and 1993 and had a further 120 planned for the following year. This would bring the number to 1950, some way short of what was required. In all the University planned to spend £11.8 million over the next five years on rationalisation and a limited amount of new building, plus £10.4 million on tackling the backlog of maintenance. The money for these operations, it was hoped, would come from reserves, from grants from DENI and the Department of Environment for the conservation of historic buildings, from property sales, from loans, and from donations.[55]

In 1995 the University still owned more than 260 building, many of them in the conservation area. Queen's was not planning new buildings apart from those required for the School of Nursing and outreach projects. Instead, it hoped to achieve a more efficient use of its space. The estates officer surprised a sceptical Academic Council in 1996 by revealing that lecture theatres were used for only half the working week and when in use were filled to only 21 per cent of capacity. Queen's therefore had a 'utilisation rate' of only 10 or 11 per cent instead of the 64 per cent recommended by the National Audit Office. Little wonder that the University's expenditure on the estate was 'well above' the national average.[56]

In the same year Queen's estimated that it would require at least £180 million up to 2002–3 for recurrent and capital building programmes. This was the equivalent to 15 per cent of total expected income. There was one particularly pressing need, which was for yet more Library space. The University had already set aside £1.7 million for the project (the Heaney Library) in the expectation that HEFCE (the successor to the UGC) would provide the remaining £600,000.[57] Two years later Queen's looked back to its 1995 strategy. It had been postulated on an increase of 4000 students over several years without a significant increase in capital expenditure. The award of the contract for educating

55 *Senate minutes, 1993*, 504–71.   56 *Senate minutes, 1997*, 24; *Academic Council minutes, 1997*.   57 *Senate minutes, 1995*, 316–17.

nurses and midwives involved absorbing 1400 students. The University could cope, 'but such expansion must be properly resourced.'[58]

The century ended with a flurry of activity as Queen's decided to spend for the future. The north-west wing of the Lanyon Building was refurbished to house some of the administrative departments (the wheel had come full circle for the administration had decamped from the Lanyon Building thirty years before). The Great Hall was restored at a cost of £2.5 million, and 'Lanyon II' on the site of the Students' Union building was being planned. The music department had been refurbished and equipped with electronic music studios. The geology building, no longer required for teaching the subject, was to be converted into a learning and teaching centre. A new centre for pharmaceutical research financed by the McClay Trust had been built at the City Hospital. A dedicated building for nursing and midwifery was under construction close to the pre-clinical building on the Lisburn Road. Another students' hall was rising at Queen's Elms. Around the main site environmental improvements were taking place including new road layouts and a curving ramp up to the door of the Lanyon building for disabled students. At the Queen's campus in Armagh extra space was being acquired for a range of academic developments.[59] Back in Belfast there were other ambitions embracing the whole of the campus and involving new buildings including a library), the demolition of some existing buildings and extensive landscaping.[60] The determination was there. All that was required was the money and planning permission.

CONCLUSION

Queen's was fortunate in having a fine purpose-built building from its foundation in 1845–9. Thereafter it put up buildings according to need and as it could afford them. Always it had to build within the constraints imposed by its location in a large and expanding city. Unlike Cambridge, say, where the city fitted around the university, Queen's had to accommodate itself to the city. This meant paying attention to the neighbours and complying with local planning regulations. In the years immediately following the end of the Second Word War there was an acute shortage of space. During the 1950s the Keir Building spread its bulk between the Malone and Stranmillis roads and at the beginning of the 1960 the Ashby thrust tentatively upwards; both buildings went a long way towards solving the shortage of space. The upsurge of civic violence at the end of the 1960s, the oil crisis of 1973, and chronic inflation added to the problems of running the estate. During the 1970s and 1980s the University had to make the best of what it already possessed. The make do and mend period extended into the 1990s, but at the end of the decade the University had embarked onto a phase of major new building.

58 *Senate minutes, 1997*, 515. 59 *Estates committee January, 1999–May 2000*, 18, 41–2, 52, 111, 159, 246, 314, 329, 330, 331 and 351–2. 60 *Queen's University estate master plan, 2001*.

7

Staff – academic and others

COUNTING HEADS

'It is not walls but men who make the state.' The words of Thulycides, quoted by Sir Richard Livingstone, sometime Vice-Chancellor, on the occasion of the Queen's centenary in 1949, gets to the heart of universities.[1] Sir Eric Ashby put the point a different way in 1950: 'the University is a society of students and teachers who voluntarily come together because they are enthusiastically and imaginatively interested in knowledge'.[2] The students – apprentice scholars as it were – are the subjects of the next chapter. Here we concentrate on the staff and particularly on the professors and lecturers without whom there can be no university.

It is easy to forget that the academic staff are a minority of the University's employees. Professors and lecturers accounted for only a quarter of the work-force at the end of the twentieth century. The position half a century earlier is not certain since information is hard to come by. In 1944–5 Queen's told the UGC it employed 8 full-time administrative staff, 3 part-time administrators (who were also academics) and 14 clerical staff plus another 9 in the Faculty of Agriculture. There was a university steward, 3 workmen, 37 technicians and laboratory assistants, 4 assistants in the in library, 12 porters, 7 gardeners, and 23 female cleaners or housekeepers.[3] They were only slightly fewer in total (118) than the academic staff. Three decades later there were 712 porters, security men, grounds men, workmen, cleaners, domestics, boiler men and miscellaneous workers who comprised 27 per cent of all employees. There were also 785 academics.[4]

From the 1980s Queen's began to record total staff numbers as part of its equal opportunities policy. The composition of the total staff at the end of the century is shown in table 7.1.

The table is interesting from various points of view, not least the light it casts on the complexity and the slightly unexpected features of the University at the end of the century, such as the fact that computing staff outnumbered library

---

1 QUB, *Centenary celebrations held 25th–30th September 1949*, 11. 2 Eric Ashby, 'A note from the Vice-Chancellor', *Q: a literary magazine*, 1 (Belfast, Michaelmas 1950), 4. 3 *Academic Council minutes, 1944–5*, Submission to the UGC 1945, pp. 1M–35M. 4 *Vice-Chancellor's report 1973–4*, 54. The figures are taken from a one-off table. The academic total does not entirely correspond with the figure elsewhere in the report.

Table 7.1: Categories of staff in 2000[5]

Category	Number	Percentage
Academic	822	25.7
Administrative	270	8.4
Technical	311	9.7
Clerical	535	16.7
Computer	108	3.4
Research	410	12.8
Library	105	3.3
Miscellaneous	532	16.6
Nursing education	105	3.3
TOTAL	3198	99.9

staff, and the large number of people employed in training women and men to become nurses. The miscellaneous category is intriguing for its size: included here are cleaners, catering assistants, crèche attendants, porters, and others. However, it is the academic work of Queen's that is our principal interest, although we will discuss the non-academic staff briefly later in the chapter.

Table 7.2 shows the numbers of academic and other senior staff between 1944 and 1999. The figures have been compiled from the annual calendars and, in the case of academic staff, from the Vice-Chancellor's annual reports. It should be remembered, though, that the final two columns of the table include only those staff senior enough to get their names and grades in the calendars. A comparison of tables 7.1 and 7.2 suggests that during the 1990s the calendars included the names of fewer than half the total work force.

The ratios between the categories in table 7.2 are as revealing as the totals. The numbers of academic and academically related staff increased eight-fold during the second half of the century, but the non-academic categories grew by a much greater extent. In the late 1940s there was one senior administrator for every twenty academics. This ratio quickly fell to one per ten academics. By the end of the 1990s one administrator supported five academics. The rising ratio of administrators to academics was an index of the growing bureaucracy that infected the University from outside and which multiplied almost exponentially inside. Academics complained continually that, notwithstanding the increasing army of administrators, they were compelled to engage in ever more paper-pushing. Parkinson's Law reigned supreme.

5 The table has been compiled from the *Fifth report on equal opportunities* (QUB, May 2001), table 1.6. The combined total of academic, research, and nurse teachers is 306 less than the total teaching staff for the year 2000 shown in appendix 2. Part of the explanation may be that the equal opportunities' figures relate to February 2000. The figures in the appendix relate to December 2000.

Table 7.2: Categories of staff, 1944–99 (five yearly averages)

Year	Academic and academically related	Library and computer	Administration and support
1944–9	173	2	5
1950–4	241	5	17
1955–9	313	7	24
1960–4	433	8	37
1965–9	591	29	63
1970–4	703	44	88
1975–9	785	70	113
1980–4	840	83	131
1985–9	939	81	129
1990–4	1047	87	127
1995–9	1330	84	169

SOME SCHOLARS: SOME SURVIVORS, AND SOME NEWCOMERS

To modify Thulycides, it is both men and women who make the state. In the case of universities it takes more than a few outstanding scholars to set the agenda for teaching and research. The quality of a university depends on the whole of its staff. For this reason this chapter concentrates on groups rather than individuals. Nevertheless, behind the headcounts were flesh-and-blood men and women whose presence helped to give a particular flavour to the place. Their teaching, their scholarship, or simply their personalities, made Queen's what it was.

In 1944–5 out of the one hundred or so lecturers and professors in post, one or two had been on the staff since before the First World War, including A.O. Belfour, Reader in English Language since 1909, and H.O. Meredith, Professor of Economics since 1911. The former had taught Helen Waddell as a student (and had escorted her to the opera), but in the 1930s undergraduates knew him only as a reclusive and pedantic scholar.[6] Although Meredith had retired in 1945, he later taught at Magee University College. He had been an outstanding student at Cambridge and was a somewhat peripheral member of the Bloomsbury Group (where he was known as H.O.M.). He had lectured at the London School of Economics and Manchester before coming to Queen's where he maintained 'a one man atmosphere of the Cambridge of Lowes Dickinson, E.M. Forster – and indeed of H.O.M.'[7] He published a study of protectionism

6 J. Boyd, *Out of my class* (Belfast, 1985), 118; D. Felicitas Corrigan, *Helen Waddell* (London, 1986, 163, 171, 172 and 174. Belfour joined the army on the first day of the war and was captured by the end of August 1914. Perhaps four years as a German prisoner of war turned him into the lonely figure observed by Boyd during the 1930s. 7 Quoted in R.S. Kidelsky, *John Maynard Keynes*, i, *Hope betrayed, 1883–1920* (London, 1983), 427–8. His history tutor at King's told him, 'You are very brilliant, but you will never do anything.'

in France in 1904 and a useful book on English economic history in 1908. Thereafter his contributions to economics were negligible except perhaps through his teaching. Even in this task a student remembered him droning 'through his notes as if he didn't think much of them himself and was delivering them only because it was his fate to teach the subject'.[8] But he was the driving spirit behind the University dramatic society and made his own translations of Euripides for performance by unemployed dock workers. A colleague wrote, he 'occupied the Chair of Economics, but ... [he] might well have held a Sofa of Classics, Philosophy, English literature, and a half-dozen other of the liberal humanities'.[9]

Several other long-serving members of staff retired at the war's end, including James Edie Todd who held the chair of modern history from 1919. He published nothing but 'carried a burden of teaching as few professors would have contemplated' and 'made it his business to give to the history of Ireland, hitherto neglected in the Queen's University of Belfast, its fitting place in the general plan'. His teaching did not impress run-of-the-mill students, but he inspired a small band of honours students to go onto distinguished academic careers.[10] Other retirements included those of Professor McCallister from the chair of education that he had occupied since 1919 and Professor Lowry after twenty-five years as professor of midwifery.

Several pre-war appointees remained in post after the war and continued to be influential in University affairs. They included two law professors. J.L. Montrose had been appointed to the chair of law in 1934. F.H. Newark was appointed to a lectureship in 1937 and promoted to a chair of jurisprudence nine years later. Montrose was dean of the faculty for thirty years and, in the words of H.G. Hanbury, Professor of English Law at Oxford, 'erected a Faculty of Law second to none in Great Britain'.[11] His scholarship was recognized by an honorary fellowship of University College, London, and an honorary doctorate from Trinity College, Dublin. Francis Newark became Secretary of the Academic Council in 1947 and, in his own words, the chair of jurisprudence became 'rather a part-time job'.[12] Montrose and Newark were involved in a clash in May 1963 that reverberated through the University, the local press and beyond, when the former was voted out of the deanship and was replaced by

8 Boyd, *Out of my class*, 139. 9 Walker and McCreary, *Degrees of excellence*, 97–8; S. Gourley Putt, 'A packet of Bloomsbury letters: the forgotten H.O. Meredith', *Encounter*, 59 (November 1982), 77–84. 10 H.A. Cronne (ed.), *Essays in British and Irish history: in honour of James Eadie Todd* (London, 1949), xiv. Todd has left a memoir outlining his career in Scotland, Canada and Belfast; it is a story of heavy teaching loads throughout his career. Uncatalogued typescript memoir in the QUB Archives. 11 H.G. Hanbury, 'Introduction', in J.L. Montrose, *Precedent in English law and other essays*, ed. H.G. Hanbury (Shannon, 1968), 1–2; A. Phang, 'Exploring and expanding horizons: the influence and scholarship of Professor J.L. Montrose', *Singapore Law Review*, 18 (1997), 15–57. 12 'Profile', in *Belfast Telegraph*, 29 June 1962.

Professor Newark. Montrose had the support of most students who regarded him as a father figure, but Newark won the day (and the deanship). At a distance of several decades the conflict reads like a clash of egos elevated in the academic hothouse into matters of principle.[13]

Scarcely less prominent in University business was Maurice Boyd, a lecturer in Latin since 1933 who succeeded R.M. Henry to the chair in 1939. He published little, taught conscientiously, and administered prodigiously. A colleague later wrote, 'those of us who loathe committee work owe a great debt to the minority who enjoyed it. Maurice Boyd belonged to the latter group. He sat on and chaired many committees, always displaying great aplomb and adroitness.'[14] A dominant figure in the world of medicine was Professor J. H. Biggart, Professor of Pathology from 1937 and dean of the faculty from 1944 to 1971. 'He was a charismatic figure among students and the hospital consultants alike.' His students and medical colleagues regarded him with awe and affection in more or less equal measure and Vice-Chancellors ensured they kept on his right side.[15]

Among others whom Ashby referred to as the old guard was Professor Charlesworth who combined his duties in the chair of geology with chairmanship of the building committee; since there was no buildings officer he was in effect the domestic bursar. Karl Emeleus had been a member of the physics department since 1927 and professor since 1933 until his retirement in 1966. He combined a heavy and effective teaching load with long periods of sustained research every summer in the Cavendish laboratories. He was respected as a shy and gentle scholar throughout the University.[16] An almost exact contemporary was Estyn Evans who came to Belfast in 1928 to take up a newly established lectureship in geography. He built up a department with an international reputation and was appointed professor in 1945. His wide interests led also to the establishment of the departments of archaeology and social anthropology, and the Institute of Irish Studies, whose first director he became in 1966. Outside Queen's he was instrumental in setting up the Ulster Folk and Transport Museum.[17]

The 'old guard' was gradually replaced by the new. These included David Bates, a Queen's graduate who returned to the University from London in 1951 as professor of applied mathematics. He made Queen's an international centre

13 There are numerous accounts of the dispute in the *Belfast News Letter* and the *Belfast Telegraph* throughout May 1963. That the local newspapers devoted so much space to an arcane academic argument is a measure of the intense interest the local community had in Queen's. A more detached, but somewhat oblique account is contained in Andrew Phang, op. cit.   14 A.B. Scott, 'Classics and Queen's, 1845–1995' (unpublished typescript, 1995), 22.   15 Among several accounts are John Bridges, *Belfast Medical Students Association* (Belfast, no date), 41 and 51–2; J.A. Weaver, 'John Henry Biggart 1905–1979, 1–19; R. Clarke, 'Giants in Ulster medicine', *Northern Ireland Medicine Today* (February, 2000), 5. Taped interview with Lord Ashby.   16 Alf McCreary. Taped interviews with Mrs Florence Emeleus (March 1992) and Professor Sir David Bates (March 1992).   17 Reminiscences made available to me by Mrs Evans. R.H. Buchanan, 'Obituary: Emyr Estyn Evans, 1905–1989', *Ulster Folklife*, 26 (1990), 1–3.

for the study of upper atmospheric physics. He was knighted for his services to science and education in 1978, and nominated for the Nobel Prize in Physics in 1990. He, in turn, recruited Alex Dalgano and Philip Burke, both of whom later became fellows of the Royal Society, the former when at Harvard and the latter at Queen's. Bernard Crossland, a Nottingham graduate, was appointed to the chair of mechanical engineering from Bristol University in 1959 and did much to transform the work of the Faculty of Applied Science. He inherited cramped premises and equipment 'which by 1959 should have found a place in a museum'. He was involved in the planning of the Ashby Building and had the task of bringing engineering from the Institute of Technology fully into Queen's. Professor Crossland was dean of the faculty between 1964 and 1967, Pro-Vice-Chancellor in 1978–82, and was appointed to a research chair in 1982. He became a fellow of the Royal Society, and was one of its vice-presidents in 1984–6. He was knighted, and in 1999 received the James Watt International Medal for his contribution to engineering.[18]

During the 1940s and 1950s most academics in the arts and social sciences were better known within Queen's than outside. But this was changing as new appointments brought fresh blood into the University. In modern history J.E. Todd was succeeded first by G.O. Sayles (who later went to the Regius chair at Aberdeen) and then, from 1954 by Michael Roberts, an Oxford trained historian appointed from South Africa. His successor was W.L. Warren, a mediaevalist and, like Roberts, a product of Oxford. Roberts and Warren were both important figures in the British historical profession. Roberts' colleague, J.C. Beckett, became one of Ireland's leading historians. He was a Queen's graduate and a school master for 'eleven years and three weeks' before returning to the University in 1945 to teach in the history department where he was appointed to a personal chair of Irish history in 1958. Philip Larkin, a sub-librarian at Queen's in the 1950s and fellow resident in Queen's Chambers, remembered him as 'a small old-maidish historian with a passion for Jane Austin and chess'. A more perceptive judgment comes from a historian of a younger generation. 'Beckett was a fair-minded and learned scholar; he was also a passionate Christian, who early in his life embraced both a religious faith and a particular vision of Irish identity.' He was a man 'who has touched so many of our lives for so long'.[19]

Influential in a different way was K.H. Connell appointed from Oxford to a senior lectureship in economic and social history in 1953 and later to a chair. When he died in 1973 his obituarist wrote, 'an historian is an important or significant historian to the extent that after he writes, or teaches students, history is not the same again ... Kenneth Connell was such a historian.' Through

18 Taped interview with Mr Alf McCreary, 1990; 'Interview' in *University of Nottingham Magazine*, 15 (autumn 2002), 12. **19** Andrew Motion, *Philip Larkin: a writer's life* (London, 1993), 198. Professor J.C. Beckett, interview with Alf McCreary, 1992. For a sensitive discussion of the importance of Beckett as a scholar see, Alvin Jackson, 'J.C. Beckett: politics, faith, scholarship', *Irish Historical Studies*, 33: 130 (2002), 129–50.

1 Queen's University, *c.*2000

2 The Quadrangle, *c.*2000

3 Old Library

4 Great Hall

5 The Old Queen's Elms, demolished in 1964

6 The New Student's Union in 1970

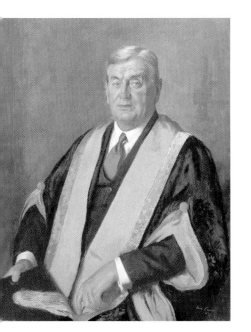

(*above left*) Sir David Lindsay Keir, Vice-Chancellor (1939–49) 8 (*above right*) Sir Eric Ashby, Vice-Chancellor (1950–9) 9 (*below left*) Dr Michael Grant, CBE, Vice-Chancellor (1959–66) 10 (*below right*) Sir Arthur Vick, Vice-Chancellor (1966–76)

11 (*above left*) Sir Peter Froggatt, Vice-Chancellor (1976–86) 12 (*above right*) Sir Gordon Beveridge, Vice-Chancellor (1986–97) 13 (*below left*) Sir George Bain, Vice-Chancellor (1998–2004) 14 (*below right*) Senator George Mitchell, Chancellor since 1999

15 (*above left*) Mary McAleese (Law). President of Ireland since 1997 **16** (*above right*) J.C. Beckett, MRIA (History). Professor of Irish History, 1958–75. **17** (*below left*) Brenda McLaughlin, CBE (Geography and Social Studies). Senior Pro-Chancellor of Queen's University since 1999. **18** (*below right*) Seamus Heaney (English), Nobel Laureate. Poet.

19 (*above left*) Estyn Evans, MRIA. Professor of Geography, 1945–66. 20 (*above right*) Sir David
Bates, FRS. Professor of Applied Mathematics and Theoretical Physics, 1951–74. 21 (*below left*)
John Blacking, Professor of Social Anthropology, 1970–90. 22 (*below right*) John McCanny, CBE
FRS. Professor of Microelectronics Engineering since 1988.

23 (*above left*) Edna Longley, MRIA. Professor of English, 1991–2003. **24** (*above right*) Dame Ingrid Allen, MRIA. Professor of Neuropathology, 1978–97. **25** (*below left*) Elizabeth Meehan, MRIA, Professor of Politics since 1997. **26** (*below right*) Margaret Mullett, FSA. Professor of Byzantine Studies since 1998.

27 (*above left*) Entering the Heaney Library. **28** (*above right*) Computer Suite. **29** (*below left*) School of Music. **30** (*below right*) Pharmacy Laboratory.

 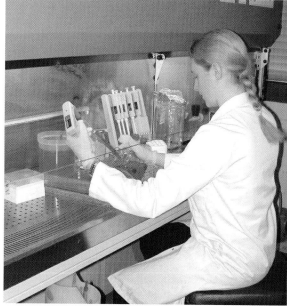

31 (*above left*) Gaelic football. 32 (*above right*) Hockey. 33 (*below left*) Netball. 34 (*below right*) The Rowing Club.

35 (*above left*) Relaxing. **36** (*above right*) The Union shop. **37** (*below left*) Coffee time. **38** (*below right*) Student crèche.

 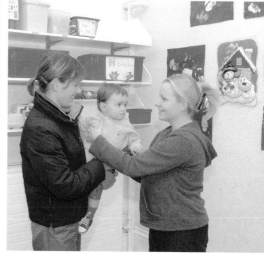

39 (*above*) Graduating.
40 (*right*) After the ceremony.
41 (*below left*) The garden party.
42 (*below right*) Champagne bar.

43 (*above left*) Queen's University of Belfast at Armagh. **44** (*above right*) The Cardinal Daly Library, Armagh. **45** (*below left*) The Art Gallery, Lanyon Building. **46** (*below right*) Festival at Queen's (Pure Movement, 2003).

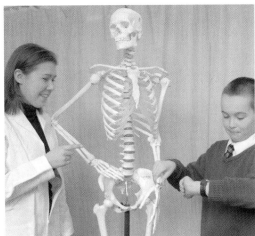

47 (*above left*) Young aeronautical engineer. 48 (*above right*) Young doctor. 49 (*below left*) Young scientist. 50 (*below right*) Young in heart. Jazz in the cloisters.

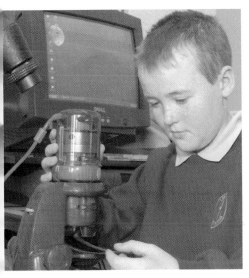

51 President Clinton, June 2000

52 Prince of Wales, January 2002

his relatively small corpus of writings on Irish population history he became one of the few truly seminal historian of Ireland in the second half of the twentieth century.[20] He was never fully appreciated in Queen's where his delight in controversy could make him an awkward colleague

Economic history developed within the Faculty of Economics and not in history. Following Professor Meredith's retirement, Keith Isles was appointed to the chair of economics, which he occupied until becoming Vice-Chancellor of the University of Tasmania in 1957. He was succeeded by S.R. Dennison (later Vice-Chancellor at Newcastle), and in 1962 by R.D.C. Black, who had joined the department in 1945 and remained at Queen's until 1985 as a world-renowned authority on the history of economic thought.[21] Charles Carter (who like Isles and Dennison also became a Vice-Chancellor) was appointed to a newly created chair of applied economics in 1951. He was followed in 1962 J.R. Parkinson who went on to the chair of economics at Nottingham.

The English department had for a long time been a weak link in the Faculty of Arts, but the appointment of a second professor in 1955 and a succession of new lecturers turned things around. In the mid 1960s Philip Hobsbaum began a poetry group that produced a line of fine young poets, the best known of whom was Seamus Heaney, a student from 1957 to 1961 and a member of staff from 1966 until 1972. Heaney acknowledged his debt to Queen's, and especially to Professor John Braidwood, in broadening his cultural horizons.[22] By the end of the century Queen's was properly regarded as one of the finest centres of creative writing in the United Kingdom.

This account so far has been exclusively about men. There were fewer than half a dozen women on the academic staff when the war ended. The first female professor (Mrs Katherine Atkinson) was appointed in 1964 and there were three more by the end of the decade. In the Faculty of Medicine Professor Mary McGeown made Belfast a world-renowned centre for the treatment of kidney disease. She became the first woman (apart from Queen Victoria) to have her portrait hung in the Great Hall. She was joined in 2003 by Mary McAleese, a Queen's graduate, who became Director of the Institute of Professional Legal Studies in 1987, professor and the first female Pro-Vice-Chancellor in 1994, and was elected President of Ireland in 1997.

In the scholarly world great importance is attached to that mysterious process known as 'peer review'. Universities prize the external recognition achieved by their staff. These include honorary degrees, although these are awarded for

20 R.M. Hartwell, 'Kenneth H. Connell: an appreciation', *Irish Economic and Social History*, 1 (1974), 7–13. 21 A.E. Murphy and R. Prendergast (eds), *Contributions to the history of economic thought: essays in honour of R.D.C. Black* (London and New York, 2000), 3–27. 22 Edna Longley, '"A foreign oasis"? English literature, Irish studies and Queen's University', *Irish Review*, 17/18 (winter 1995), 28–9 and 38–7; typescript memoir of Seamus Heaney by Eammon Hughes, School of English; Seamus Heaney, Introduction to *Beowolf: a new translation* (London, 1999), xxii–xxiv; Walker and McCreary, *Degrees of excellence*, 109.

status as well as academic success (Vice-Chancellors become weighed down by them). For scientists the ultimate accolade is a fellowship of the Royal Society. Queen's has had only a few fellows between 1945 and 2000. They included Professors Alan Wells and Sir Bernard Crossland in engineering, Sir David Bates and Philip Burke in applied mathematics and theoretical physics, and Alwyn Williams in geology. In the humanities and social sciences the equivalent is a fellowship of the British Academy. FBAs in Queen's have included Michael Roberts (history), Martin Jope (archaeology), R.D.C. Black, (economics), and David Livingstone (geography). Ireland has its own learned society, the Royal Irish Academy established in 1785, which embraces both science and 'polite literature'. At any on time around half a dozen staff have been members. Two Queen's graduates, both former members of staff have become Nobel laureates, David Trimble, a former law lecturer (peace), and Seamus Heaney (literature).

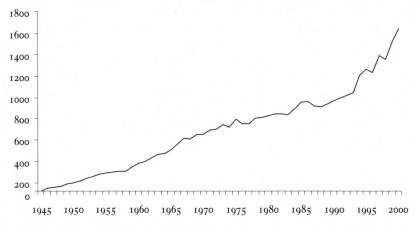

Graph 7.1: Full-time academic staff (teaching and research), 1945-2000

This discussion has covered only a small faction of academic men and women in Queen's. In singling them out we have overlooked the many who pursued careers in the University. Not all became fellows of learned societies or authors of seminal books, but through teaching, research, or administration – or all three – they contributed to the work of the University. Their numbers increased substantially between 1945 and 2000 (see graph 7.1) although during the last quarter of the century at a slower rate than the increase in student numbers.

ACADEMIC APPOINTMENTS, 1945–2000: A PROFILE

Between 1945 and 2000 the University made over 2300 full-time permanent appointments to the lecturing staff (see graph 7.2).[23] The years immediately

23 The data are taken from the *Senate minutes*, which until the end of the 1980s reported in considerable detail the *curriculum vitae* of appointees. Excluded are part-time and temporary

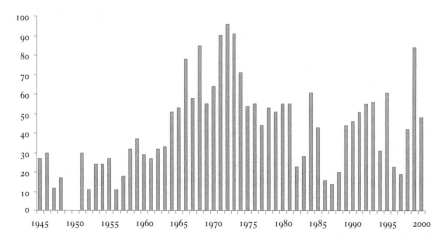

Graph 7.2: Annual full-time permanent lecturing appointments, 1945–2000

after the war were busy as vacant and newly established posts were filled. The flurry of activity dwindled at the end of the 1940s as staff numbers were brought back to pre-war levels. But the student population was growing and during the 1950s the pace of staff recruitment accelerated, fuelled by increased funding and driven by the missionary efforts of the Vice-Chancellor (Sir Eric Ashby). It quickened still more during the 1960s and continued unabated into the mid-1970s. A different Vice-Chancellor in 1964 complained it was difficult for Queen's to recruit good staff because of its remoteness from the London-Oxbridge triangle. Nevertheless, young scholars continued to find their way to Belfast. The peak years for appointments were 1971, 1972 and 1973 when 90, 96, and 91 academic posts were filled. Thereafter, annual appointments settled down at roughly 50 a year for the rest of the decade.

During the cash-strapped years of the late 1970s and the 1980s the trend in appointments was downwards. In addition to tight budgets the Troubles depressed recruitment. New appointments dropped sharply in 1982 and 1983. There was some recovery in 1984, 1985, and 1986, but fewer appointments were made in 1987, 1988, and 1989 than at any time since the early 1950s. Staff already in post became accustomed to receiving letters from the personnel office inviting them to lay down their careers for the good of the University. A

appointments. Also excluded are assistant lecturers, a grade that was abolished in the early 1960s. Most assistant lecturers were appointed to supernumerary lectureships within two or three years. When this happened they have been included in the calculations. Junior lecture-ships (six-year appointments created in 1924 and which survived into the 1950s) are included, as are fixed-term appointments. Personal chairs have been included when the Board of Curators reported them to the Senate, a practice that was not always followed during the 1990s. By the early 1990s, personal chairs had been superseded by promotional chairs. Academically related staff (i.e. research officers, etc.) are not included in the statistics.

premature retirement compensation scheme (PRCS) was introduced in 1982 to encourage staff over the age of 55 to leave, and there was a similar scheme for younger staff.[24] As a result there was a continual outflow of people and the total number of academic staff declined (although not student numbers). The retirement schemes were continued into the 1990s with further losses of academic men and women.[25]

Such a chronic haemorrhaging could not continue without damage to the work of the University. The level of appointments picked up in the early 1990s, reaching a peak of 61 in 1995 (well below the heights of the early 1970s). This was followed by another sharp retrenchment; only 19 appointments were made in 1997. The University was marking time between one regime and the next. In 1998 there was a new Vice-Chancellor and an ambitious plan to spend £25 million on academic restructuring. This involved the retirement or redeployment of around one hundred academics and the recruitment of new staff who, it was hoped, would be active researchers. There were 84 new appointments in 1999 and 48 in 2000.

In every year there was an outflow of staff through resignations and retirements; over the half-century such losses averaged roughly half the number of newcomers.[26] George Cowie, the Secretary of the University, calculated that between 1950 and 1960 24 lecturers moved from Queen's to chairs elsewhere, nine professors went to chairs in Britain and four became Vice-Chancellors.[27] There was an increase in resignations during the 1970s. At the end of the 1980s departures as a result of natural retirements or under PRCS sometimes outnumbered the inflow. Had it not been for a relatively young age structure of the staff, the net losses would have been even greater. During the boom years 1965–74 the average age of appointees was 32.[28] In late 1980s and 1990s, therefore, there were many academics in their low to mid-fifties for whom PRCS was not attractive.

What of the newcomers? On average nearly 50 men and women joined Queen's every year between 1945 and 2000. Their motives for coming were varied. Queen's was one of many universities in the United Kingdom; and universities in the Republic of Ireland, the USA and the Commonwealth also attracted British and Ulster-born academics. Queen's was admittedly distant from the centres of scholarship, although it had attractions of its own and com-

---

24 *Senate minutes, 1983*, 75–61, 86 and 205–6; *1986*, 319.   25 *Senate minutes, 1995*, 585–7.
26 Retirements and resignations were recorded in some detail in the *Senate minutes* until the 1970s. Thereafter only names were noted but it is not always possible to distinguish between academic and non-academic staff.   27 Taped interview with Alf McCreary, March 1991. The Vice-Chancellors included Keith Isles (Tasmania), Charles Carter (Lancaster, via the chair of economics at Manchester), H.R. Pitt (Reading, from the chair of mathematics at Nottingham), and S.R. Dennison (economics) to Newcastle. Later Vice-Chancellors recruited directly from Queen's included Alwyn Williams (Glasgow), Gareth Owen (Wales), and Colin Campbell (Nottingham).   28 The *Senate minutes* recorded the ages of appointees until 1997.

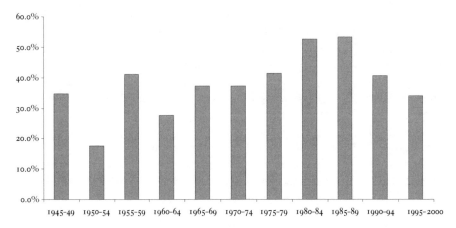

Graph 7.3: Proportion of academic staff qualifications from QUB

pared well with some English provincial universities. Philip Larkin arrived in 1950 as sub-librarian from Leicester and liked what he saw. 'Set beyond lawns and elm trees, and approached through impressive wrought-iron gates, [the Victorian buildings] evoked an academic atmosphere more like Oxford than Leicester.' When he left five years later he remembered 'a perfect little paradise of a library' (this was before the tower had reared its ugly head).[29]

A clue to the origins of the academic community is to be found by examining where individuals gained their qualifications. Graph 7.3 shows the proportion of qualifications gained at Queen's and, by implication, from other universities.[30] Thirty-eight per cent of qualifications were home grown and 62 per cent were from other universities. The proportion was not constant over time. From the early 1960s through to the late 1980s there was a rising trend in degrees obtained from Queen's,. At the peak, in 1987, Queen's awarded 68 per cent of the qualifications possessed by new appointees.

The rising trend of Queen's qualifications became pronounced during the 1970s as new appointments declined. The disturbed political climate of the 1970s and 1980s frightened some people off; the small number of candidates for senior posts was a constant worry to the boards of curators. There were one or two instances of individuals withdrawing from positions after initially accepting

---

29 Motion, *Philip Larkin*, 197–8; 247. The Lanyon Building similarly charmed Dr Godin when he arrived from Cardiff in 1934 to take up a lectureship in French. He contrasted it with the 'classical austerities' of University College London where he had studied, and the 'rather uninteresting modern style of the Cardiff College'.   **30** The table is compiled from information published in the *Senate minutes*. It uses the first three qualifications of an individual. Few persons possessed more than three on appointment but if they did, the first three have been used. The qualifications included are degrees and postgraduate diplomas except for teaching certificates. The medical degrees of MB, BCh, BAO are treated as a single qualification. Profession qualifications (e.g. memberships and fellowships) are excluded. The source of qualifications is only a proxy for the origins of the individual.

them. In one case a new professor took up his post and was welcomed to his first meeting of Academic Council, but quickly left the University in the face of terrorist threats. The point should not be exaggerated. It was not unknown in universities for a person to turn down an appointment after it had been offered, usually because he or she had received what was perceived to be better offer from elsewhere. But television images of bombs and bullets went down badly in Britain.

During the 1990s a succession of cease-fires made Northern Ireland seem a less unappealing place and the University became more attractive to aspiring academics. The total number of appointments climbed once again and the recruitment net was becoming spread more widely. The proportion of qualifications from universities other than Queen's rose, especially at the end of the decade.

All in all, the academic community of Queen's was reasonably cosmopolitan, with more than 60 per cent of its staff holding qualifications gained somewhere else. One-fifth of new appointees had been educated at some point in their careers at Oxford, Cambridge, or London. The proportion was highest in the 1950s and 1960s, after which the red bricks and glass plates made a greater contribution. During the 1980s and 1990s a sprinkling of appointees began to arrive from the New University of Ulster and its successor, the University of Ulster, especially in subjects such as business and nursing where Queen's had no strong tradition of producing graduates. Scottish qualifications were fairly numerous in the immediate post-war years but as the years passed the proportion of academics educated in Scotland (and Wales) declined.

Trinity College Dublin and the National University of Ireland together supplied only around 6 per cent of academic qualifications and there was no clear trend over time. The UK and Irish universities were separate systems, although with similar academic traditions, but Belfast was very much part of the former. Europe and the USA each supplied 2 per cent of academic qualifications. Other foreign countries and the Commonwealth provided about 4 per cent. Towards the end of the twentieth century there was a growing number of academics recruited from Russia and China. This trend was probably linked with the break-up of the Soviet Union and the political unrest in China. Whatever the reasons, such foreign appointments confirmed the place of Queen's in the international world of scholarship.

Recruitment was affected by custom and practice within the University as well as by supply conditions outside. Until the late 1980s, when employment legislation in Northern Ireland imposed strict appointment procedures, Queen's operated much as other universities, with information about vacant posts and promising scholars passing along the academic grapevine. The telephone, the postal service, the conference circuit, and personal contacts were great recruiters.[31]

31 A good example was that of D.R. Bates, who in 1951 was invited by Sir Eric Ashby to

There were marked differences across the disciplines. The most cosmopolitan faculties were arts and the social sciences.[32] Queen's awarded only 18 per cent of the qualifications held by scholars in these areas. Even during the 1980s, the proportion rose only to about a quarter. Scholars in the humanities were traditionally footloose. For many arts graduates making direct use of their expertise were few. Most arts departments in the Queen's were similar to dozens throughout the United Kingdom and they attracted people because of the opportunities they offered of working in a university. Occasionally the reputation of an individual academic exerted a pulling-power. Under John Backing, for example, the Department of Social Anthropology became an international centre for the study of ethnomusicology.

Lecturers in the faculties of law and education were more likely to be Queen's graduates than those in the humanities. Both professions relied on Queen's for trained men and women and there was a close relationship between the University and practising lawyers and teachers. In the natural sciences the proportion of degrees from Queen's was roughly the same as the University average. Many Queen's science graduates also had qualifications or had gained experience elsewhere. The University did not recruit actively in the applied sciences (engineering) until the mid-1950s. Up to that time most subjects were taught at the College of Technology where there was a definite emphasis on Queen's qualifications. Thereafter recruitment was spread more widely.

The tradition of appointing from among its own was long established in medicine where there was almost an apostolic succession of bright young graduates joining the staff.[33] Many of them, though, had spent time in hospitals in England, Scotland, or North America, before settling at Queen's. Clinical work took up a lot of time of the medical staff and for a long time there was no strong research ethos among the Queen's-trained staff and the most active research areas were often headed outsiders. Gradually, though, a growing number of non-Ulster trained professors and lecturers joined the medical faculty. The Faculty of Agriculture employed a high proportion of Queen's graduates. Possibly the civil service conditions of appointment were not attractive to outsiders seeking university appointments. The trend in appointments in the faculty also was different from those in the rest of the University.

return to Queen's from Imperial College, London to take up a chair of applied mathematics. An assistant lectureship was also created and Professor Bates wrote to Professor Massey at Imperial College asking for the name of a candidate. He recommended Alex Dalgarno who became 'probably the greatest figure in this field'. Interview with Mr Alf McCreary, February 1992. **32** The groupings follow the traditional faculty structures. Thus, geography and psychology are classified as sciences. Computer science is included in the natural sciences even though it was later transferred to engineering. Comparative pathology is included in agriculture but other branches are in medicine. Pharmacy is included in science and pharmacology in medicine. **33** Moody and Beckett, *Queen's, Belfast, 1845–1949*, ii, 505. Sir Eric Ashby recalled that when Sir William Thompson, Professor of Medicine, died in 1950, there was some resentment among consultants that his successor was chosen from the London Postgraduate Medical School.

THE PROFESSORIATE

Professors occupy a peculiar place in the British academic community. The status is normally gained by scholarly achievement (occasionally by promise) and professors in the Scottish and red brick universities traditionally served as heads of departments. This was the practice in Queen's for many years. With the increasing burdens of administration, and in acknowledgement of the fact that good scholars did not always make good administrators, the University gradually uncoupled the role of professor from that of departmental head. Personal chairs as recognitions of scholarship were instituted in 1956–7.[34] They were awarded sparingly until the 1980s, but personal chairs thereafter became a promotional grade and lost some of their former cachet.

More than 330 men and women were appointed or promoted to chairs between 1945 and 2000, the equivalent of 14 per cent of total academic appointments. Judging by their qualifications, they had a more varied background than the academic population as a whole. Only 30 per cent of their qualifications were gained in Queen's, compared with 38 per cent for all academics. The faculty distribution was similar to that for all staff, with the medical faculty heavily populated by professors holding Queen's degrees. The faculty also had proportionately more chairs than the other faculties. Nearly a quarter of all medical appointments were professorial. In engineering and science 14 or 15 per cent of appointments were professorial and in the humanities and social sciences 13 per cent. Professorial appointments were thin on the ground in agriculture where barely one person in ten was a professor. There are no obvious explanations for these differences, although in medicine it was probably necessary to offer senior appointments with professorial and consultant status in order to attract high quality medical graduates into academic life.

The greatest barrier to professorial status was gender, although the barrier operated principally lower down the academic hierarchy at the point where women entered the profession. Only 23 women were appointed to chairs between 1945 and 2000. Of these, 13 were appointed or promoted after 1990. The first female professor was Mrs Kathleen Atkinson, a member of staff since 1948, who was appointed to the newly established chair of ancient history in 1964 against external competition. The Vice-Chancellor, Dr Michael Grant, thought the event sufficiently noteworthy to draw it to the attention of the Senate. Dr Margaret Pelan was awarded a personal chair of medieval French in 1966. She had been a lecturer since 1938 (and a student before that). In 1967 another long serving member of staff, Dr Florence McGowan, was given a personal chair of morbid anatomy. In 1970 Dr Clare Palley, already on the staff, was appointed to the chair of public and comparative law after the first choice candidate withdrew (she was a most distinguished appointment). The first woman

34 *Academic Council minutes, 1957–8*, 93.

from outside Queen's to be appointed to a chair was Dr Kate Carr of Glasgow University, who became Professor of Anatomy in 1984. In 2000 the University had 17 female and 141 male professors.

GENDER

The small number of female professors touches on the wider issue of the small number of women appointed to academic posts at any level. Graph 7.4 summarizes the trends between 1945 and 2000. Between 1945 and 2000 just over 300 women joined the academic staff. This was an undistinguished record, although it was better than pre-war and no worse than the record of many British universities.[35] Throughout the 1950s and 1960s only two or three women, at most, and in several years none at all, jumped successfully through the curatorial hoops. There was a sudden surge of ten in 1966, only for appointments to decline to single figures again until another peak of 20 in 1974. These sporadic spurts, like the British Empire, were acquired in a fit of absence of mind, not as a result of policy. It was only in the 1990s that women were appointed in some numbers. During this decade the proportion of academic women increased by 11 percentage points from 13 in 1990 to 24 in 2000.[36]

The increase in the proportion of female appointments during the 1990s raises the question why there had been so few appointments earlier. It is possible that curators, overwhelmingly male, were wary of women and particularly of married women. In one case soon after the war they were brave enough to recommend a married woman for a lectureship, but they reassured the Senate she had no children. Gradually, though, the number of female appointments increased and the pool of women on the academic staff became larger. Between 1990 and 1994 the number of grade A lectureships (i.e. on the first three points of the salary scale) held by women went up by nearly 8 per cent. In 2000 women accounted for 40 per cent of grade A lecturers, 29 per cent of grade B lecturers, 22 per cent of readers or senior lecturers, and 11 per cent of the professors.[37] There were no female Pro-Vice-Chancellors in 2000 (Mary McAleese had been appointed in 1994) or deans, although earlier there had been three female deans, two in law and one in the social sciences.

The distribution of female academics across the faculties during the second half of the twentieth century was much as we might expect. Just over 60 per cent

35 According to Moody and Beckett, nine women were appointed to lectureships between 1931 and 1949, only three of these before 1945. These figures exclude temporary appointments and junior lecturers (Moody and Beckett, *Queen's, Belfast*, ii, 645–57). In 1998–9 Queen's was ranked by *The Times* as 45th out of 81 universities in its proportion of women professors: QUB, Women's Forum, *Report on gender imbalance at Queen's* (May, 2000), 4. 36 *Fifth report on equal opportunities* (QUB, 2000), 14. 37 QUB, Women's Forum, *Report on gender imbalance*, 5. See also *Senate minutes, 1996*, 308.

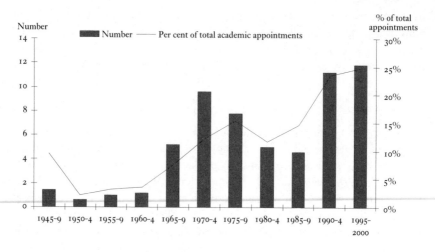

Graph 7.4: Annual average female full-time appointments

(190) were in the broad area of arts and social sciences. Women were relatively well represented in law, English, and other languages, as well as in sociology, social work, and social anthropology. It is striking how many young women there were on the staff of the Faculty of Law. We can only guess at the explanation. The legal profession was male-dominated and it may be its culture was uncongenial to female barristers and solicitors who therefore found academia more attractive. The medical school was proportionally the next largest employer of females, although a long way behind the humanities and social sciences. Women made up 16 per cent of all appointments in medicine. Their numbers were boosted in the late 1990s by the creation of the School of Nursing. The medical faculty was slightly more likely than some others to promote women to professorial positions.

The natural sciences could muster only forty-one female appointments between 1945 and 2000. Most were in psychology and the biological sciences. There were very few in chemistry, physics, mathematics, and geography. Generally the sciences were a male domain until the 1990s, although less so than agriculture and food science (fourteen female appointments over half a century) and engineering (six appointments). No woman breached its portals of engineering before 1989.

In 1996 the Director of Human Resources told the Senate, 'female employment at QUB reflected patterns in the labour market generally, with concentrations in administrative, clerical and library grades'.[38] In other words, conditions outside Queen's were responsible for the small number of women on the academic staff. The clerical staff were overwhelmingly female (98.5 per cent

---

38 *Senate minutes, 1996,* 308.

in 1994), and women were well represented in the Library. More than half the miscellaneous employees were women. These proportions were in contrast to the low representation of women among the academic grades.[39]

The University could not appoint women to lectureships unless they applied in the first place, and for many years there were no female candidates for academic posts. However applications gradually rose and in 1992–3 women accounted for 30 per cent of all academic applicants.[40] For senior positions the proportion was lower.[41] The distribution of applications reflected patterns of study by female undergraduates. As long as few women studied the sciences and engineering in schools and universities the supply of qualified female applicants in these disciples was bound to be small.

During the 1950s and 1960s marriage and motherhood kept many women out of the labour market, although much less so in later decades. In 1989 women made up 44 per cent of the work force in the United Kingdom, a proportion that increased throughout the 1990s. More strikingly still, 70 per cent of married women were in paid employment in the 1990s, many of them on a part-time basis. In Northern Ireland 46 per cent of all females were economically active in 1986, a rise of 11 percentage points since 1971, and 40 per cent of married women in 1986 worked outside the home.[42]

Superficially, conditions of employment in Queen's were identical for men and women. In 1994 the personnel office produced a gender report identifying attitudes that in society militated against women in employment, but the report was based on theoretical literature and not on an investigation of the position in Queen's. Not until 1999 with the establishment of the women's forum and the gender initiative did the University ask its female employees whether they found Queen's a congenial place in which to work. Almost to a woman they complained of a culture of isolation. The problem was not so much personal relationships – although there were occasional frictions – as the structures of the University. The working day, with lectures, tutorials and laboratory supervisions, preparation and marking, and committee meetings, was long. The main grievance was the lack of promotion opportunities. A long way behind was the absence of family-friendly policies. For example, committee meetings were often held at unsociable hours, making it difficult for women with families to attend. Unequal pay, limited crèche facilities and a lack of 'voice' were problems identified by women at all levels of the University.

There is no way of knowing whether the women on the staff in, say, the 1950s or 1970s shared the attitudes of their successors. The practice during the 1960s and 1970s of the Academic Council holding its meetings at 5 p.m. on Friday

39 *Fifth report on equal opportunities*, 14. **40** QUB, Personnel Department, *Gender report, third draft* (May 1994), 26. **41** E. McLaughlin and J. Trewsdale, *Gender equality at Queen's: a policy paper prepared for the Vice-Chancellor* (QUB, April 2000), 25. **42** M.J. Davidson and C.L. Cooper, *Shattering the glass ceiling: the woman manager* (London, 1992), 1; R.I.D. Harris et al. (eds), *The Northern Ireland economy*, 153 and 192–8.

evening hardly encouraged women to seek election (males, too, tended to value their Friday nights). Women suffered from restricted promotion opportunities throughout the whole period. The issue of unequal pay is a tricky one to pin down. Women in all categories of employment were concentrated in the lower grades and their average earnings were below those of men. They were also more likely than men to be on fixed-term contracts. The position was much the same throughout the United Kingdom universities.[43]

In January 1998 the Equal Opportunities Commission told Queen's that it was 'minded' to investigate the salaries of females in the Faculty of Law, suspecting that women were being appointed at lower salaries than men and remained on lower salaries even though doing work of equal value. The commission believed that the practice was not confined to law. The University was able to claim successfully, but 'only by the creative application of statistical techniques', that it was not discriminating against women, but it remained open to charge of a 'lack of transparency' in determining salaries on appointment.[44]

The gender initiative and the women's forum after 1998 helped to boost female employment, but the trend towards greater female participation had set in earlier. Social and legal pressures to open up female employment had been building up for several years and there were issues of social justice that the University could not ignore. At the end of 1989 the University was accused of discriminating against Roman Catholics in its employment policies. In the summer of the following year the Vice-Chancellor commissioned an inquiry to examine its employment procedures. The ensuing report concentrated on religion and at first diverted attention away from the much greater gender imbalance.[45] But it led to the implementation of procedures designed to avoid discrimination on grounds of religion, and if it could be done for religion it could be done for gender. During the 1990s there was plenty of good will towards appointing women, but positive measures were not put into place until the end of the century. Much of the credit for this was due to the new Vice-Chancellor, an expert in the workings of labour markets.

RELIGION

Universities elsewhere in the United Kingdom have little idea of the religious beliefs of their employees. Not so in Northern Ireland. Ever since the six-county Ulster was created as a political unit, discrimination in employment on grounds of religion (more precisely, of denomination) was widespread. The practice was one of many grievances that fed into the Troubles and from 1976 there was a raft

---

43 Sir Michael Bett, *Independent review of higher education pay and conditions* (London, 1999), D23–D24.   44 McLaughlin and Trewsdale, *Gender equality*, 5 and 22–3.   45 See chapter ten for a discussion.

of legislation in Northern Ireland prohibiting discrimination 'on grounds of religion, political opinion, gender and married status. Also included in the prohibition ... is discrimination on grounds of pregnancy and family status.'[46] Under the Fair Employment acts of 1976 and 1989 all bodies with more than ten employees were required to make annual returns to the Fair Employment Commission of the religious composition of their workforces and of applicants for employment. The monitoring was at first done according to which primary school in Northern Ireland persons attended. People educated outside Northern Ireland were categorised as XNI (later defined as 'not determined').

The *Fifth report on Equal Opportunities* published by Queen's in May 2001 offers a perspective on the trends in perceived religious allegiance of staff over the previous decade. The position is summarized in Table 7.3.

Table 7.3: Religious composition of staff, 1987–2000[47] (%)

	Protestant	Roman Catholic	Non-determined/other
1987	61.1	16.0	23.0
1990	60.9	19.2	19.8
1992	57.7	22.1	20.2
1994	55.5	23.0	21.3
1996	52.8	24.6	22.6
1998	54.9	28.8	16.3
2000	54.1	30.8	15.1

The most obvious feature of the table was the increase in the proportion of Roman Catholic staff. The large rise in 1998 and 2000 may be explained partly by a change in the monitoring method, from the schools test to direct questioning.[48] This suggests that there were more Roman Catholics among the academic staff in 1987 (and earlier) than the previous method revealed. However, this is not the full explanation. This becomes clear by examining the trends in each of the employment categories (see table 7.4).

Between 1987 and 2000 there was little change in the proportion of academic staff described as Protestant. There was, however, a 16-percentage point increase in the proportion of Roman Catholics, matched by an 18-percentage point fall in the proportion of those labelled non-determined. Lecturers were more likely to be recruited from outside Northern Ireland than other kinds of staff. When the Protestant/Catholic divide was determined by which primary school in Northern Ireland a person attended, nearly half of academics had been assigned to no denomination (XNI). Direct questioning in 1998 revealed that many of them were at least nominally Roman Catholic.[49]

46 The definition is quoted from Employment Equality Services, *Review of the structures, procedures and practices of the Queen's University of Belfast as they relate to the provision for and application of the equality of opportunity and fair participation in employment* (QUB, February 1993), 12.   47 *Fifth report*, 11.   48 *Fifth report*, 12 and 19.   49 We can only speculate why

Table 7.4: Representation by religion in each employment category (%)

| | 1987 | | | 2000 | | |
	Protestant	*RC*	*ND & Other*	*Protestant*	*RC*	*ND & Other*
Academic	42.5	9.3	48.1	44.5	25.7	29.8
Admin.	71.7	8.7	19.5	57.8	34.8	7.4
Technical	70.2	19.2	10.5	66.6	28.6	4.8
Clerical	73.0	17.6	9.5	62.8	34.2	3.0
Computer	57.8	31.9	10.3	52.8	41.7	5.6
Research	53.4	18.8	27.8	36.6	34.1	29.3
Library	56.0	20.0	23.3	67.6	23.8	8.6
Misc.	74.6	18.4	7.0	63.2	28.0	8.8

There were considerable differences among faculties. The proportions of Roman Catholic academics were lowest in medicine and engineering, and highest in the humanities and social sciences. During the enflamed sensibilities in Northern Ireland in the 1990s the high proportion of Protestants among the medics and engineers gave the critics of Queen's plenty to feed upon. The faculty differences reflected the patterns of academic recruitment discussed earlier whereby the humanities and social sciences cast their nets more widely than the others.

The non-academic categories display increases in the proportion of Roman Catholics during the 1990s that cannot be explained by a reclassification of the XNIs. There was, for example, a 26 percentage point increase in the proportion of Roman Catholic administrators, but only a 12 percentage point decline in the non-determined group. In two categories, research, and miscellaneous, the proportion of non-determined staff actually increased slightly at the same time as the Roman Catholic category grew substantially. In the case of the Library, more of the previously undefined staff seem to have been Protestants not Roman Catholics,

The most plausible interpretation of the patterns shown in table 7.4 is that a conscious policy of avoiding discrimination was being followed during the 1990s, whereas in earlier decades there may have been unintentional discrimination when making non-academic appointments. There is anecdotal evidence that Roman Catholics were reluctant to apply for clerical or maintenance posts, believing that they would not be appointed, but positive evidence is hard to find.[50]

a large number of XNIs were probably Roman Catholics. Some had been born in the Republic of Ireland and it is probable they were Catholic. There were also English- and Scottish-born Roman Catholics on the staff.   50 A fuller discussion will be found in chapter ten.

THE NON-ACADEMIC STAFF

The discussion of religious affiliations has led us back to the non-academic staff without whom the academic business would stutter to a halt. In the immediate post war years the senior administrative staff could be accommodated – almost – in two or three reasonably sized rooms.[51] The administrative structure was much as it had been in 1908. Apart from the Vice-Chancellor, whose role was more academic than administrative, the most important officers in the University were the Secretary of the Academic Council (who was also an academic), the Bursar, the Secretary of the University, and the Librarian. By 1950 the Bursar had an assistant and the Secretary had two assistants, and there were four assistant librarians.[52] The administration was beginning to multiply like agitated amoeba. By the end of the century the Bursar (now re-designated as the Director of Finance) had nineteen assistant administrators plus several secretaries. The most spectacular growth occurred in the personnel office. The University did not have a Personnel Officer until 1971. Twenty years later he had a staff of eleven; and at the end of the 1990s the Personnel Officer had become the Director of Human Resources and was supported by a staff a staff of seventeen, including an equal opportunities unit required under the Northern Ireland fair employment legislation.

Matching the growth in administration was a multiplication in the number of services intended to assist staff and students such as University Health Service, the Physical Education Centre and the careers office. By the end of the 1950s the University had a buildings office and a catering unit. These were joined in the 1960s by the data processing office and the capital development office. The scrutiny of academic standards spawned its own structures staffed by their own administrators. So there emerged the Centre for Academic Practice, the Enterprise Office, and the Research Office. Training courses for newly appointed lecturers were introduced in the mid-1970s. They were greeted without enthusiasm, but came to be accepted as a rite of initiation. A staff training and development unit was set up in 1989 offering a range of courses. At the end of the century, to select at random, there was a two-day programme for academic staff covering such mysteries as human resources, financial management, personal development, library and computer resources, as well as the mundane matter of how to teach. There were induction courses for research and clerical staff and advanced classes for established staff on interviewing techniques. A course on 'writing plain English in a professional context' was deemed to be

51 Dr Godin recalled arriving in Belfast in 1934. He went to see the Bursar, John Green. He was 'a tall man with spats, standing at an equally tall desk. His staff of two ladies also stood at tall desks.' Address to QUB Association of Women Graduates, March 1983. 52 There are intriguing glimpses of the library staff in the early 1950s in Motion, *Philip Larkin*, 200–1, 209, including a photograph of the male library staff including Larkin and 'Ernest the stack boy' between pp 268 and 269.

desirable for 'Secretarial and Administrative Staff, in particular'.[53] This was a long way from a memorandum circulated by the Vice-Chancellor to administrators in the 1950s setting out the correct use of capital letters, commas, and semi-colons.

The need for a strong public image was a further reason for the growth of administrative numbers. A flurry of university newspapers came and went until in October 2000 *Queen's Now* emerged in a tabloid format. The newspaper was produced by the Communications Office whose jurisdiction included the annual festival of the arts, the film theatre, a shop selling momentoes, the art gallery, and the organization of 'events' (that is, graduation ceremonies, public lectures, and the like). Finally, the University developed closer links with its alumni (it needed their money) by means of a Development and Alumni Office.

We do not have statistics of the numbers of secretaries, cleaners and others employed by the University for most of the time. At the end of the century there were 535 clerical staff. One hundred and seventy-eight cleaners (including 58 men) kept the University tidy. There were gardeners, caterers, crèche attendants, 'tradespeople' (all males) and 36 porters. For many visitors to the University a porter was likely to be the first person he or she met.

Just occasionally one of these anonymous employees emerges from the shadows such as Miss Darragh, a part-time glass washer in the Department of Biochemistry from 1932 to 1968. When she finally retired aged 82, the University awarded her a discretionary pension of £1 a week. It wanted to give her more but that would have reduced her state pension.[54]

CONCLUSION

At the end of the twentieth century Queen's was one of the largest employers in Northern Ireland with more than 3,200 employees. Except perhaps in ethnicity (more than 80 per cent of the workforce were defined as 'white/European') the employees formed a diverse group. Nearly two-thirds were Protestant and just over half of them were male.[55] The gathering of such statistics was important for satisfying the requirements of employment legislation, but they do not capture the essence of the University. The men and women who were at the heart of Queen's were the professors and lecturers who did the teaching and carried out the research. Among them were some who would have been outstanding in any institution of higher learning in the world. There were one or two, no doubt, whose appointments in retrospect might be thought of as mistaken. As for the rest, John Henry Newman once wrote:

53 The Staff Training & Development Unit, *Training and development opportunities for all university staff, 1999–2000* (QUB, 1999). 54 *Senate minutes, 1968*, 207. 55 *Fifth report*, 1 and 5.

A University is not a birthplace of poets or of immortal authors, of founders of schools, leaders of colonies, or conquerors. It does not promise a generation of Aristotles or Newtons, of Napoleons or Washingtons, of Raphaels or Shakespeares, though such miracles of nature it has before now contained within its precincts. Nor is it content on the other hand with forming the critic or the experimentalist, the economist or the engineer, though such too it includes within its scope. But a University training is the great ordinary means to a great but ordinary end; it aims at raising the intellectual tone of society, at cultivating the public mind, at purifying the national taste, at supplying true principles to popular enthusiasm and fixed aims to popular aspiration, at giving enlargement and sobriety to the ideas of the age, at facilitating the exercise of political power, and refining the intercourse of private life.[56]

This is a fair description of the nature and purpose of the body of scholars who worked in Queen's between 1945 and 2000.

56 Quoted in I. Ker, *The genius of John Henry Newman: selections from his writings* (Oxford, 1989), 25.1973–4.

8

Students

Students are the backbone of Queen's. The metaphor is perhaps not quite appropriate since most students are passing through, staying for three or four years before moving on. But they are the reason for the University's existence. For all the stress currently put upon research, universities came into being in order to educate students.

Major changes occurred in the composition of the student body during the half-century after the war. The number of full-time students increased seven-fold, and part-time students studying in what was eventually known as the Institute of Life Long Learning (originally Extra-Mural Studies and then Continuing Education) grew from insignificant totals to several thousand. Female students rose as a proportion of the total and eventually outnumbered males. Roman Catholic students became increasingly numerous. The faculty distribution of students changed dramatically. Queen's was at one time known as 'a medical school with a university attached'.[1] At the end of the 1950s this was no longer true. Nevertheless, the medical faculty remained large and by the late 1990s it became larger still as it embraced nursing as well as its traditional disciplines of medicine and dentistry. The social sciences flourished and within its broad church business studies and accounting boomed, alongside the more venerable disciplines of sociology, politics and economics. In the humanities there was an inexorable dwindling of the classics, but history, English, and the major European languages, except for Italian and Russian, prospered. In the sciences there was a major growth in computer-related studies. The most noticeable development in the Faculty of Engineering was the advance of women into what had been almost a male monopoly.

The social and support services provided for students expanded faster than their growth of numbers. The halls at Queen's Elms and student houses replaced Queen's Chambers, Riddel Hall and Aquinas Hall. The glass and concrete slab of the Students' Union building on University Road took over from the late Victorian premises in University Square as the focus of social activities. Within the Union the nature of student life altered out of recognition. By the end of the century, if students were in difficulties academically, financially, or personally, there was a plethora of institutional shoulders for them to weep on.

1 The description has a considerable currency. It is quoted by Edna Longley in '"A foreign oasis"?', 28. Walker and McCreary in *Degrees of excellence* (Belfast, 1994), 65, attributed it to Dr D.B. McNeill, an engineering student in the 1930s, but he may have been using a phrase current at the time.

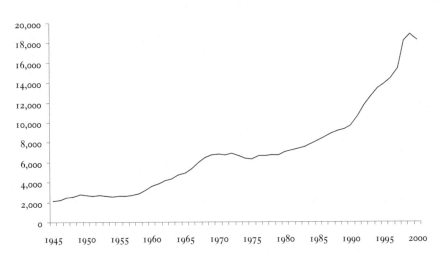

Graph 8.1: Student numbers, 1945–2000

STUDENT NUMBERS

Graph 8.1 shows the increase in student numbers from 1945 to the end of the twentieth century. Numbers rose for a few years immediately after the war as ex-servicemen joined school leavers in the University. Thereafter the student population stayed more or less static until the mid-1950s. Numbers then increased again, possibly reflecting the introduction of the eleven-plus examination into Northern Ireland in 1948 and the consequential growth in the grammar school population. In 1950–1 fewer than 4 per cent of 17- to 20-year-olds in Northern Ireland entered Queen's.[2] A few also went to Oxford, Cambridge, or Trinity College, Dublin. There were, though, growing concerns in Britain about the small numbers of university-educated men and women, concerns that eventually found expression in the Robbins report in Britain and Lockwood report in Northern Ireland.

There was a sustained increase in student numbers during the 1960s when the student population doubled. Queen's shared to a limited extent in the expansion of higher education throughout Northern Ireland following the report of the Lockwood committee; the New University never succeeded in attracting students in the numbers that had been planned. Mandatory grants for undergraduates, introduced in 1962, eased some of the financial burdens on students. According to the Vice-Chancellor they resulted in many weak students 'flocking' to Queen's thus pushing up failure rates in First Arts (to 50 per cent in one subject).[3] He did not consider an alternative explanation, that poor teaching

2 *Vice-Chancellor's report, 1950–1*, 15.   3 *Gown*, 12 October 1962.

might be partly to blame. Grants notwithstanding, entry into higher education remained skewed towards the higher social classes. As late as 1973 three-quarters of the Province's full-time undergraduates came from non-manual backgrounds.[4]

The rate of growth slackened during the 1970s; indeed there was a slight dip in the mid-1970s. The New University of Ulster was taking a few students and the post-Robbins universities in Britain were attracting growing numbers of undergraduates, particularly as the Troubles bit into everyday life. At its peak in the early 1970s the outflow accounted for over 40 per cent of Northern Ireland's entrants to higher education. Thereafter it settled down to around one-third.[5] In the other direction, the once substantial movement of Ulster students to Trinity College, Dublin dwindled to insignificance. Student numbers in Queen's began to rise again in the late 1970s and the 1980s. The student population grew rapidly during the 1990s although with a temporary stutter at the end of the century, possibly associated with the growing burden of costs of higher education falling once more on students or their parents.

At the end of the century more than 60 per cent of grammar school leavers in Northern Ireland went on to higher education (the proportion from the secondary schools was only 5 per cent), and 80 per cent of all school leavers with two or more A-levels moved into universities or polytechnics. In 1956 Sir Eric Ashby told undergraduates to prepare for 'a strenuous intellectual adventure' and advised them 'it is unwise ... to rely on vacation employment as a source of income' because 'vacations are primarily intervals between classes for solitary and essential study – not holiday periods.'[6] Four decades later when there were no grants and they had to pay fees, most students needed vacation earnings to pay off overdrafts and possessed pragmatic expectations about their courses. Their motives, as revealed in a survey of student attitudes published in 1996, were to get a job qualification, to find time to grow up ('self development'), and 'to meet people from the other religion'.[7]

There was an expansion of part-time undergraduate education. Between 1950 and 1980 part-time students accounted for less than 15 per cent of the total. Some of the were undergraduates repeating a year and enrolled for examinations only because of previous failure. Most of the rest were postgraduates. The Faculty of Economics was the only one that offered a primary degree by part-time study in the evening. The introduction of the BA (General Studies) degree in 1984–5 and modular course structure pushed up the proportion of part-time students to a fifth of the total during the 1990s. Of the part-timers 60 per cent were now undergraduates.

4 Osborne, *Higher education in Ireland North and South*, 33. By 1991 the proportion coming from the manual had risen to 35 per cent. Even so, social classes I and II, which accounted for 25 per cent of the population, supplied 58 per of entrants to higher education (ibid., 34). 5 Ibid., 18–19. 6 *A fresher's guide to Queen's*, 1956. QUB archives, P/870. 7 A.M. Gallagher, R.D. Osborne, R.J. Cormack, *Attitudes to higher education: report to CCRU and DENI* (Belfast, 1996), 2–3 and 63–4.

A consequence of increasing part-time numbers was to raise the number of so-called mature students (i.e. aged 21 and over) in Queen's. In 1965–6 only 12 per cent of new undergraduates were aged 21 or over; by the 1990s the proportion had risen to over 17 per cent. The opposite end of the age structure of undergraduates had worried the University in the early 1950s when nearly a third of students entering Queen's were under 18 years of age, compared to only 9 per cent in British universities. The Northern Ireland senior leaving certificate normally lasted for one year only, whereas in England sixth-form studies extended over two years. As a result, boys and girls in Northern Ireland 'leave school earlier and they enter the University younger in years and less mature intellectually.' High failure rates in the first year were attracting critical comments from the University Grants Committee. The Vice-Chancellor described the position as 'a perplexing educational problem.' The solution, he suggested, was for the schools to extend sixth form studies over two years, not for the University to lower standards.[8] By the end the decade many grammar schools in the Province had introduced a second year in the sixth form. The problem disappeared when the Northern Ireland schools adopted A-levels.

GENDER AND DENOMINATION

The most striking change in the composition of the student population was the increasing proportion of females entering Queen's from the mid-1960s (see graph 8.2). During the 1950s and 1960s they accounted for 20 to 25 per cent of the population, much the same as before the war. Thereafter their numbers rose steadily and in 1997 women outnumbered men for the first time. The establishment of the School of Nursing, a predominately female profession, carried the proportion of women up to nearly 60 per cent of the total by the end of the century. Part of the explanation for the increase was that girls out-performed boys at A-level.[9] But the reasons go deeper than this. The girls' grammar schools were getting better at teaching the sciences, thus adding to the flow of females into subjects such as physics, chemistry, and engineering.[10] More important still, society's assumptions of what females could do were changing; careers once regarded as exclusively male were opening up to women. Females were coming to Queen', and indeed to all universities, in the expectation that after graduation they would compete in the job market on the same terms as men.

8 *Vice-Chancellor's report, 1952–3*, 167–8.   9 Osborne, *Higher education in Ireland*, 33. 10 On the traditional weakness of girls' schools in the teaching of science see A. McEwen and C. Curry, 'Girls' access to science: single sex versus co-educational schools'), in R.D. Osborne et al. (eds), *Education and policy in Northern Ireland*, 137–49. In 1972 the number of girls sitting mathematics A-level was 335, compared to 1,138 boys. For physics the numbers were 298 and 1,091; and for chemistry 310 and 853. These figures are taken from Lynda Egerton, 'Social and economic discrimination against women in Northern Ireland', typescript produced by the Welfare Committee of the Students' Union (*c.* 1975). QUB archives, P/879.

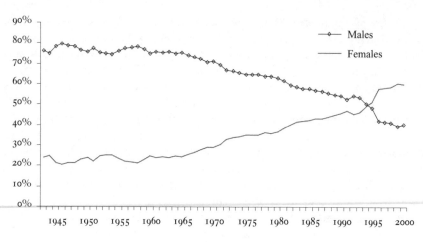

Graph 8.2: Percentage of students by sex, 1945–2002

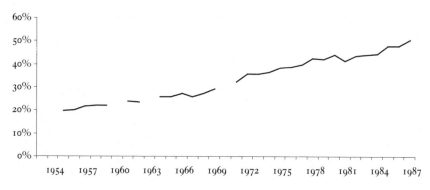

Graph 8.3: Roman Catholic students as a percentage of total students

A second important shift was the growing proportion of Roman Catholic students (see graph 8.3[11]). When Queen's became independent in 1908–9 Roman Catholics accounted for fewer than 6 per cent of all students. At that point the University stopped collecting denominational information. However, the Catholic bishops had decided that Queen's was a place suitable for its flock and by 1915 just over a quarter of students were Roman Catholics. During the inter-war years the proportion hovered around 20 per cent. But the proportion started to rise during the 1950s. The biggest increases were in arts, followed by economics and medicine. By the end of the 1980s Catholics accounted for half the students in Queen's and they were in a majority in arts, law, and the social sciences. The lowest share was in medicine (42 per cent). In the mid-1990s

11 *Academic Council minutes, 1990*, insertion after p. 36. The data were supplied by the Roman Catholic chaplaincy.

Queen's resumed the gathering of denominational data. At the end of the century 54 per cent of the student population was Roman Catholic and 46 per cent Protestant. The Catholic proportion was now greater than the proportion of Roman Catholics in the population at large aged 18–24 (48 per cent in 1991) from which the bulk of university entrants was drawn.

The changing balance between Protestant and Roman Catholic students reflected major social changes in the Province. In 1963 the President of the Catholic Secondary Teachers' Association claimed the low social status of many Roman Catholics made it difficult for their children to get into universities, although he blamed the Catholic schools for showing 'timidity' when it came to encouraging their pupils to train for the professions.[12] But the schools were changing and so were the aspirations of their pupils and their parents. School leavers were now moving into higher education in increasing numbers. They were often the children of manual workers, and 'there is clear evidence that Catholics have been using higher education as a route to social mobility in circumstances where both historically and in more recent times job opportunities have not always be open to Catholics.'[13]

During the 1990s there was a heated and not very enlightened discussion about why Roman Catholic students had become a majority in Queen's. Some unionist politicians alleged there was a 'chill factor' in the University, and especially in the Students' Union, deterring Protestant students. As a result Queen's was becoming a 'Catholic', even a republican, university. The evidence is unclear. Sixth-formers were aware of the tensions within the Students' Union, but a survey of the attitudes of school leavers failed to show that 'significant numbers' were thereby affected in their choice of university.[14]

In one respect Queen's retained a stoutly Ulster face. Throughout the second half of the twentieth century between 85 and 95 per cent of all students came from Northern Ireland. In the immediate post-war years there were around 150 students a year in residence from other parts of the United Kingdom, constituting about 6 per cent of the total. Many were ex-servicemen taking the opportunity of post-war demobilization schemes and their numbers soon declined.[15] When Queen's joined the United Kingdom universities' clearing system (UCCA) in 1967 there was a temporary increase in the number of British students. But their numbers fell to between 1 and 2 per cent of the total as the civil unrest scared them off. Even in the more settled 1990s the proportion of students from Britain remained low and overseas students outnumbered British students by almost two to one.

During the 1980s and early 1990s there was a small but rising number of

12 *Irish News*, 9 March 1963.   13 Osborne, *Higher education in Ireland*, 34–7; Gallagher et al., *Attitudes to higher education*, 66–70.   14 Gallagher et al., *Attitudes to higher education*, 43–7.   15 One of these was Peter Benham who after an interlude at Imperial College, London, returned to Queen's where he became Professor of Civil Engineering and then of Aeronautical Engineering, and Pro-Vice-Chancellor.

students from the Republic of Ireland. By coming from a country within the European community they could enrol in Queen's without paying fees at a time when universities in Ireland charged fees. The re-introduction of student fees into United Kingdom universities put a stop to this modest influx.

FACULTY AND SUBJECT DISTRIBUTION

In 1945 students were enrolled into one of eight faculties: agriculture, applied science (later engineering), arts, commerce (later economics), law, medicine, science, and theology (education came later). In 1996 the nine faculties were reduced to five. Theology was merged with arts to form humanities; economics, social sciences, law, and education had been lumped into an omnibus faculty of law, social, and educational sciences (LSES). Science had absorbed agriculture. Applied science had been renamed engineering. Medicine had gained a school of nursing and was renamed the Faculty of Medicine and Health Sciences (surely there was not a suggestion that medicine was not a health science?). The student numbers shown in table 8.1 (below) have been arranged according to the structures in place since 1996.[16]

The immediate post-war figures were distorted by ex-servicemen, many of them reading medicine or applied science. Comparing the 1950s with the 1990s, the biggest percentage gains were in the social sciences. These were a conglomeration of economics, economic and social history, sociology, social work, politics, management, accounting, and information management. The biggest loser in percentage terms (although not numbers) until the arrival of the nursing students, was medicine. Student numbers in the humanities almost quadrupled between the mid-1950s and mid-1990s, although their share of the total fell. Science and agriculture grew both in numbers and in percentage terms. Engineering experienced a fall as a per cent of the total, but a four-fold increase in numbers.

Students enrolled in a single faculty, but this was essentially an administrative convenience and many of them read combinations of subjects that crossed faculty boundaries. For example, in 1965–6 combinations of arts, economics, and social science courses accounted for 16 per cent of all enrolments, and various arts combinations for another 8 per cent. A further 10 per cent of enrolments were made up of permutations of arts, social sciences, the natural sciences, or engineering.[17] To put the point another way, single subject enrolments in law, civil engineering, mathematics and physics, and medicine, each

16 The category, 'academic general' includes a small number of exchange students pursuing *ad hoc* courses. After 2000 they were allocated to faculties according to the subjects they studied. From 1984 to 2000 students reading for the BA(General Studies) degree were counted with LSES; thereafter they were distributed among faculties.   17 These proportions have been calculated from the University's returns to the UGC. Earlier figures are not available.

Table 8.1: Distribution of students by faculty

(i) number

	Humanities	LSES	Science/ agriculture	Applied science (engineering)	Medicine/ health sciences	Academic general	Total
1945–9	504	309	352	517	759		2441
1950–4	649	342	447	508	705		2651
1955–9	755	432	540	484	588		2798
1960–4	1159	658	958	639	650		4064
1965–9	1686	1070	1305	1051	778		5891
1970–4	1998	1239	1656	994	803		6689
1975–9	1899	1486	1434	848	961		6627
1980–4	1930	1730	1740	1080	926		7406
1985–9	2089	2322	2139	1340	953		8842
1990–4	2455	3447	2810	1677	1214		11603
1995–2000	2664	4964	3568	2294	2932	132	16553

(ii) per cent

	Humanities	LSES	Science/ agriculture	Applied science (engineering)	Medicine/ health sciences	Academic general	Total
1945–9	20.7	12.7	14.4	21.2	31.1		100
1950–4	24.5	12.9	16.9	19.2	26.6		100
1955–9	27.0	15.4	19.3	17.3	21.0		100
1960–4	28.5	16.2	23.6	15.7	16.0		100
1965–9	28.6	18.2	22.2	17.8	13.2		100
1970–4	29.9	18.5	24.7	14.9	12.0		100
1975–9	28.6	22.4	21.6	12.8	14.5		100
1980–4	26.1	23.4	23.5	14.6	12.5		100
1985–9	23.6	26.3	24.2	15.2	10.8		100
1990–4	21.2	29.7	24.2	14.4	10.5		100
1995–2000	16.1	30.0	21.6	13.9	17.7	0.8	100

claimed around 4 per cent of undergraduate enrolments. There were two consequences of this pattern of study. The first was that students graduating with primary degrees were broadly, although not always deeply, educated. Secondly, small subjects thrived. There might not be many students wishing to specialize in, say, Greek or the history and philosophy of science, but such subjects prospered as part of a bundle of studies.

Substantial shifts in student preferences occurred as the decades passed. The general degree was phased out during the 1980s and most degrees, whether general or honours, now lasted for three years.[18] There remained, nevertheless, a great deal of choice for students. At the end of the twentieth century the most heavily subscribed subject, as measured by 'student load' was medicine[19]

18 See chapter nine.   19 Student load was a planning statistic that attempted to relate student numbers to staff numbers. An honours student was weighted more than a subsidiary or 'minor' student, a final year student differently from a first-year student, a postgraduate stu-

But this was a special case created by the length of the degree (five years) and the high weighting given to students engaged in clinical work. Otherwise, the most popular subjects were law, biology and biochemistry, the social sciences, engineering, geography, English, computer science, chemistry, physics, applied mathematics, modern history, and the major modern languages.

Students generally chose subjects with an eye on the job market. Those hoping to enter business enrolled in economics, business studies and accounting. The colonization of the world by computers and information technology created a demand for courses in those areas. Careers in medicine, dentistry, social work, architecture or law all required relevant degrees. Undergraduates with ideals, or perhaps with no clear sense of what they wanted to do after graduation, looked to politics or sociology for salvation or inspiration. There were many subjects that had no particular relevance for future employments. Students who chose to read English, or history often did so because they had been good at them at school and had a generalized understanding that an arts degree might open up opportunities in teaching, management, journalism, management, or administration.

Beyond the possibilities of employment, there were random influences of parents, friends, and school teachers. There were dynasties of doctors and lawyers in Northern Ireland whose sons and daughters followed their fathers (and occasionally their mothers) into these professions almost by a process of apostolic succession. From time to time the government tried to influence demand ('the nation needs more engineers'), although it stopped short of direct demand management. Demand was determined also by what the University was prepared to offer. Nobody was able to read theatre and film studies, for example, until Queen's taught the subjects at the end of the century. It is sometimes argued that universities should teach subjects such as classics, no matter the level of demand, because they are the foundations of western civilization. The problem for Queen's was that maintaining subjects regardless of the level of demand could only be done at the cost of not doing something else.

STUDENT SUPPORT

The facilities in Queen's designed to ease undergraduates their way through their studies were few at the end of the Second World War. Most lived at home or in lodgings. The Students' Union (men only, except for the dining room) operated in a building too small for the purpose at the end of University Square. There were scarcely adequate athletics facilities at Cherryvale on the Ravenhill road and a small Physical Education Centre in Sans Souci Park. A student

dent more than an undergraduate student, and so on. The number of staff as well as the numbers of students studying in a department affected the measure.

health service had begun in 1948. Undergraduates were the passive recipients of lectures and they had little influence on the scope and content of their courses or on the performance of their lecturers. The Library was too small for the needs of two thousand students and the science laboratories were cramped.

Fifty years later much had changed. A new Union Building had been built in the 1960s, although thirty years later it was bursting at the seams. Sports' facilities included the playing fields at Upper Malone and the Physical Education Centre in Botanic Gardens. An expanded University Health Service attended to the physical and mental welfare of students (and staff), and a Careers and Appointments Service eased graduates into the world of work. Students had become members of the Academic Council and the Academic Board, sat on staff-student committees, and wrote (confidential) reports about their courses and their teachers. The Library had been supplemented by a battery of computer facilities that enabled students to search the world-wide-web for information although not necessarily for understanding.

A pressing at the end of the war was the lack of residential accommodation. It had long been an article of faith among university thinkers that living in a community added to the richness of the experience. Throughout his tenure as Vice-Chancellor between 1924 and 1933 Sir Richard Livingstone had advocated the building of halls for men, because, 'residential halls are obviously better for boys from 17–20, for they combine supervision with freedom'.[20] Little had been achieved until the opening of Queen's Chambers in 1936. A decade later there were only 42 residential places for men, plus a total of 81 for women in Riddel Hall for Protestant students, and Aquinas Hall for Catholic women, neither of them owned by Queen's.

In 1946 the Vice-Chancellor hoped 'the advantage of the residential system ought ultimately to be made available to every student of the University.'[21] Three years later Queen's declared its ideal of providing at least one year's residence for every student.[22] At the time there were places for only 5 per cent of students. In 1953 nearly a half of all students still lived at home and most of the rest were in lodgings or lived with relations. In 1960 the University bought a site on the Malone Road and construction of four halls began in the following year.[23] Two were ready in 1964–5 and a third was finished two years later. By 1968 over 600 students lived in the halls; two-thirds of them came from Northern Ireland, 22 per cent from Britain and Ireland, and the rest from elsewhere.[24] A fourth hall was ready in 1970. A decade later there were over 800 students in residence.

As the halls went up so some of the conventions that shaped society for generations came down. At the beginning of 1969 the Committee of Deans reported the outcome of a meeting with the Students' Representative Council.

20 *Senate minutes, 1923–4*, 173. 21 *Vice-Chancellor's report, 1945–6*, 164. 22 *Vice-Chancellor's report, 1948–9*, 190–1. 23 *Vice-Chancellor's report, 1960–1*, 308. 24 *Vice-Chancellor's report, 1967–8*, 23.

The students had asked that Queen's should stop acting *in loco parentis*. The deans agreed: 'as a general principle, the Deans supported the view that the concept of *loco parentis* is no longer valid.'[25] A further sign of changing times was that one of the halls (Hamilton Hall) became a mixed hall in 1975–6, a move that was reported to be very popular among students.[26] Queen's was also extending its stock of approved lodgings. A lodgings committee had been formed in 1946 and a part-time lodgings officer appointed two years later. Approved lodgings were registered and the University held an annual tea party for its landladies. In the mid-1950s there were 500 registered lodgings on the books, housing 700 students.[27] The University also provided self-catering houses that by 1970 offered 320 places.[28] Three years later the first of the custom-built self-catering blocks was opened at San Souci Park and others soon followed.[29]

Between 1988 and 1995 the University added over 600 residential places to its stock of residences. One hundred of these were catered places in Brunswick House near the city centre, which the University rented to ease its accommodation problems. The rest were self-catering rooms preferred by most students. Many were in purpose-built premises – Guthrie House, Grant House, and Sir Rowland Wright Hall – and the remainder in refurbished houses in San Souci Park and Mount Charles. In 1998 Queen's proposed to increase its stock of residences to 2100 places at a cost of £11.6 million. Included in the plans was the refurbishment of the 1960s halls at Queen's Elms site. The University was also giving preliminary thoughts to the construction of a 'student village' incorporating shops and the other accruements of life that had become necessary to the late twentieth century student.[30]

By the end of the century Queen's had more or less achieved its objective of being able to offer all students a year's residence in university accommodation. Many students also rented houses from private landlords. Styles of living had changed greatly. A sign of the times was the closure of Riddel Hall in 1975. It had been opened sixty years earlier for 'young Protestant girls coming from the country who would be under proper supervision'. Supervision was no longer in fashion and self-catering was cheaper.[31] There was a price attached to independence. In the year Riddel Hall closed its doors, the University's medical officer reported that, 'the increasing number of students living in unsupervised accommodation, as economic pressures are felt, is also tending to create a health hazard. Some of them appear to have little or no knowledge of the basic rules of nutrition or personal hygiene.'[32]

25 *Academic Council minutes, 1968–9*, 140. **26** *Vice-Chancellor's report, 1975–6*, 49; *1980–81*, 57. **27** *Vice-Chancellor's report, 1956–7*, 13. **28** *Vice-Chancellor's report, 1969–70*, 31. **29** *Vice-Chancellor's report, 1972–3*, 59. **30** *Vice-Chancellor's report, 1994*, 150; *1997*, 129; *1998*, 586–9. **31** In 1997, for example the cost of catered accommodation in Queen's Elms was £57 a week. Self-catering in a converted Queen's house cost £38.50 (*Senate minutes, 1997*, 129). Private rentals *per head* depended on the condition of the property, which was often not good, and the size of the renting group. **32** *Vice-Chancellor's*

Fortunately there was a health service to look after them and to attend to the usual staples of coughs, colds, and acne, sports injuries, and examination stress. An embryonic student health service began in 1943 by Professor J.H. Biggart.[33] The concept of health care free at the point of contact was then being advocated by the Beveridge report. The particular needs of students were considered in two reports produced by the Royal College of Physicians in London in 1943 and 1946. In 1948, coinciding with the introduction of the national health service into Northern Ireland, Queen's appointed its first full-time medical officer, Dr Wilson Johnston.

The development of the health service mirrored the growth of Queen's from a large village of 2500 souls to a small town of more than 20,000 people including staff. In 1971 there were three full-time, and two half-time medical officers, four full-time nurses, and five secretaries. A counselling service was introduced in the 1970s. The service also expanded into occupational health care. A first step had been taken in 1958 with the formation of the radiation protection sub-committee, and in 1981 the University created an occupational health service. The Student Health Service then became the University Health Service. By 1991–2 it employed five doctors, three counsellors, six nurses and five secretaries and was handling 60,000 patient contacts a year.[34] It had outgrown its accommodation in University Square and in 2000 it migrated to more spacious premises in Lennoxvale.

When the University practice opened in 1948 all undergraduates were required to have an annual chest X-ray and there were routine medical examinations for all first year students. The need for the former was soon demonstrated when fifty-two cases of pulmonary tuberculosis were diagnosed among a student population of just over 2000. Thirty years later tuberculosis was practically a disease of the past and screening was discontinued in 1982–3. One and a half thousand polio vaccinations were administered in 1959–60, but polio too was receding into history. Instead students were requiring travel inoculations as vacation work overseas, inter-railing, and foreign study scattered them far and wide. In 1985–6 14 per cent of undergraduate women were prescribed oral contraception, a much lower proportion than in British universities.[35]

At an early stage in its history Queen's accepted it had an obligation to assist the transition of students into paid employment. In 1976 the Appointments Board claimed the first meeting of its predecessor had occurred in July 1926 and it was therefore fifty years old.[36] Evidence of the early activities is scant,

report, 1974–5, 49, 51. **33** The following paragraphs are based on an unpublished history of the University Health Service written by Dr Robin Harland, the second University medical officer. The Student Health Service was renamed the University Health Service in 1981 when it extended its activities into occupational health. **34** *Vice-Chancellor's report, 1991–2*, 8. **35** *Vice-Chancellor's report, 1985–6*, 47. **36** *Senate minutes, 1976*, 253.

although in October 1939 Queen's briefly appointed a warden to Queen's Chambers and he doubled up as secretary the committee.[37] Immediately after the war the clerk of admissions carried out the duties of an appointments' officer on a part-time basis, but in 1960 the Queen's made the post full-time. Mr Norman Buller was appointed the following year from the University of Sheffield.[38] Over the years the Careers and Appointments Service grew to three advisers. It organized visits from prospective employers (the 'milk round'), and kept statistics of the employment destinations of students after graduation. There was a minor crisis in 1987–8 when financial retrenchment in the University left the service under-staffed and barely able to cope with demand. But following a report from an external consultant it was brought up to strength and provided with a satisfactory computer system.[39]

In 1998 the annual report of the Careers and Appointments' Service recorded changes in educational philosophy and in the market for graduates. More graduates than ever were seeking employment as the numbers of universities multiplied. There were also more employers looking for graduates, with the large ones recruiting bright young men and women regardless of the subjects they studied, and the smaller ones looking for specific skills. The old employment staples for arts graduates, such as teaching, were no longer buoyant. There were other changes, too, as employers simplified their management structures, resulting in fewer jobs at the top of the tree. Graduates needed to be open-minded about careers. The service told the Senate it had begun experimenting with 'the development of careers management skills into the curriculum'.[40] This somewhat gnomic statement referred to the fact that undergraduate courses were now supposed to embody 'employability skills'. The University had come a long way since the days when the official who admitted students gave them advice about jobs on the way out.

THE STUDENTS' UNION AND STUDENT PARTICIPATION

In the 1940s student affairs were in the hands of three organizations: the Students' Representative Council (the SRC), the Students' Union Society (the SUS), and the committee running the Women's Students Hall (the WSH). The SRC was composed of members elected from faculty constituencies. Its president was chosen from among its number and, if a graduate, he or she was a member of the Senate. The function of the SUS was to manage the affairs of the union building in University Square. It described itself grandly in 1953: 'the members of the SUS include all gentlemen undergraduates of the University

37 Moody and Beckett, *Queen's Belfast*, ii, 520. The appointment was quickly terminated when the holder of the post joined the navy. 38 *Senate minutes, 1960*, 187; *1961*, 87. 39 *Senate minutes, 1988*, 5, 506. 40 *Senate minutes, 1998*, 52–3.

and such graduates and members of Staff as wish to join'.[41] Women had their own hall squeezed into two houses in University Square. In 1952 these arrangements were described as 'untidy and inefficient', but students voted to leave them as they were.[42] In 1959 the Vice-Chancellor wrote of the 'rich and diverse world' of student activities. But there was a cost.

> It is essential that there should be a group of students prepared to devote themselves to student-administration: pressing for better local authority awards, arranging vacation employment, managing the amenities of the University, and the like. But it is a pity that this service should involve so many dreary hours of committee work (the rate at which committees do business seems to be inversely proportional to the age of their members!) and (more and more) paper work. This year SRC revised its constitution. The number of square feet of paper and student-hours required for this not very vital operation do not bear thinking about. There is a real danger in permitting student clerical work to proliferate: we are already reaching a point where very few students can afford the time to take office in the SRC Executive; and it would be a pity if high office in the SRC became closed to a student who wanted to distinguish himself in academic work.[43]

In 1963 the relationships between the SRC the SUS and the WSH committee were again reviewed.[44] The separation of male and female unions was out of tune with the times, but the impulse for change was the completion of the new Union Building. The three bodies came together in 1965 to devise a joint constitution. This was revised in 1968 (and many times thereafter). The outcome was a restructured SRC executive consisting of a president, a deputy-president, a lady vice-president, and a growing army of sabbatical officers and other officials. Its functions were to promote the interest of students, to mediate between the students and the University, to maintain contacts with other places of higher education, to organize social events and, a reflection of emerging political tensions in the wider community, to 'promote a spirit of unity.'[45] The united body was known as the Students' Representative Council of the Students' Union (SRCSU), shortened in 1975 to the Students' Union.

By now student leaders were demanding an active role in running the University. In October 1969 Rory McShane, the president, demanded that students should be members of the Academic Council and faculty boards.[46] But the SRCSU was itself under attack for being unrepresentative of the student body. Sometime in 1969 or early 1970 an undated pamphlet circulated in the Union

41 *Students' Union Society book, 1953–4.* QUB archives, P/872. 42 *Vice-Chancellor's report, 1951–2*, 11. 43 *Vice-Chancellor's report, 1958–9*, 11. 44 *Vice-Chancellor's report, 1962–3*, 343–4. 45 Constitution and laws of the SRCSU, 1965, 1968. QUB archives, P/871. 46 *Gown* 21 October 1969.

entitled SRCULAR. It was edited by Nick Ross, 'with and despite the assistance of Dave Montgomery', and denounced the SRCSU as 'a clique with all the pretensions of representing the study body'.[47] The pamphlet demanded universal suffrage in the election of union officers and decision-making given to a general meeting with a quorum of 10 per cent. The Academic Council, which had the final authority of ratifying the constitution of the SRCSU, would not agree to the 10 per cent rule because it could result in policy being manipulated by a small and unrepresentative group. The issue rumbled on for some time.

The demand for a share in university management was happening in all British universities. For the first half century of its existence students in Queen's seemingly had been content with a passive role in the affairs of the University. In 1945 the SRC had politely asked the Committee of Deans if the University would establish staff-student committees to discuss matters of common interest.[48] It outlined the successful operation of such a committee in the medical faculty since 1943. The committee contacted the faculties. The then dean of arts failed to respond, but his successor agreed to meet the students, although he would not agree to the setting up of staff-student committees even though the SRC told him of the 'complete dissatisfaction with the present first course in English literature' and that, 'many lectures were a complete waste of time.' Somewhat defensively, the dean replied he had no authority to interfere with the internal affairs of a department ('why not?' the students asked). The SRC did not get very far with other faculties either. Science was 'not enthusiastic'; the Faculty of Agriculture thought staff-student committees were 'unnecessary'; and applied science was 'too busy' to consider the matter.

Thereafter the issue seems to have died, but the first shots in what turned out to be a protracted campaign were fired in April 1968 when the SRCSU asked the Committee of Deans for representation on departmental boards. The deans suggested instead that it might be a good idea to set up staff-student consultative committees. A few weeks later the SRCSU created the post of educational secretary 'to represent the interests of the ordinary members of the Union, in matters relating to their academic studies.'[49] Staff-student consultative committees were subsequently established in most departments.[50]They did not satisfy students for long. The authors of SRCULAR demanded that the Senate and the Academic Council should be composed of representatives of staff, students, and providers of finance 'in approximately equal proportions'. Joint committees of staff and students should run faculties and departments, and 'a few students' should sit on progress committees 'so that justice may be seen to be done.' They

47 SRCULAR, QUB archives, P/871. Thirty years later the former was well known to watchers of television and the latter had become chairman of Mirror Group Newspapers following the watery demise of Robert Maxwell. See also *Gown*, 4 February 1969.   48 *Staff-student committees and the position in Queen's* (SRC, May 1945) QUB archive, P/871. 49 *Academic Council minutes, 1967–8*, 151,215.   50 *Academic Council minutes, 1969–70*, 186–7.

should also have a 'major' representation on committees and be members of boards of curators responsible for academic appointments.

A more moderate case for student representation was presented to the Academic Council in 1970.[51] Its text was taken from a speech by the president of the National Union of Students, Jack Straw, who denounced the universities as 'the last great unreformed institution of our time.'[52] The student argument quoted from the writings of Sir Eric Ashby:

> The paradigm for a graduate forty years ago was the conventional man, ready to take responsibility for preserving a set of values which he felt no need to question, deferring to his elders because they were older, not because they were wiser; obedient to principle, constitutions, traditions. That sort of young man cannot cope with the flux of the modern world. The contemporary paradigm is a man educated for insecurity, who can innovate, solve problems with no precedents. He must have expert knowledge. That is what he gets from his lecturers and laboratories. He must also have the confidence which comes from participation in community living. That is what he gets from belonging, as a co-equal, to a society of Chancellor, Masters, and Scholars.

It was an ingenious ploy to invoke the authority of a previous Vice-Chancellor and one of the most powerful thinkers of the time on university education. When it came to specific points, the students asked for representation on the Academic Council, the Senate, the faculties, most committees, and the boards of curators. 'We do not believe', the document continued, 'in ... a system where staff and students are equal to the point of synonymity [*sic*]. But nor do can we accept a paternal and undemocratic system.'

The Academic Council set up a working party with the SRCSU to consider the memorandum. In the meantime it summoned a special meeting to discuss the matter. There was not much initial sympathy. Professor Alwyn Williams, later Principal of Glasgow University, 'would not counter widening student access to satisfy the student ego or avert demonstrations', although he conceded that students could be effective in scrutinizing teaching methods. Another member was alarmed that students wanted power and not merely representation. A third member thought that students misunderstood the nature of

---

51 'Student representation. A memorandum from the executive of the SRCSU to Academic Council, January 1970'. *Academic Council minutes, 1969–70*, 16 January 1970. QUB archives, P/871. 52 At the time of writing Jack Straw is the foreign secretary of the United Kingdom. It is matter of interest, if not of significance, that the campaign for increased student participation in Queen's was inspired in various degrees by three men (Ross, Montgomery, and – from a distance – Straw) who later became well known for quite other things. Perhaps the only conclusion that can be drawn is that the outcome of a university education is unpredictable.

university administration, which he defined, idealistically, as supplying 'the minimum essential machinery to allow the teaching and research function of a university to proceed.'[53]

The working party issued an interim report proposing student membership on fourteen committees, but on the main points the students and the University were miles apart. The former was seeking power; the latter was offering consultative status only. The report was sent to the faculties for consideration.[54] There then followed eighteen months of discussions. The outcome, which was finally accepted by all parties in April 1972, was that departmental staff-student committees remained consultative. Student membership of the Senate would be enlarged when the statutes were changed. The most important innovation was the creation of an Academic Board consisting of 20 students elected by the SRCSU and 40 staff members elected from the Academic Council. The Board had a wide remit to comment on 'general matters' and to make recommendations to the Academic Council.[55]

The Academic Board got off to an uncertain start. A meeting in January 1974 was gate-crashed by a student denouncing the University for carrying out research on biological weapons and rifle barrels for the Ministry of Defence. The University denied the allegations.[56] At the end of the year students boycotted the Board because they were unhappy with its limited powers and for two years refused to elect representatives. Months of intense wrangling at last produced a revised constitution and the Academic Board settled into a useful role of scrutinizing changes in regulations, syllabuses and curricula, and examination methods.[57]

The Academic Board did not satisfy the more vocal student politicians. In 1976 the Union criticized changes being planned to the University's charter and statutes, which in its view did not go far enough. The Union urged Queen's to take account of the 'social milieu of 1976, with the growth of concepts such as industrial democracy'. The Senate was condemned as 'self-perpetuating' and 'quasi-incestuous', while the 'Better Equipment Fund [a body that had existed since 1901] is merely a pretext to permit back-door entry to Senate of private enterprise gnomes.'[58] The Senate was interested neither in exterminating private enterprise gnomes nor embracing notions of industrial democracy. It did agree, though, that the Better Equipment Fund had outlived its usefulness.

The Academic Board functioned peacefully for the rest of the decade. But it nearly collapsed in 1982–3 when a dispute emerged between the University and the Students' Union over whether a student, who had been required to with-

53 *Academic Council minutes, 1969–70*, 115–16.   **54** *Academic Council minutes, 1970–1* 15–8; 52–6.   **55** *Academic Council minutes, 1971–2* 18–28, 187–80 and 219–21.   **56** *Academic Board minutes*, 30 January 1974, 11 March 1974. The charges had been published first in *Gown* on 29 January 1974.   **57** *Academic Board minutes*, 12 December 1974; 5 March 1975; 24 January 1977; *Academic Council minutes, 1976–7*, 55–9.   **58** *Academic Council minutes, 1976*, appendix, 'submission from the Students' Union'.

draw from Queen's because of academic failure, could hold sabbatical office to which he had been elected before his failure. The students said 'yes' and the Academic Council said 'no'. The issue became caught up in a renewed demand for membership of Academic Council and faculties. There was a two-day sit-in in the council offices in March 1983 and in June the University resorted to the trusty device of appointing another working party on student representation. Eventually the students achieved part of what they had been seeking for years. The working party recommended they should have five representatives on the Academic Council although they still had no membership of faculties.[59]

Amidst the noisy demands for power it is easy to forget that the Union was involved in day-to-day matters. Some of these were trivial, such as the publication in 1951 of the *Ulster Student Song Book*, which claimed 'no pretence to intellectual eminence or scholarship sublime' and is best left undisturbed in the archives.[60] In April 1955 there appeared the first edition of *Gown* edited by an American student in Queen's. It was greeted by the Vice-Chancellor as a 'welcome relief from its predecessor, *Qubis*, and as a credible organ of student opinion'.[61] The Vice-Chancellor's judgement of *Qubis* was only slightly harsh. It had started life in 1949 as dismal sheaf of typed foolscap sheets, but it sold for a penny a copy in old money (later increased to three old pence) and was moderately informative. *Gown*, by contrast, was professionally produced and looked like a newspaper, complete with photographs, feature articles, and gossip columns (who was taking whom to the union dances was a topic of abiding interest). It recorded the ebbing and flowing of student life and, indeed of the University more widely, over the next four decades. It was originally published fortnightly, although in the late 1990s its appearance became somewhat erratic.

Until the early 1960s *Gown* was well written, generally deferential to the University authorities, and occasionally pompous. At the end of 1963 it almost went out of business when it published an alleged libel on a member of the academic staff. It was saved by a new editor (Alf McCreary) and almost simultaneously was judged to be the best student newspaper in Ireland. Later in the decade *Gown* turned itself into a tabloid, written in the style of tabloids. In October 1977 a correspondent complained, not without justification, of the superfluity of profanities and lavatorial language littering its pages.[62] *Gown* also became more critical of the University's administration. During the 1960s and 1970s its columns became filled with the political problems of the Province. In the 1980s and 1990s *Gown* reverted to its more traditional role of criticizing the Front, campaigning for student grants, and reporting the mundane matters of student life.

---

59 *Academic Council minutes, 1982–3*, 138–9, 237–8; *1983–4*, 234–9; *Academic Board minutes* 15 December, 1981, 20 April, 1982, 25 May, 1982, 28 February, 1983; 19 April 1983; 1 May 1984. **60** *Ulster students' songbook*, QUB archives, P/879. **61** *Vice-Chancellor's report, 1954–5*, 168. **62** *Gown*, 26 October 1977.

A subject frequently discussed in *Gown* during the 1950s and 1960s were the activities of the Literary and Scientific Society (the Literific). This was a venerable society founded in 1850 with the purpose 'of affording students of the Queen's College and others an opportunity of improving themselves by writing papers on literary and scientific subjects, to be read and discussed before the Society.'[63] It conducted its business along parliamentary lines with private members' business and set-piece debates addressed by prominent political or literary figures from all parts of the United Kingdom and from Ireland. During the 1960s the Literific was in trouble. In October 1963 its president, together with a former president of the Law Society, were suspended from Queen's for a year 'for behaviour prejudicial to the good name of the University'. The prejudicial behaviour was an 'incident' during a debate at Stranmillis College organized by the Students' Christian Society and the New Ireland Society (a political ginger group)[64] A few months later an editorial in *Gown* claimed that proceedings at the Literific had become little more than angry diatribes and were doing 'enormous damage' to Queen's. In October 1964 a briefly famous playwright dropped his trousers during a debate, creating a rumpus in the local press in inverse proportion to the momentary glimpse of his posterior. A new president contrived to get himself arrested after too convivial a dinner at a local hotel. By April 1966 the Literific had 'degenerated into a collection of clique-forming and self-glorifying poltroons'. It struggled on for another year or so when it was replaced by the Union Debating Society, which the Vice-Chancellor hoped 'may be better suited to the expanded community than the traditional Literific'. The Union Debating Society survived for a few years before drowning in a sea of apathy.[65] The Troubles engendered in many students a desire to be home before dark and the nightly rioting started.

Apart from *Gown* most student publications flickered intermittently like sun in a Belfast summer. An exception was *PTQ* that enjoyed a continuous publication history from 1928. It early issues were models of decorum and included jokes and cartoons syndicated from *Punch* and similar sources, as well as some gentle home-grown japes. In 1956 the University made students responsible for censoring its contents: 'good humour should prevail'.[66] In 1962 it cartoons were too crude for the citizens of Omagh whose council wrote a letter of protest to the Chancellor. Two years later a bishop of the Church of Ireland condemned *PTQ* as 'crude, vulgar and obscene'; his Catholic counterpart stood shoulder to shoulder in ecumenical support. An 'angry *PTQ* seller' retorted that obscenity existed only in the mind of the bishops and a magazine with a higher moral tone

63 *The book of the fete: Queen's College Belfast* (Belfast, 1907), 73.   64 The incident was an alleged assault, but the evidence was very confused.   65 *Northern Whig*, 7 March 1963, 8 March 1963, 6 March 1964, 30 October 1964, 26 April 1966, 2 February 1967, 6 February 1973; *Northern Whig*, 7 March 1963; *Belfast Telegraph*, 28, 30, 31 October 1964, 2 November 1964, 9 March 1965; *News Letter*, 10 March 1965; *Vice-Chancellor's report, 1966–7*, 444. 66 *Academic Council minutes, 1955–6*, 80.

would seller fewer copies.[67] And so *PTQ* proceeded on it saucy way year by year raising money and ire in unequal measure.

Literary magazines trod a stony path between apathy and pretension. Between 1950 and 1963 a journal called simply *Q* appeared every year and published items of remarkably high quality, including reviews and poems by Philip Larkin (then a sub-librarian), John Betjeman, and others, as well as by students. In 1964 *Q* failed to appear and was not heard of again. Two decades later, in June 1985, *Gown* included a literary supplement that contained contributions from Seamus Heaney and Bernard McLaverty, but the experiment was not repeated. Subject-based magazines such as *Gradule* (geography), *Snakes Alive* (medicine), and *Spectrum* (engineering and science) prospered during the 1950s and 1960s but then disappeared. The mid-1960s were graveyard years for most student publications.

Sporting activities remained in a much healthier condition. They revolved around athletics, hockey, rugby, rowing, Gaelic football, and hurling.[68] Political societies represented mainstream politics in the Province as well as capturing the international issues of the time such as the Suez and Hungarian crises of 1956, the troubles in Biafra, and apartheid in South Africa.

Beyond sport and politics the Union concerned itself with matters close to the lives of students: grants, the cost of food and residences, whether there should be a bar in the Union and contraceptive machines in the cloakrooms (both achieved in 1967), and the perennial problems of study and examinations. For some students participation in the business of the Union was as much an education as the academic courses they started.

CONCLUSION

During the second half of the twentieth century student life in Queen's was similar in many ways to student life in British and Irish universities. Everywhere numbers increased rapidly and women came to constitute a large proportion of the total. Everywhere the social mores that shaped student behaviour in the 1950s were dissolving as the century progressed. In common with most universities, Queen's offered a wide range of subjects from which students could choose. Their choices changed over time, and as once popular disciplines disappeared and new ones became popular. The relationships between students at Queen's and the Front went through similar phases of deference and challenge, formality and informality, respect and hostility as those that occurred between students and administrations elsewhere.

67 *Northern Whig,* 13 February 1962; *Belfast Telegraph,* 23 March 1965; 24 March 1965.
68 There are excellent accounts of Queen's sporting achievements in Walker and McCreary, *Degrees of excellence, 1845–1995.*

Yet there was an important difference between student life in Belfast and student life in universities in Britain and in Ireland. Queen's University drew most of its students from the Province, and their attitudes were those of the society that reared them. For many young Protestants, coming to Queen's gave them their first opportunity of socializing with Roman Catholics. The same was true, in reverse, for Catholic students. The exposure to people holding different ideas was a heady experience. By the mid-1960s Ulster students, in line with their British and Irish compatriots, wanted a greater share in the running of their university. But the voices of the student reformers in Queen's were quiet in comparison with those elsewhere. When there was real revolution in the streets and the city echoed with the sounds of bombs and bullets, civil rights marches were more compelling than occupying the offices of the Vice-Chancellor for a day or two. We return to these issues in a later chapter.

9

Scholarship

In the first chapter we considered the purpose of universities and identified two philosophies of higher education: the liberal and the vocational. Queen's embraced both. The Queen's College had been founded in 1845 to educate the sons and (later) daughters of Ulster to become clergymen, school teachers, civil servants, social workers, business men and women, or just good citizens, and its teaching had evolved accordingly. When the University gained its independence in 1908–9 it included faculties of medicine, law, and commerce, all dedicated to vocational training, and it was soon to acquire a Faculty of Agriculture. The Faculty of Arts alone was centred primarily in the liberal tradition, and even here most undergraduates read the humanities with the intention of entering a profession.

In 1957 the Vice-Chancellor, Sir Eric Ashby, surveyed the debate about the purpose of university education. 'In one article', he remarked, 'the reader is stunned by statistics about Soviet technologists into accepting the view that universities must devote their resources principally to producing scientists and engineers. In another article the reader is lured by such words as "culture", "humanities" and "values", into believing that universities exist mainly to perpetuate some esoteric tradition, very precious but very vague, which can be acquired only through disinterested study, for its own sake, of subjects which have no obvious relevance to the contemporary world.' The reality is:

Universities are viable in the twentieth century precisely because they have learnt how to integrate what is permanent with what is contemporary. They offer opportunities both to the student who wishes to acquire self-fulfilment without reference to any professional training and to the student who wishes to acquire professional skill and nothing more. This is as it should be. The country needs both kinds of people ... If one reflects on the work of our own Senate in the last seven years a clear pattern of policy emerges. On the one hand the University has prepared itself vigorously for the demands which society is making on it for experts in fields as far apart as philology and aeronautics, microbiology and law. On the other hand Queen's remains a place where a young man who really cares for the humanities – for literature, music, philosophy, and art – finds a congenial atmosphere which favours these pursuits. The Senate has preserved a balance between these interests. There has been an apparent preoccupation with science and technology, but when one comes to analyse the figures one finds that the proportion of the University's resources which has been devoted to what are collectively known as the "arts subjects" is in fact higher than it is in many other British universities. Any notion that the University is pursuing technology at the expense of the humanities and that the arts subjects are being starved is simply not in accordance with the facts.[1]

Notwithstanding the Vice-Chancellor's reassuring words, the Faculty of Arts feared its importance was being eroded. It submitted a memorandum to the Academic Council arguing, 'university education is not (or should not be) purely vocational.' The purpose of universities was not to impart techniques; 'their business is rather to study and reflect upon the principles that underlie the techniques, and they must not confine their attention to what is immediately or obviously useful.' The University should not react to every change in 'public demand'. The role of the Faculty of Arts was to pursue the study of 'man in society', a role that was 'not obsolete'. The faculty urged the University to pay more attention to a liberal education, and it offered to provide mind-enhancing courses for students in other faculties. The memorandum was circulated for comment. The responses were sympathetic but indicated no strong desire to take up the offer of civilizing courses. The Faculty of Law responded stiffly that the study of 'man in society' was not the monopoly of the Faculty of Arts and it had no business to tell others how to conduct their affairs.[2]

A related issue was the balance between teaching and research. In Queen's the academic advancement of scholars has come to depend principally on research and publications. Although most lecturers were clear that teaching and research were activities of equal importance, the issue was less clear-cut to students. Their first priority was teaching that would get them through their examinations. In 1952 a debate at the Literary and Scientific Society argued that lecturers should be appointed for their teaching ability as well as for their learning.[3] Queen's paid no immediate heed, but three years later, Professor Newark, the Secretary to the Academic Council, pointed out to students the error of their thinking.

[A] common assumption is that a university teacher is no good if he cannot lecture. In one sense, of course, this is obviously true, but the fallacy lies in the supposition that a member of university staff is simply a 'university teacher'. If histrionic performance in front of a blackboard were all that were required we should probably recruit out staff from the Old Vic.

1 *Vice-Chancellor's report, 1956–7*, 164–5. 2 *Academic Council minutes, 1957–8*, 65–6 and 95–6. 3 *Qubis*, 38, 1 February 1952.

As it is those who have the duty of making appointments to university staff look for scholarship, and if sometimes the scholar has a weak voice and a tendency to be incoherent it is unfortunate. Unfortunate, but not fatal. It would be both unfortunate and fatal if the person appointed were silver-tongued but shallow and second rate.[4]

The University did not turn to the Old Vic for its lecturers and for many years it did not regard the training of university teachers as important. Lecturers coped with their classes as best they could and students did the same with their lecturers. Most of the latter taught conscientiously and did not give research precedence over teaching, at least during term-time. When, in October 1978 a professor well-known for his commitment to research was granted a two-week extension to a full year's leave in order to complete a project, a fellow professor reminded the Academic Council of 'the contractual requirement for an academic member of staff to engage in teaching as well as in research.'[5] Most conflicts in the professional lives of academics were between scholarship and administration, not between the obligation to lecture and the requirement to publish books and articles.

UNDERGRADUATE STUDIES

With the exception of medicine and dentistry, the bachelors' courses after the war normally followed the pattern of three years for a pass or general degree, with a fourth year for honours. The pass degree in arts was unsatisfactory. In March 1951 a letter to the student newspaper complained, 'the Pass Arts students have no roots in any departments, no sense of common interests, and spend their University careers with small cliques of co-religionists.'[6] The last part of this complaint revealed a sense of dissatisfaction with more than the academic content of the degree. The programme consisted of eight courses studied over three years. English literature or modern history were compulsory subjects in the first year, as were two of Greek, Latin, a modern language, or mathematics. Since many students found the instruction in English and mathematics unsatisfactory these requirements were irksome. As the Vice-Chancellor put it, the pass BA introduced a student

> to several subjects [but] without giving him sufficient familiarity with any one of them. It lacked continuity: a student would 'finish' a subject in June and begin a new one in October ... It took no account of increasing maturity: the same class might contain third year students on the eve of

4 *Gown*, 12 May 1955. 5 *Academic Council minutes, 1978–9*, 72. 6 *Qubis*, 26, 2 March 1951.

graduating and young people fresh from school. It made no provision for initiating the freshman into academic life and for watching how he adapts himself to his unfamiliar liberties.[7]

A new structure was introduced in 1955. Students now read three subjects in the first year before embarking during years two and three on the study of two main subjects, together with a subsidiary subject that ran for one year. At least one of the first-year subjects was normally continued into the second and third years. A minority of students was accepted for honours and remained for a fourth year. This pattern remained in force, with minor modifications, until 1986.

In 1948–9 the bachelor of commercial science degree was revised and renamed as the BSc(Econ) to reflect the wider academic agenda it now contained. The pass course in economics lasted for three years and was available also by part-time study in the evening over five years. There was a four-year honours programme composed principally of economics courses, but with limited room for other social science subjects or accounting. Degrees in the natural and applied sciences and in law could be achieved at an honours level within three years, but four years was the usual route. The science faculties also had an intermediate year, sometimes known as level zero, designed to bring weak school leavers up to the required university standard. In medicine the regulations for the combined degrees of MB, BCh and BAO allowed them to be taken 'in not less than five years', but since teaching continued into the sixth year it was difficult to graduate in under six years. After 1980 medical students were normally exempted from the first pre-clinical year and five years of study became the normal pattern. The degree in dentistry extended over four years but in 1990 a fifth year was added.

Queen's had followed the Scottish pattern of four-year honours degrees. The Northern Ireland higher leaving certificate lasted for only one year and students needed the extra year at Queen's. The case for the four-year degree was weakened when the Ulster schools shifted to A-levels during the 1960s. This led to pressure from the government for Queen's to come into line with England. The Faculty of Economics started the shift toward three-year honours degrees when in 1967–8 it introduced the bachelor of social science degree to accommodate a range of social sciences subjects. Many social science graduates competed for jobs in the United Kingdom and were at a disadvantage with a three-year pass degree. The BSc(Econ) followed suit in 1972–3.

In 1982 the Chilver review group suggested that Queen's should be funded only for three-year honours degrees, and a year later the Northern Ireland Working Party challenged the University to justify its four-year courses. Queen's rose to their defence although it was in a difficulty because the Faculty of Economics and Social Sciences had already introduced three-year degrees. The University could hardly concede that a social science honours degree was inferior

7 *Vice-Chancellor's report, 1954–5*, 159.

to one in arts. It came up with a not totally convincing explanation of its mixed menu. 'The retention of four year honours courses [in arts] was a matter of conscious decision after careful deliberation. The four-year honours arts degree offered "breadth and sound specialisation". The lawyers also needed four years in order to combine the study of law with professional training. The same careful deliberation led to the introduction of three year degrees in the Faculty of Economics and Social Sciences and for selected students in Science and Engineering.'[8]

The Faculty of Arts retained its four-year structure until 1986 at which point the UGC refused to fund it any more; law managed to hang on for another couple of years, but the establishment of the Institute of Professional Legal Studies, which added practical legal skills to law degrees, made the four-year course difficult to justify. The science and engineering faculties also moved to three-year honours degrees. The exceptions were medicine and dentistry, degrees in modern languages requiring a year abroad, and some enhanced science and engineering courses that included a year in industry.

Further major changes to degree structures occurred during the 1990s. In 1989 the UGC asked the University to set out its plans for the next five years and whether it intended to introduce modular degrees.[9] This was a 'have you stopped beating your wife yet' type of question that strongly implied a positive answer would be welcomed. Many one-time polytechnics operated modular degrees that provided undergraduates with considerable flexibility in the choice of subjects. They were a boon to part-time students, who could accumulate sufficient modules over several years, and fitted in with the current philosophy of widening access to higher education.

Queen's pointed to its part-time BA (General Studies) degree which worked on a modular pattern and told the UGC it intended to 'go modular' in the next year or two. At the same time the traditional academic year of three terms was re-shaped into two semesters. There followed two hectic years of planning. In the pattern that emerged students studied eighteen modules over six semesters (i.e. three years). The first six were treated as qualifying modules, leading to honours courses in years two and three. In theory a student could study modules chosen from eighteen different disciplines. In practice there were restrictions on choice in order to create coherent pathways of study. Courses were examined module by module and the results banked until students had accumulated a sufficient number to qualify for a degree.

As we noted in an earlier chapter, students were offered a wide range of studies. The choice broadened over time as new subjects were introduced and a few were withdrawn. In humanities English, history, French and Spanish remained

8 *Academic Council minutes, 1981–2*, appendix; *1983–4*, additional paper AC/R/84/8/iv.
9 It was known as 39/89, being the thirteenth circular received from the UGC during 1989. By now the UGC was sending circulars to universities almost on a daily basis.

heavily in demand. Celtic attracted a relatively small numbers of students but was important because of its central place in Irish studies. Italian and German both suffered from falling student numbers during the 1970s and 1980s. The University established a Department of Slavonic Studies in 1967–8 but the small number of students coming from the schools restricted its development and teaching ended in 1995.[10] The position of Greek and Latin was weakened by new regulations in 1954–5. In February 1959 *Gown*, asked, 'Is Latin going out?' The paper conducted a survey among the professors. The professor of Greek thought that Latin should not be an entrance requirement (presumably he did not think the same about Greek); children between twelve and fifteen should 'dabble' in Latin, but they should be exposed to a range of other languages, including Russian. The professor of French declared that entrance Latin was of 'no use'; the newly appointed professor of English thought Latin was not necessary and professors Evans (geography) and Naylor (engineering) argued German was more useful for their students.[11] When the chair of Latin became vacant in 1976 the University considered leaving it unfilled, but decided to make a new appointment.[12] In 1983 it proposed amalgamating Greek and Latin, a suggestion that provoked an outraged debate in the Academic Council. The traditionalists were only reluctantly comforted by Queen's assurance that it intended to 'maintain the study of Greek as a fundamental cultural tradition of the western world.'[13] Had they been able to look a few years into the future they would have shuddered to see the UGC advocating the advantages of a combined department of classics and ancient history.[14] The chair was not filled when it again became vacant in 1992 and at the end of the decade Queen's decided to end the teaching of both classical languages.

Three arts subjects, social anthropology, education, and, for a time, library studies prospered. Social anthropology emerged from within geography and became an independent department in 1962. When the lecturer in charge left two years later Queen's found it difficult to find a replacement and the Committee of Deans suggested merging it with sociology, but the Academic Council rejected the idea.[15] In 1970 the University appointed Professor John Blacking, an ethnomusicologist with an international reputation, and the subject flourished thereafter.

Education had been a subject of the Faculty of Arts since 1914. The department offered an arts degree plus a diploma for students holding training scholarships from the Ministry of Education. It also provided one-year training courses for non-scholarship holders.[16] Following the Lockwood report, Queen's set up a Faculty of Education to oversee a new four-year Bachelor of Education taught in the colleges and established an Institute of Education.[17] There was a

10 *Academic Council minutes, 1995*, 104. 11 *Gown*, 27 February 1959. 12 *Academic Council minutes, 1975–6*, 147 and 149. 13 *Academic Council minutes, 1982–3*, 152–9. 14 *Academic Council minutes, 1987–8*, 45. 15 *Academic Council minutes, 1968–9*, 199; *1969–70*, 34–5. 16 *Academic Council minutes, 1960–1*, 24–5. 17 *Academic Council minutes,*

major reorganization a decade later as a result of the Lelievre report into teacher training in Northern Ireland. The Institute was abolished and two additional chairs (educational studies and further professional studies in education) were created.[18] Six years later, following the Chilver report, the BEd was restructured to differentiate paths for primary and secondary teachers, and one of the chairs was abolished. In 1986 the faculty was reorganized yet again into a single school of education responsible for initial teaching training, further professional training and physical education.[19]

The school of librarianship originated in 1963 from an agreement between the University and the Library Association. Funding was available from the Leverhulme Trust. and the Northern Ireland Ministry of Finance provided start-up costs. There were three members of staff and the University Librarian acted as part-time director. The school offered a graduate diploma and the first students were admitted in October 1965.[20] When business studies moved to the University of Ulster library studies was transferred to the Faculty of Economics and Social Sciences. In 1995 the scope of the subject was broadened into information management and the library component was discontinued.[21]

There were two major trends in the social sciences during the second half of the twentieth century. The first was the bachelor of social sciences degree introduced in 1967.[22] Now economic history, politics and social studies had the opportunity of developing their own honours programmes. The freedom was particularly liberating for politics and social studies. The former expanded rapidly, especially in the area of Irish politics. Social studies included sociology, social policy and social work. Since 1942 a board of social studies had acted almost as an independent faculty offering diplomas and certificates to students intending to become social workers.[23] As social work expanded a chair of social work was established in 1973 with financial support from the Department of Health and Social Services. In 1991 social work became a separate department concentrating on postgraduate training.[24]

The second trend was the expansion into management and accounting. In 1964–5 Rothmans of Pall Mall endowed a chair of management for seven years.[25] The chair was quickly re-designated as a chair of business studies. The department began teaching postgraduate diplomas and masters' degrees and soon branched out into undergraduate courses. At the same time accounting, which for decades was an option within the economics degree, expanded. The part-time lectureship became a full-time appointment and in 1978 a chair was established. An independent department was created two years later.[26]

1966–7, 107–8, plus inserted pages, 203–5. **18** *Academic Council minutes, 1976–7*, 137–42. **19** *Academic Council minutes, 1979–80*, AC/R/79/ 13/XIII; *1982–3*, 266–7; *1985–6*, 256–7. **20** *Academic Council minutes, 1963–4*, 144–7. **21** *Academic Council minutes, 1995*, 325. **22** *Academic Council minutes, 1966–7*, 83. **23** *Academic Council minutes, 1944–5*, XII, Submission to the UCG, p. 32. **24** *Academic Council minutes, 1972–3*, 10 and 38. **25** *Academic Council minutes, 1964–5*, 11–13. **26** *Academic Council minutes, 1949–50*, XIV,

The report of the Butler committee at the end of 1986 brought an abrupt end
to the further development of business studies by concentrating studies at the
University of Ulster. The Academic Council protested vigorously but ineffec-
tively at the loss. The mistake Queen's had made was to expand at the
undergraduate and immediate postgraduate level, where the University of
Ulster already had a large presence, instead of concentrating on advanced training for middle managers. Accounting might have been lost at the same time,
except that Queen's had strong ties with the Irish Institute of Chartered
Accountants and so was able to regroup business courses around accounting,
finance, law, and information management.[27]

The law faculty had long trained men and women to become barristers or
solicitors for generations. The normal route to the bar was a four-year degree
followed by a period at the Law Library in Belfast, or one of the Inns of Court
in London or Dublin. For solicitors the path after graduation was an appren-
ticeship in a solicitor's office. In 1971 the Northern Ireland Department of
Education set up a committee (the Armitage committee) to examine legal education in the Province. The outcome was the creation of the Institute of
Professional Legal Studies, with financial support from DENI and the Law
Society, providing a one-year postgraduate professional certificate and a two-
year certificate for non-legal graduates.[28] There were now many law graduates
going into business or government service. The Faculty of Law developed specialized courses for such students.

Courses in science, applied science (engineering), and agriculture were continually modified as advances occurred in the disciplines. A chair of inorganic
and analytical chemistry was established in 1960 and a second chair of physics
five years later. In 1968 Queen's created a department of computer science (a
professor had been appointed two earlier). The Faculty of Agriculture diversi-
fied into food science in 1969–70.[29] In 1971 Queen's took over the teaching of
pharmacy from the College of Technology and appointed a professor. Twenty-
five years later Queen's became a regional centre for postgraduate
pharmaceutical education.[30] In 1979–80 the University set up a palaeoecology
centre that became one of the leading centres in the world.[31]

There were losses in science, most notably in geology, a long-established and
distinguished discipline in the University. At the end of the 1980s the department was considered too small to be economically viable and it failed to recruit
an outstanding scholar to fill the vacant chair. Queen's therefore decided to
merge geology, geography, archaeology and palaeoecology. Geology survived in
this form until the end of the century, when teaching was phased out amidst

226; *1978–9*, 68; *1979–80*, 265–6.   **27** *Academic Council minutes, 1987–8*, 10, 132; 1989, 24.
28 *Academic Council minutes, 1971–2*, 10; *1973–4*, 63–4; *1974–5*, 99, 101–4 and 237; *1975–6*,
6–7 and 56–7; *1976–7*, 31 and 318–23.   **29** *Academic Council minutes, 1969–70*, 327.
30 *Academic Council minutes, 1960–1*, 38; *1965–6*, 112; *1967–8*, 21; *1970–1*, 101; *1996*, 82.
31 *Academic Council minutes 1979–80*, 201–4.

loud controversy as part of the restructuring plan implemented by the new Vice-Chancellor.[32] On a more expansive note, in 1992 and 1993 the Faculty of Science followed a national trend by introducing enhanced degrees in physics and mathematics consisting of three years of academic study and one year's placement.[33]

Turning to engineering, by 1960 most courses had moved from the College of Technology into Queen's. Thereafter the faculty expanded in several directions. The first discussions about a school of architecture took place in 1960 and a chair was established three years later. Twenty years later the Esher committee recommended the department should be closed as part of a UK rationalization of the teaching of architecture. Queen's, with the help of the local profession, successfully resisted the proposal, but architecture was merged with the department of town and country planning and eventually became part of a school of the built environment.[34] A chair and department of industrial chemistry was established in 1970. A decade later, following the publication of the Finniston report into engineering education, the faculty developed a range of enhanced undergraduate courses taken over four years. A chair of aerospace engineering was established in 1989 with financial support from Shorts PLC.[35] The consequence of these initiatives was to bring the teaching of engineering closer still to the requirements of industry.

The Faculty of Medicine had a long tradition of clinical training.[36] The most important initiative in the faculty came in 1997 when the school of nursing and midwifery was established. The first steps had been taken some years earlier with the introduction of a diploma of nursing as part of a nation-wide reorganization of nursing education. This was accompanied by the appointment of Jean Orr as professor of nursing studies in 1991. In 1996 the University negotiated a contract with the DHSS worth £40 million to provide pre-registration and post-registration training for nurses. To do this required the appointment of more than fifty members of staff, most of them as nurse-teachers, plus a core of full-time academic staff.[37]

There were other developments of a less prominent kind. On the medical side, a bachelor of medical science degree (a non-clinical qualification) was introduced in 1991 and five years later a medical education centre was established to oversee the introduction of a new medical curriculum.[38] Clinical dentistry was threatened with closure in 1983 when the General Dental Council

---

32 *Academic Council minutes, 1989*, report of the Academic Planning Group. **33** *Academic Council minutes, 1992*, 221; *1993*, 167. **34** *Academic Council minutes 1959–60*, 116; *1960–1*, 44; *1961–2*, 75; *1962–3*, 103–5; *1985–6*, 3, 76 and 252–6. **35** *Academic Council minutes, 1979–80*, 116 and 266–8; *1981–2*, 189 and 222; *1982–3*, 143; *1987–8*, appendix A. **36** Peter Froggatt, 'The distinctiveness of Belfast medicine and its medical school', *Ulster Medical Journal*, 54: 3 (1985), 89–108. **37** *Academic Council minutes, 1996*, 140–1; *1997*, appendix B of a paper on collaboration with other institutions. **38** *Academic Council minutes, 1990*, 44; *1996*, 134.

had concerns about the quality of teaching, and the school was too small to be economically viable. But at the end of the decade the Dental Council judged the teaching to be excellent. The curriculum had been modified and efforts made to strengthen research.[39] The school was still small, but it was maintained because of its regional importance.

Viewing developments in undergraduate teaching, a common theme emerges. There was a pronounced shift towards vocational programmes of study. This was true even in the humanities where at the end of the century all courses, no matter how liberal, were required to develop 'employability' skills (the ability to think and communicate clearly). There remained nevertheless, a wide range of subjects in the humanities that had no specific vocational focus. And it remained possible for students to study, say, physics for no reason other than intellectual curiosity. They became graduates in physics rather than physicists. Many science graduates, like their arts counterparts, went on to careers that did not make direct use of their specialized knowledge.

THE QUALITY OF TEACHING

In 1956 the Vice-Chancellor told new students, 'it is not the duty of a professor to make you work.'[40] Did it follow, though, that it was not the business of professors to lecture effectively? It is difficult to judge what teaching was like in the 1940s and 1950s because the evidence is fragmentary. John Boyd the Belfast author and Rodney Green, later Director of the Institute of Irish Studies, both read history at Queen's just before the war, the latter albeit briefly in 1937–8. Their opinion about the teaching was unflattering but also unrepresentative.[41] Academic survival in the University could be uncertain, especially in the arts faculty during the first year. Between 1946 and 1949 the failure rate was 18 per cent; in science it was 16 per cent, but in medicine only 7 per cent.[42] Poor teaching was a chronic problem in one or two areas. The SRC complained, 'the first course in Mathematics and English have been a sore point with students for a long time.' A mordant poem published by a former student in *Gown* in 1959 showed no respect for the ability or dedication of lecturers, describing them as:

---

39 *Academic Council minutes, 1987–8*, 35 and 211; *1989*, appendix A.   **40** *A fresher's guide to Queen's*, 1956, 2.   **41** Boyd and Green were discussing Queen's in 1942 or 1943. Green dismissed the history teaching as 'garbage' and Boyd thought it a waste of time: John Boyd, *The middle of my journey* (Belfast, 1990), 10. But an earlier student (Harry Cronne) wrote in 1944 that Professor J.E. Todd was the most inspiring teacher he had met anywhere (uncatalogued letter, QUB archives). Cronne became professor of medieval history at the University of Birmingham. John Boyd had also a low opinion of the teaching in English and economics. **42** Michael Forster, *An audit of academic performance: a study of the prediction of academic success in the Queen's University of Belfast* (QUB, 1959), 11 and 15–17.

Reading the Manchester Guardian and the Daily Worker
From ten-fifteen to quarter-past-eleven,
Through Michaelmas and Hilary to Trinity;
Accumulating ignorance fact by fact ...[43]

In 1968 the SRC carried out a survey of student opinion. Nine hundred students responded. They had mixed feelings about lectures and a majority wanted more tutorials, more continuous assessment and fewer examinations. Most students said they needed more guidance about their courses. Sixty per cent judged staff relationships to be satisfactory or good, although 10 per cent thought they were poor.[44] Twenty-five years later a survey of nearly 1300 graduating students conducted by the Centre for Academic Practice revealed a high level of satisfaction with the quality of lectures but considerably less with tutorials, seminars, and practicals. Many students were unhappy about the overcrowding in the Library and the 'feedback' they received from their teachers. Although they were generally happy with their education, many had doubts about the 'employability' of their degrees.[45]

In 1990 the Committee of Vice-Chancellors and Principals introduced a nation-wide system of audit designed to test the quality of university teaching. Teams of subject auditors visited universities and departments were ranked according to whether they were 'below average', 'satisfactory', or 'excellent'. Queen's notched up six 'satisfactories' and six 'excellents'.[46] This crude method of assessment was later replaced by a six-point assessment covering various aspects of the curriculum, teaching and learning. These were marked on a scale of 1 to 4, giving a maximum of 24 points. Between 1994 and 2001 fourteen subject areas in Queen's were assessed, producing two scores of 19, one of 20, three of 21, three of 22, three of 23, and two of 24.[47] Queen's had become one of the most highly rated teaching universities in the United Kingdom.

Another indicator of the effectiveness of teaching may be the proportion of degrees falling into the various classes. Graph 9.1 shows the trend of 1sts and 2.1 degrees between 1954 and 2000 (data for the previous decade are not available). The most striking feature is the rising proportion of 2.1 degrees, except for a slump between 1974 and 1978. No obvious explanation offers itself for the

43 *Gown*, 27 February 1959. The author was James Scott, a former dental student and lecturer in the dental school since 1946. He was appointed professor of dental anatomy in 1964. His inaugural lecture is remembered for being in the form of a 5000-word poem. 44 SRC, 'Student opinion on aspects of University education', 1968. QUB archives, P/871. 45 *Academic Council minutes, 1994*, 112–13. 46 The satisfactory subjects were mechanical engineering, computer science, architecture, chemistry, geography and social anthropology. The excellent departments were law, social work, history, geology, music, and English. *Academic Council minutes, 1997*, appendix 2 to QUB planning statement. It was generally possible to avoid a visit by claiming 'satisfactory'. 47 *Academic Council minutes, 1998*, 36, and appendix 3, of the academic plan; *2000*, 19, 127; *2001*, 7.

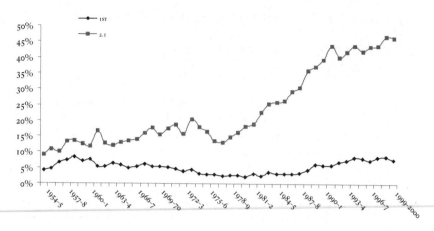

Graph 9.1: Proportion of 1sts and 2.1 degrees (all subjects)

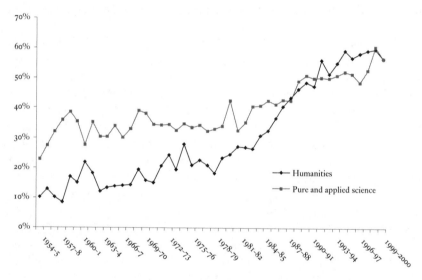

Graph 9.2: Proportion of 1sts and 2.1 degrees
(humanities, and pure and applied science)

fall, but possibly the Troubles had a depressing effect on student performance. From 1978–9, however, there was an almost uninterrupted increase in the proportion of 2.1 degrees and at the end of the century they accounted for 46 per cent of the total. The trend in the proportion of first class degrees was slightly different. It rose in the later 1950s but then drifted downwards for more than two decades until it was only a little over 2 per cent in 1980–1. During the 1980s and 1990s the proportion of first class degrees increased three-fold.

There were differences between the faculties, shown most conveniently in graph 9.2 where the combined totals of 1sts and 2.1 degrees have been plotted. Until the mid-1980s it seemed to be easier to achieve the higher classifications in the pure or applied sciences than in the humanities. Thereafter there proportions were similar. It is unlikely that science students were brighter than arts students (were they better taught?). We must look instead for other explanations. Objective judgments (the ability to recognize high or low quality performance) were probably easier in the pure and applied sciences than in arts subjects; in the latter marks were often squeezed into the 30–70 range rather than being spread throughout the scale from zero to one hundred. For many years academics in the humanities liked to mark scripts in Greek ('beta-plus with a touch of alpha-minus'), which made the achievement of high honours an Olympian effort. Until 1986 many arts students chose to read for general degrees and by definition this kept them out of the honours classifications. However there was a pronounced swing towards honours courses in arts from the mid-1970s, a full decade before the general degree was abolished. The demise of the general degree was as much an acknowledgement of the wishes of students as the result of the unwillingness of the UGC to finance four-year courses.

There were sceptics throughout the university system who argued that the rising proportion of good honours degrees was the result of falling standards. The worries were discussed in the national press. In June 1993, for example, the London *Times* reported that the proportion of first class degrees in British universities had increased by fifty per cent 'prompting' fears that standards were falling.[48] Critics pointed to the effects of modularization, which, in their view, enabled students to assemble bits and pieces of poorly related knowledge. But it was up to examiners to reward quality regardless of how degree programmes were constructed, and as can be seen from graphs 9.1 and 9.2, the upward trend in good honours results began fifteen years before the introduction of the modular structure. A shift towards continuous assessment enabled many students to perform better than the traditional examination system had allowed. In 1990 the University established the Centre for Academic Practice (and later the Teaching and Learning Committee and the Committee for Enterprise, Learning and Teaching) intended to improve the quality of teaching and assessment. It also introduced university-wide rules for marking and classification of examinations and course work.[49] These devices added to burdens of the academic staff and they occurred at the same time as student/staff ratios doubled. There was plenty of ammunition for those who doubted that standards really were rising but the objective evidence was against them.

48 *The Times*, 28 June 1993.   49 *Academic Council minutes, 1990*, appendix A following p. 38; *1994*, 8–12 and 124; *1996*, 36–7; *1998*, 187.

POSTGRADUATE TRAINING

Postgraduate courses formed the bridge between undergraduate teaching and research. During the 1960s 15 to 20 per cent of students in Queen's were post-graduates; the proportion rose to about a quarter in the 1990s. Many of them studied part-time and more than half followed programmes of professional training. For example, the Institute of Professional Legal Studies prepared men and women to become barristers and solicitors. The School of Social Work taught masters courses for professional social workers; and the School of Education provided the graduate certificate of education as well as diplomas and masters degrees in specialized areas of education. Many schools and departments offered postgraduate courses in specialized areas of their disciplines, in addition to undergraduate teaching.

Research students typically wrote theses leading to a master's degree or to a PhD. The majority of them were in the natural and applied sciences where they worked under the direction of a supervisor and were members of research teams. Research in the humanities was usually of a more free-wheeling nature and the student followed his or her own topic, which may have been suggested by the supervisor but which, equally, may have been the student's own idea. There were fewer research students in arts than in the sciences; unless they were studying aspects of Irish society they generally needed to get away from Belfast. The Institute of Irish Studies was established in 1966 in order to attract scholars to Belfast. It was not impossible, though, to study societies distant from Queen's. During the 1970s and 1980s Professor Blacking, such was his reputation, had a host of ethnomusicology students scattered through Africa and Asia. In 1992 DENI recognized the difficulties caused by the distance from the major research laboratories and libraries and established a pool of postgraduate scholarships of relatively high value to attract students to Northern Ireland and to be shared by both universities.

In 1995 the Higher Education Funding Council asked all universities for their views of the purpose of postgraduate education. Queen's identified two important aims. The first was to enhance the pool of knowledge; the second was to provide training in research skills. In the humanities the former was the more important; the PhD in history, for example, was intended either to be telling us something we did not know before or offering a different explanation for something that had been known. In the sciences the development of research techniques was often as important as pushing back the boundaries of knowledge. But there was no hard and fast difference between the arts and sciences. The purpose of the taught postgraduate qualifications was different. They were designed to add specialist knowledge to that acquired when studying for the primary degree. They also served as 'conversion' courses. The department of computer science, for example, offered both a masters degree and a diploma for graduates in the arts with no computer experience.[50]

50 *Academic Council minutes, 1995*, appendix 2 after p. 315.

A problem with all postgraduate studies, and especially with research degrees, was a high dropout rate. Part-time students usually had jobs and families and many found they did not have the time to attend to their studies. Even a full-time student might find his or her research topic was leading nowhere. During the 1980s the research councils and DENI, all of which funded research students, became worried by high dropout rates. The Economic and Social Research Council blacklisted universities that had submission rates below 40 per cent within four years. Queen's was on the list for a short while, even though the ESRC funded only one or two students in Queen's. Nevertheless, the University tightened up its regulations governing theses to prevent studying dragging on for decades and introduced codes of practice for supervisors and students to prevent the latter from withering from neglect.

RESEARCH

In 1955 the Secretary to the Academic Council told students that university research was 'organised curiosity'.[51] Whether they were impressed is unclear. The definition captures the almost gentlemanly attitude to research that was prevalent at the time. Research was what scholars chose to do during the long months between May and October. As the Vice-Chancellor put it in 1954, 'a willingness on the part of academic men to publish under the exacting conditions demanded by scholarly journals is an assurance that they have that mental vigour essential for the health of their university.' What should be the objects of their organized curiosity was a matter for the individual researcher. Some research was directly related to the needs of local industry and agriculture or for the health and social services. In 1957 the Vice-Chancellor singled out Isles and Cuthbert's study of the Northern Ireland economy as a particularly prominent example.[52] Thirty years later the Vice-Chancellor's report carried accounts of research in such diverse areas as microelectronics, computer-aided aircraft design, Irish place names, the rotational moulding of plastics, the attitudes of nurses towards smoking, food irradiation, and osteoporosis.[53]

Whether research was the product of the curiosity of individuals, which was the normal case in the humanities, or the activity of teams, as in science, it needed time and money. The costs were compounded in Queen's by its location remote from the major archives, libraries and research laboratories. The University did its best to compensate by making travel and subsistence grants available to staff to attend conferences and visit archives and laboratories. As early as 1945, when money was very tight, the University established a

51 *Gown*, 12 May 1955. 52 *Vice-Chancellor's report, 1953–4*, 167; *1956–7*, 167. The work referred to was Isles and Cuthbert, *An economic survey of Northern Ireland*. 53 *Vice-Chancellor's report, 1988–9*, 6–7.

Committee on Higher Studies and Research, set up a distinguished scholars' fund, and created research fellowships of £600 (then a substantial sum) for established scholars to study at Queen's. It introduced a system of sabbatical leave for lecturers, and gave annual grants to departments that helped pay for essential equipment.[54] This set the tone for the next fifty years. By the end of the century financial support had to be given more selectively than in the past because Queen's needed to back winners in order to boost its research reputation.

Research grants and contracts became increasing important ways of financing research. As we noted in chapter four, the University accounts do not record research grants until 1967. Thereafter the proportion rose until by the end of the century roughly 15 per cent of income came from research grants and contracts. This was a substantial achievement. Even so, Queen's received substantially less from contracts and research grants as a proportion of total income than did many British universities of similar size. This was both a financial weakness and a drag on the reputation of Queen's as a research institution.

For many years the only measures of the quality of research emanating from Queen's were the reputations enjoyed by its staff and the lists of publications appended to the annual reports of the Vice-Chancellor. In 1986 the UGC conducted the first national assessment of the quality of research in universities throughout the United Kingdom. Research areas were graded as 'below average', 'average,' 'above average', or 'excellent'. Queen's submitted a comprehensive list of its activities, pointing out the high quality of them all and the excellence of many.[55] It was a shock, therefore, when the assessors did not agree. Only social anthropology was rated as excellent and only seven subjects as above average. Fifteen areas were judged to be average, and twenty-six as below average. Applied mathematics and theoretical physics, a subject widely regarded both within the University and outside as outstandingly good, was described as below average. The UGC privately admitted this was a mistake and the department received a 'letter of comfort' from the chief executive; but it did little to mend dented pride. Appeals to the special circumstances affecting the University, such as its remoteness from national archives and laboratories, or the debilitating effects of the Troubles, as explanation of research weakness had no effect. Emphasizing the responsibilities of Queen's to the local community cut little ice either with assessors. Their judgments were based on the numbers of articles appearing in academic journals and books bearing the imprint of a distinguished publishing house. The University had to live with the results of the assessment and endure headlines in the local press proclaiming, 'QUB research below average'.[56]

The UGC and its successors continued with the research assessment exercise

---

54 *Academic Council minutes, 1944–5*, XII, 7–9.   55 *Academic Council minutes, 1985–6*, 38–43.   56 *Belfast Telegraph*, 30 May 1986.

(the RAE) and the acronym served as the lodestone for every Vice-Chancellor ambitious for the reputation of his or her university. The assessment process became more refined over time. Universities were now required to submit profiles of the research conducted in subject areas over the previous three or four years. The profiles included lists of publications, research grants awarded and numbers of postgraduate students. The assessment panels, composed of academics, ranked them on a scale of five to one. Five indicated that the majority of research in the subject area had reached international standards and the rest was of national standard. A ranking of four suggested a good mix of international and national research. A score of three pointed to research mainly of a national standard, with a touch of international quality. The lower grades reflected research effort of generally low quality.

Queen's performed better in 1989 than in 1986 (the letter of comfort in the possession of applied mathematics and physics had turned into a five), although it lagged well behind its UK comparators. But improvement was on its way as can be seen in table 9.1.[57] Like a maturing tadpole Queen's was shedding its tail and fattening up its head. As with Alice though, to mix the metaphor, it needed to run (or swim) faster to stand still since all universities were achieving 'grade shift', not least because they were all learning how to play the RAE game.

Table 9.1: Research assessments results, 1989–2001

Grade	1989	1992	1996	2001
5*	NA	NA	1	1
5	1	2	6	13
4	7	6	13	16
3a and 3b	11	23	24	4
2	18	16	3	1
1	12	2	0	0
Total subject areas submitted	49	49	47	35

Full evolution into frog status was not possible without a major change in tactics. For the 1989 assessment departments had been largely left to prepare their own profiles. In 1992 the Academic Council vetted submissions, although the degree of supervision was slight by later standards. The results of the 1992 RAE were encouraging, although more than a third of subjects were still in the two lowest categories. After they were published the Northern Ireland Higher Education Committee (NIHEC) made a fund available to both universities in the Province to strengthen their research. Queen's received nearly £3 million in

---

57 The detailed statistics are contained in the relevant years of the minutes of Academic Council. Universities could choose whether or not to submit subjects; those not submitted were rated as 1. The 5* grade was introduced in 1996. In that year also the grade 3 was divided into 3a and 3b. The smaller number of units submitted in 2001 was mainly the result of amalgamation of small subjects into larger units.

the first instance, followed by another £1.5 million. The University set up its own research committee to allocate the money selectively, mainly to subject areas that were already strong, but also to boost subjects such as chemistry, English and economics that were essential to any self-respecting university.[58] There was a counter argument, which was the money should be used to strengthen weak areas, but it made little headway. The 1996 results justified the strategy. The fattening head had become nicely rounded, and the tail had withered to a stump.

But it was not enough. Now it was necessary to transform the frog into a prince. To achieve this the University moved into full management mode in a fashion unthinkable even a decade earlier. It set up a research office. The research committee was chaired by a Pro-Vice-Chancellor and was given powers to set a strategy for the next assessment that was to take place in 2001. Money and additional appointments were focused on the subject areas that had achieved grades five and four in 1996, with limited funding for the grade threes. The ones and twos were left to fend for themselves; if they could improve their research performance without support, this was a bonus. There were to be 'urgent reviews' of areas deemed to be weak in research. The target for 2001 was to get more than half the staff working in research areas ranked as four, five, or five-star.[59]

A problem identified by the research committee was that Queen's had omitted around a quarter of the academic staff in 1996 because they were not 'research active'. Some of these were recent appointees who had hardly had time to get into establish a research reputation, but the remainder were people whose research careers (like the tadpole's tail) had dwindled into insignificance. Sir George Professor Bain was appointed Vice-Chancellor in 1998 as an Aladdin with a lamp, which if polished hard enough, might spirit up a prince of shining research performance. He quickly embarked on a major restructuring of academic activities aimed at raising the research profile. Queen's offered early retirement to over one hundred members of staff. They were to be replaced by new staff in areas likely to benefit from investment in research.

The results of the RAE in 2001 were a vindication of the plan (see table 9.1). Between 1989 and 2001 the average score almost doubled from 2.2 to 4.2. The frog had become a prince, not yet a monarch, but one who could stand tall among the generality of British universities. Queen's was not likely to achieve the general excellence of an Oxford or a Cambridge or an Imperial College, but it could match them in many areas and justifiably claim to be a university of national and international standing.

The improvement was not achieved without heartache. Many academics were sceptical about the entire assessment process, arguing that it measured

---

58 *Academic Council minutes, 1993,* 69–70; AC/P/93/28 appendix 2, 299; *1994,* appendix 1 after p. 96, 115. 59 *Academic Council minutes, 1997,* 2, 70–2.

quantity – the number of publications – rather than their quality. Scholars in the humanities were unhappy with the target of producing four published pieces within the assessment period; this was a science culture where frequent research papers and conference presentations were necessary ways of advancing knowledge. In the arts the scholarly monograph maturing over several years was the normal way of extending knowledge; the danger with this method was that sometimes the period of maturation was never completed. The RAE speeded up the process; whether the result was always worth having, was questionable. An academic at Warwick University in 1995 denounced the RAE for generating 'a mountain of wasted words' and distorting the nature of academic work.[60] He was articulating what many people in Queen's and elsewhere were thinking.

The charge of distortion goes to the very nature of universities. A central duty of a university teacher was to educate undergraduates in the fundamentals of their subjects and in the ways of clear and logical thinking. The stress put on research by the RAE strained this principle almost to breaking point. More worryingly, many academics in Queen's became aware of a decline of collegiality because of the pressures generated by the RAE. Collegiality is a quality more easily sensed than defined, but its essence was a shared sense of purpose. Teaching and research formed a seamless web requiring just sufficient administration necessary to carry them out well. Some people did more of one than of the other and the most successful were rewarded by promotion. But the RAE set department against department and colleague against colleague. Those who did not publish by the yard weakened the performance of the whole department. Teaching remained important in the lives of lecturers but administration was shunned by academics because it got in the way of research. The prized achievements for an academic became than of winning a grant from one of the research councils and to have articles accepted by highly rated scholarly journals, or published by a major academic publisher. Whether anybody read them was a secondary matter.

Why then did Queen's bother so much about the RAE? There were two answers. The first was that it needed the money. The government funded highly rated universities more generously than the weaker ones; unfortunately, as most universities improved their ratings, so the financial rewards were spread more thinly. The second was prestige. No self-respecting university in the late twentieth century was prepared to admit that it concentrated on teaching, leaving research to look after itself.

CONCLUSION

The mark of a university is the quality of its scholarship. Scholarship however is not easily measured. We have a clear idea of the numbers of students who

60 *Daily Telegraph*, 10 May 1995.

passed through Queen's and the classes of degrees they earned. We know how many academic staff were in post from year to year. Their publications were once listed in the Vice-Chancellor's reports and more recently have been counted for the RAE. But quality still remains elusive. Nevertheless a number of points about the scholarship in Queen's are clear. The first is that by the end of the twentieth century Queen's was educating far more students than it had been fifty years earlier and over a greatly increased range of disciplines and sub-disciplines. Secondly, the standard of the degrees students were achieving was rising when judged by the proportions of good honours grades being awarded. Thirdly, on all the external measures invented in the 1980s and 1990s, the quality of teaching was high that that of the research was rising rapidly.

10

Queen's and community

When Sir Richard Livingstone became Vice-Chancellor at the beginning of 1924 many people in the Province regarded Queen's almost as a foreign country. Only a few years before the funding of the University had come from Dublin; now it was the responsibility of the new Northern Ireland state, which had many pressing claims on its budget. When he tried to persuade the six county councils to contribute to the University's income they dismissed Queen's as a Belfast responsibility; Londonderry told him it had its own 'starving college' to think of. Still, he managed to persuade them to contribute a modest amount from the rates; and the formation of the Graduates' Association in 1929 and the Queen's University Guild (composed of non-graduates as well as graduates) the following year helped to identify the University with the infant six-county Province.[1]

A quarter of a century later an article in the student newspaper, *Qubist*, took issue with the presence of English ex-servicemen who stood out because of their maturity, their accents and their attitudes; they were most evidently not Ulstermen. The author instructed his readers to 'remember, it is Queen's University, <u>Belfast</u> – not England.'[2] It was as though Livingstone had been too successful in creating a sense of local identity.

It is easy to dismiss the injunction as a piece of careless journalism, but unguarded remarks can reveal deeply held beliefs. Perhaps by 'England', the writer meant Britain, or did he really believe that Scotsmen and Welshmen were welcome, but not Englishmen? He did not know his Queen's very well. The University was distinctively 'English' at the top. Every Vice-Chancellor since Hamilton had been Oxford men and nearly two-thirds of its professors were from England or Wales.[3] The University's annual grant came from Stormont but the amount was determined on the advice of the UGC, a body based in London. The Vice-Chancellor and his colleagues thought of Queen's as part of the UK system of universities. It was, however, a semi-detached part. This was obviously so geographically, but also in other ways. For the people of Northern Ireland Queen's was 'our' University.

Here then was a conundrum. The scholarly sights of Queen's were set beyond the borders of Ulster. Local perceptions, though, were different. For them the University's duty was to the Province. Previous chapters have examined how the Queen's exercised it responsibilities within its classrooms and

---

1 Moody and Beckett, *Queen's, Belfast*, ii, 494–8. 2 *Quibis*, 17 February 1950. 3 Moody and Beckett, *Queen's, Belfast*, ii, 627.

laboratories. The present chapter is concerned with activities in the wider community. It is concerned also with how the community reacted to what the University did and how it behaved.

EXTRA-MURAL STUDIES, CONTINUING EDUCATION, AND OUTREACH

In addition to its programmes of undergraduate and graduate studies Queen's offered lectures to men and women beyond its walls. There had been a committee for the extension of university teaching established by the Senate as early as 1910 and several of the earlier professors such H.O. Meredith, R.M. Henry and I.M.G. Llubera were active in extension work. Sir Richard Livingstone, was a well-known advocate of extension lecturing as a means of raising the moral tone of society.[4] Queen's established a Department of Extra-Mural Studies in 1928 with a responsibility for providing lectures in Belfast and the provincial towns. For many years it worked closely with the Workers' Educational Association (WEA) and the Young Farmers' Clubs, and its funding came partly from the Ministry of Education and partly from the local authorities, plus contributions from class fees.[5] These arrangements remained in place until after the Second World War.

Queen's reviewed its extra-mural activities in July 1963 in response to an inquiry into adult education in Northern Ireland by the Ministry of Education. Its programmes fell into three categories. There were short courses provided for members of the armed services; these had been a major activity during the 1940s and 1950s, but they were now of declining importance. Secondly there were vocational classes, for example for the diploma in government administration intended for civil servants. However, the department had few resources to devote to vocational education. Its main business was the teaching of the liberal arts where it aimed 'not at pure popularization but at sustained work of an intellectually demanding kind.' The department recognized there was a demand for low-level courses ('the stimulation of passing interest, pioneer work in political education in factories, elementary vocational training of various kinds') but did not consider it was its responsibility to satisfy it. Low-level courses were best left to the WEA. Relations between the department and the WEA worked well in Belfast where the latter attended to organizational matters and the University provided the intellectual content. In the countryside, though, the WEA often had no regular presence and Queen's was left to do everything itself. The funding arrangements were complicated. The department believed that core funding should be part of Stormont's annual grant to the University.[6]

---

4 J. Field, 'Educating active citizens: the contribution of Richard Livingstone', in M. Friedenthal-Haase (ed.), *Personality and biography: proceedings of the sixth international conference on the history of adult education*, ii (Berlin and Oxford, 1998), 831–45.   5 Moody and Beckett, *Queen's Belfast*, ii, 501; *Academic Council minutes, 1944–5*, XII, submission to the UGC, p. 31.   6 *Academic Council minutes, 1962–3*, between pp 162 and 163. Report of the

As a result of the Ministry's inquiry (published as the Morris report) the responsibilities of the Queen's department and the WEA were separated and the department was located in the newly created Faculty of Education. The University's concept of extra-mural studies remained conservative, with a concentration on liberal studies and recreational classes rather than vocational courses. But it was gradually developing a wider view and acknowledged that vocational teaching was a function 'appropriate to an extra-mural department as the main channel of communication between internal university departments and those in the outside community who are professionally interested in the relevant disciplines.'[7]

At the same times Queen's was experimenting with new ways of reaching out to the community. In 1963 it established a working party to consider the use of television in education. The working party included two members of the Independent Television Authority. They devised a scheme run jointly by Queen's and Ulster Television. For three years UTV broadcast a series entitled 'Midnight Oil', which drew on expertise from the University' departments. The intention of the programmes was to stimulate thought, provoke discussion and spread ideas, but not to impart particular skills. They were designed as sustained courses covering a wide range of academic disciplines. Not surprisingly, the University was an enthusiastic partner since the UTA supplied the equipment and technical skills, and met the capital and running cost.[8]

Over the next two decades extra-mural activities expanded in several directions. A new director (E.C. Read) was appointed in 1965 and there were seven additional appointments over the next decade. At this stage the department still concentrated on recreational classes, making use of its core staff and also the expertise of members of the intra-mural departments. But its thoughts were turning towards offering credit-bearing courses. In 1968 the department introduced a certificate in extra-mural studies. There were no specific entry requirements but the regulations were written so as to be 'sufficiently severe' to deter all but serious students. The certificate extended over three annual sessions each consisting of twenty-four classes of two hours. The standard of the certificate was intended to approximate to the BA general degree. So as not to deter students not interested in qualifications, the certificate courses were open to non-examination candidates.[9] Queen's had put a tentative toe into the water of continuing education.

committee set up to investigate the relationship between the WEA and the Department of Extra-Mural Studies.   7 Report, para. 6; *Academic Council minutes, 1965–6*, 29 and 42.   8 *Academic Council minutes, 1963–4*. 'Report of the working party on educational television', between pp. 12–3. The Pilkington Committee in the UK had recommended the development of educational television and Northern Ireland was chosen to pilot a scheme. The Northern Ireland member of the Independent Television Authority was Sir Lucius O'Brien who was also a member of the Senate.   9 *Academic Council minutes, 1968–9*, 46–7.

A decade later Queen's no longer saw the task of the extra-mural department principally as one of offering cultural lectures to a mainly middle class audience. The Northern Ireland Department of Education, which provided much of the money, was becoming reluctant to finance teaching that did not lead to a specific outcome. The concept of extra-mural studies was broadening into that of continuing education. In 1982 the Chilver review group asked about the University's plans for continuing education. The University was then offering one or two part-time degrees courses, but it told the committee 'not all disciplines are suited to this mode of study and it would therefore be inappropriate to talk of part-time degrees across the board.'[10] Two years later a working party produced the first plans for the part-time BA (General Studies) open to students without formal entry qualifications. The degree was administered by the Institute of Continuing Education and the academic departments supplied the modules. The Academic Council hoped, 'the concept of continuing education would spread through all the faculties'.[11] It did so slowly; many departments found it difficult to cope with rising numbers of intra-mural students and expand into continuing education at the same time.

In February 1989 the Council of Continuing Education submitted a report to the Academic Council that became the basis of developments during the next decade. Its basic premise was that continuing education should be part of the normal academic work of the University, and that there should be a 'permeable membrane' between continuing education and degree teaching. The BA (General Studies) was central to the plan. The Institute of Continuing Education was now organizing degrees at masters and bachelors level and also offering certificate courses aimed at updating the professions. The amount of recreational teaching the institute could offer depended on the demand. Recreational teaching required skills of a high order from lecturers and a specialized department of continuing education staffed by specialized teachers was therefore needed to carry it out and attract fee-paying students. Even so, student fees would cover only half the costs of continuing education. The Council for Continuing Education argued that University needed to accept its responsibilities to provide core funding and the necessary administrative support.[12]

Queen's had come a long way in fifty years. The most important development had been the opening up of degree programmes through part-time study to mature students. But they still had to come to Queen's. The final step was to take the University into the countryside. In his graduation address in 1994 the Vice-Chancellor, Sir Gordon Beveridge, referred to the 'barren landscape of university provision' in the south and west of the Province. For several years some of the foundation modules of the BA (General Studies) could be taken at approved provincial centres, including Omagh and Armagh, but the degrees

10 *Academic Council minutes, 1979–80*, AC/P/80/3/XI/A.   11 *Academic Council minutes, 1982–3*, 175–85; *1985–6*, 258.   12 *Academic Council minutes, 1989*, after p. 76.

had to be completed in Belfast. The Vice-Chancellor's idea was that Queen's should have campuses in the provincial towns. The first possibility was in Omagh where a disused mental hospital was available, but the building was too costly to convert to university use. However, the late eighteenth-century county infirmary in Armagh was no longer being used. With the enthusiastic support of the local city and district council, including a levy on the rates, it was adapted for use as the Queen's University at Armagh. The choice was an appropriate one historically, for Armagh had harboured aspirations for a university since 1795. The Tomas Ó Fiaich library was being constructed in the grounds of St Patrick's cathedral, and Queen's was soon to acquire the library of Cardinal Cahal Daly. The first part-time students were enrolled in September 1995. Meanwhile, in Omagh a master's degree in migration studies was instigated at the Irish-American Folk Park and postgraduate courses in rural development were started at the Rural College in Draperstown.[13]

PUBLIC LECTURES, THE ARTS, AND THE FESTIVAL AT QUEEN'S

Public lectures after the Second World War were reflections of the University's normal activities. They included inaugural lectures given by newly appointed professors, annual lectures on fine art, theology, agriculture and other subjects. There were occasional lectures ranging over the humanities, natural, medical and applied sciences. Visiting academics came under the distinguished scholars scheme to deliver public lectures. The departments of music and extra-mural studies arranged music recitals and the extension committee collaborated with the British Music Society in organizing concerts in the Great Hall.[14] From the 1930s Queen's had joined with the British Film Institute Society and the Scientific Film Society in showing films that did not get onto on the commercial circuit. In 1951 the Director of Extra-Mural Studies brought these bodies together to form the Queen's University of Belfast film society. The society screened world cinema films in the Whitla Hall. It published a magazine and generally promoted interest in cinema as an art form.[15] It was the forerunner of the QUB Film Theatre.

With the exception of music, the University had no performing arts among its degree programmes to draw upon. It owned a large collection of paintings, many of them portraits of university worthies, but had no art gallery. Pictures were hung obscurely in offices and corridors; there was a Lavery in the old common room, a Luke in an administrator's office, and unseen treasures in the basement. Until the collection was catalogued in 1995 the University was really not

13 *Vice-Chancellor's report, 1994–5*, 4–5.   14 *Vice-Chancellor's report, 1947–8*, 207; *1948–9*, 192.   15 *Academic Council minutes, 1962–3*. 'Report of the committee set up to investigate the relationship between the WEA and the Department of Extra-Mural Studies', appendix B.   16 E. Black, *A sesquicentennial celebration: art from the Queen's University Collection*

sure what it owned.[16] There was, however, a lively visual arts group started in 1956 by Dr (later Professor) Godin that organized exhibitions in the Lanyon Building and later in the foyer the Social Science Building. Its first exhibition was of the works of Stanley Spencer, described in the local press as a 'controversial choice'.[17] Queen's owned a fine collection of silver, which spent most of its time locked in a strong room, until the opening of the Visitors' Centre in 1993 provided a limited display venue. There were theatrical performances given by the students' dramatic society but no academic study of drama in the University and no theatre. There were several decisions 'in principle' over the years to build a theatre, but until the end of the century there were always more pressing demands for the money.

A change came in February 1964 when Queen's held an arts festival. There had been precursors in 1962 and 1963 but this was a more ambitious affair. The instigator was a student, Michael Emmerson, who obtained a modest grant of £600 from the University and he enjoyed the enthusiastic support of an army of volunteers. Over the years the Festival at Queen's grew into an annual event of international standing, second in size in the United Kingdom only to the Edinburgh Festival.[18] It attracted financial support from the Arts Council, the Belfast City Council, BT, Guinness's, and other sponsors, as well as from the University. At the end of the century its gross income exceeded £600,000. It brought orchestras, theatre and dance companies, and performers from all parts of the world. It spread out of the Whitla Hall and lecture theatres (the first venues) into theatres and halls throughout Belfast. Michael Emmerson left in 1972 and was succeeded briefly by David Laing and then by Michael Barnes, a history lecturer. He was appointed temporarily as a part-time director, but he remained the director for two decades.

In the light of the success of the Festival at Queen's and the Film Theatre, also started by Michael Emmerson, it is a surprise to read a report to the Academic Council in April 1997 claiming that 'while individual members of staff at Queen's have made substantial contributions to the arts, the University's institutional attitudes have ranged from half-hearted support at best to overt hostility at worst.'[19] This judgment stemmed from a worry that financial constraints were forcing the University to concentrate on money-making activities, but the report also drew attention to the absence of an art gallery and a theatre. There was a limited amount of teaching in art history in the Institute of Continuing Education At the end of the century a degree course in theatre studies was introduced in the school of modern languages, there was an art gallery and a proper theatre was about to be built.

(Ulster Museum 1995).   17 The catalogues of the exhibitions and press coverage between 1956 and 1977 are among uncatalogued papers in the QUB archives.   18 I am grateful to Ms Stella Hall, the current festival director, for information about the festival. See also Walker and McCreary, *Degrees of excellence*, 126–7 and 141–3.   19 *Academic Council minutes, 1997*, appendix, 'Queen's University and the arts'.

The report is best read as a manifesto for the future rather than as a judgment on the previous forty years. The Festival at Queen's had been a spectacularly successful attempt to uphold the civilizing values of the performing and visual arts throughout the community. Its success coincided with a period when Northern Ireland was contriving to make itself appear ungovernable. The Festival demonstrated there were human qualities in Northern Ireland other than those of bigotry and hate.

TROUBLED TIMES

Queen's worked under a public scrutiny unique among all UK universities The local press followed its activities more avidly than provincial newspapers elsewhere reported the performance of their football teams. From 1953 to 1968 the University had its own fortnightly spot in the *Belfast Telegraph* ('A Letter from Queen's') written anonymously by a member of staff, which it found useful for providing an official view of what was happening in the University. All three local newspapers regularly contained features on its activities: public lectures, appointments, resignations and retirements, academic and sporting achievements. Their letters pages were open to every person who wished to tell the University what it ought be doing. The publicity was welcome when things were going well but was distinctly uncomfortable in troubled times.[20] The civil strife that erupted in the 1960s created for Queen's the most difficult decades in its history. The essence of the conflict was starkly simple. A minority of the population wanted an end to the British presence in the north of Ireland; the majority wanted to preserve it. Lacking a peaceful resolution, violence burst onto the streets. The University was embroiled by the turmoil.[21]

The growing proportion of Roman Catholic students in the University increased their involvement in student affairs. The first Roman Catholic President of the SRC was elected in 1955. He was John Savage, a medical student from Monmouthshire, although of Northern Ireland parents. He remarked later, 'I don't think people cared very much in those days whether you were Roman Catholic or a Protestant when voting for the Students' Representative Council.'[22] But attitudes were changing. Six years later a member of the Catholic Students Society, in an article in *Gown*, entitled 'Sectarianism', complained that Union elections were rigged on sectarian lines. He was quickly contradicted by the President of the SCR who was himself a Catholic.[23]

---

20 The 'Letters from Queen's' were at first written by a student but they quickly became the responsibility of a member of staff with the assistance of a student 'winger'. 21 For a discussion of the political background of this period see J.J. Lee, *Ireland 1912–22: politics and society* (Cambridge, 1989), 411–57; P. Buckland, *A history of Northern Ireland* (Dublin 1981), 106–73; A. Jackson, *Ireland, 1798–1998* (Oxford, 1999), 396–414. 22 *Gown*, 12 October 1956; Walker and McCreary, *Degrees of excellence*, 144–5. Dr Savage later emigrated to Canada and in 1993 became premier of Nova Scotia. 23 *Gown*, 2 and 16 February 1962.

This was a domestic squabble confined to the University. But the outside world had its eye on Queen's. In 1957 the *Irish News* criticized *Gown* for covering extensively a mission to the University conducted by a well known Protestant evangelical clergyman but of ignoring the Catholic students' annual spiritual retreat, a charge that *Gown* denied. Three years later another student publication was in trouble when the printers refused to print an edition of the literary magazine *Q* because it included an article attacking the Revd Ian Paisley. *Gown* claimed the printer yielded to pressure from the Ulster Protestant Association. A few months earlier Dr Paisley had 'caused uproar' at a meeting of the Queen's Labour Party by declaring 'the Roman Catholic Church is not a Christian church.'[24] Debates at the Literific began to be concentrated on what one commentator described as the 'orange and the green'. In March 1961 the society elected a president well known for his nationalist views. The the 'Letter from Queen's' pontificated, 'no one denies the right of a President to hold this opinion provided he does not use the Literific as an organ of political propaganda.'[25]

Sporadic troubles increased. In March 1964 there was an 'undignified scuffle' at a meeting of the Tory Club addressed by Captain Terence O'Neill the Prime Minister of Northern Ireland. In October *Gown* accused the Literific of becoming 'too political', a charge its president dismissed without much conviction.[26] Organizations representing hardening political opinions outside were established in the University. The Ulster Constitutional Defence Group (a Paisleyite group) was formed in May 1966 and the incongruously named Republican Club of the Queen's University Belfast a year or so later. The University was unable to recognize the republican club because its legal advisors deemed it to be an unlawful organization under security legislation introduced in 1967.[27] The club's thwarted but probably not disappointed organizers promptly accused the University of bias. In May 1968 *Gown* published a worried editorial complaining of the injection of party politics into Union affairs.[28]

Nevertheless, when Bernadette Devlin, who became briefly the most famous Queen's undergraduate of all time when she was elected to the House of Commons, arrived in Queen's in 1965, she found most students politically naive. She epitomized a new kind of Catholic student, intelligent, working-class, articulate, and angry. In her own words, 'we were born into an unjust system; we were not prepared to grow old in it.'[29] The civil rights marches of 1967 and 1968, with their banner, 'one man one vote', transformed the atmosphere among students. A minority supported the marches and some had taken part in them. But there was a larger group who disapproved of the marches. According to Bernadette Devlin, 'the five per cent intellectual cream of the country who got

24 *Gown*, 2 February 1957, 11 March 1960, 25 November 1960, 9 December 1960. 25 *Belfast Telegraph*, 14 March 1961. 26 *Gown*, 6 March 1964, 30 October 1964, 13 November 1964. 27 *Gown*, 6 May 1966, 9, 23 November 1967; *Academic Council minutes*, 1967–8, 39. 28 *Gown*, 2 May 1968. 29 Bernadette Devlin, *Price of my soul* (London, 1969), 9.

to Queen's had its extreme right-wing element, so there were students saying, "They [the marchers] didn't get enough [police brutality]. It's a pity the police didn't kill half a dozen of them."[30] In October 1968, following a civil rights march in Derry that ended in violence, a group of Queen's students picketed the home of the Minister of Home Affairs, Mr William Craig. When a large number of students (2000 according to some reports) marched to the City Hall despite obstruction by the police and loyalist groups, he responded by accusing the President-elect of the SRCSU of inciting a riot. Soon after a group of students, with the support of one or two members of staff, formed People's Democracy, described rather grandly by Bernadette Devlin as an 'experiment in mass democracy'.[31] For a time it enjoyed the support of many moderate students concerned about the events being enacted out on the streets, but it was soon taken over by radical socialist and republican leaders.

By now the University and the SRCSU were both worried that matters were getting out of hand. In April 1969, after a meeting attended by more than 2000 students, the SRC issued a statement to the press:

> The Students' Union of the Queen's University of Belfast, being concerned at the present situation in Northern Ireland, feel it is our duty to what we can to prevent any escalation of the present civil unrest. We hereby resolve never to allow religious differences to divide us. We call on all students to refrain from any militant activities in the present situation.

Together with the University, the SRCSU agreed that 'until further notice, participation in and attendance at meetings of a political nature in the Students' Union Building shall be restricted to those who are enrolled students or members of staff.'[32] The University was anxious not to restrict political debate but it became concerned when actions verged on the unlawful (even if it believed the law was unjust). Its position was not always understood. In November 1964 the president of Literific condemned the academic staff of being out of touch because of their 'English middle class background'. A year later he accused the 'Front' of stifling free speech and implied the University had removed posters belonging to the Gaelic Society because they were in Irish. Bernadette Devlin, on the other hand, found that the Vice-Chancellor (Sir Arthur Vick) tried to turn a blind eye to student involvement in demonstrations.[33] In October 1970 the President of the SRCSU blamed the Vice-Chancellor for the deterioration in relations between students and the Front, but at his death in 1998 he 'was widely credited with plotting an independent course for Queen's University which helped to protect its intellectual freedoms during the troubles in

30 Ibid., 99–100. 31 *Gown*, 8 October, 22 October, 19 November 1968; Devlin, *Price of my soul*, 100, 101–2, 106. Professor Lee's judgment was less favourable: 'neither popular nor democratic' (Lee, *Ireland*, 422). 32 *Academic Council minutes, 1969–70*, 5. 33 *Gown*, 27 November 1964, 5 November 1965; Devlin, *Price of my soul*, 108.

Northern Ireland.'[34] The President was particularly critical of the two members of the University (Sir John Biggart and Mr J.J. Campbell) for their comments while serving on the Cameron Commission inquiring into disturbances in Northern Ireland, including the ambush of the civil rights march at Burntollet on the outskirts of Derry in January 1969.[35]

A kind of peace came over the Union after Burntollet. Most students decided marching was too dangerous a pastime. An attempt to assassinate a former President of the Union at his home served as a warning that local politics could be dangerous.[36] Strains remained below the surface, nevertheless. The *Times Higher Education Supplement* detected an 'uneasy neutrality' in the Union, with Roman Catholics and Protestant not socialising with one another.[37] There may be some journalistic embroidery at work here. When Professor Mary McAleese was a candidate for the Irish presidency in 1997 she recalled her time as a student between 1969 and 1973. Catholic and Protestants students mixed with one another. 'We were all as young people coping with this for the first time. We were realising there was a layer underneath our society we hadn't been aware of when we were growing up. There was enormous generosity among the students and friendships spanned the divide.'[38]

Not everybody felt the same. In October 1970 a first year student wrote to a local newspaper complaining socialist and republican students were denying free speech in Queen's.[39] The Monday Club alleged the Ulster Volunteer Force had organized a coup in the election for officers of the QUB Unionist Association. William Craig, now the former Minister of Home Affairs, was shouted down while addressing a meeting of the Monday Club. Elections for student offices were routinely conducted along sectarian or political lines.[40]

Many people outside Queen's did not distinguish between the Union and the University, and student politics brought Queen's firmly into the public eye. The University was criticised both from within and from without. An interned student wrote to the *Irish Times* in November 1971 complaining bitterly about the University's silence at his detention. In the same month the SRCSU organized a vigil in the Union protesting against internment. The Ulster Unionist Association immediately called for the suspension of the SRCSU, alleging the

34 *The Times*, 29 September 1998.   **35** *Irish News*, 7 October 1970. A march organized by the Civil Rights Association and People's Democracy from Belfast to Derry was harried by opponents throughout its route and was attacked by a mob armed with stones and sticks at Burntollet Bridge. Some of the marchers were students. For an account by two student participants see B. Egan and V. McCormack, *Burntollet* (London, 1969). The official account is *Disturbances in Northern Ireland. Report of the commission appointed by the Governor of Northern Ireland [the Cameron Commission]* (Belfast, 1969). Professor Biggatt and Mr J.J. Campbell were the only members of the commission apart from the chairman.   **36** *Irish Times*, 23 March 1973.   **37** *Times Higher Education Supplement*, 8 December 1972.   **38** *Guardian Higher*, 28 October 1997.   **39** *Belfast Telegraph*, 12 October 1970. The writer was David Burnside, later an Ulster Unionist MP at Westminster.   **40** *Belfast Telegraph*, 28 April, 2 May 1970; *Irish News*, 10 March 1970.

vigil had become violent.[41] The University itself handled the internment issue discretely by providing teaching for interned students and also for those who had been charged with offences but not convicted.

The press reported the effects of the Troubles on the academic life of the University. Whether or not the reports were accurate – they were sometimes exaggerated – was less important than the unappealing image of Queen's and Belfast they created. In May 1972 the Professor of Sociology wrote to the *Times Higher Education Supplement* regretting that colleagues in Britain and Holland had refused to come to lecture in Belfast because of the security situation.[42] A year later a newspaper reported 'student concern' at the high turnover of senior staff in the Faculty of Law because of the Troubles.[43]

As we saw in an earlier chapter, at the same time as some students were trying to overturn the state, others (or the same) were also seeking a greater involvement in University affairs. The two campaigns coalesced late in 1974 when a group of students were angered by the failure of the University to appoint an American graduate student to a permanent lectureship. He had endeared himself to them by his radical views and so he was obviously the man for the job. His supporters organized a 'general meeting' of the Union (such meetings were usually hastily convened and poorly attended) that issued a press statement condemning the non-appointment, which was 'for reasons other than academic incompetence and inability to teach'. His rejection exemplified 'the undemocratic and unjust nature of Queen's University'. The statement continued by declaring that 'Queen's University's official policy of "non-involvement" in Northern Ireland Affairs coupled with individuals' and individual Departments' links with Stormont have led to the University helping to preserve an unjust society in Northern Ireland'. It demanded that Queen's 'takes a stand on community issues and interests', 'speaks out against inhumanity and discrimination', and 'stands up for civil and human rights'. The University was not pleased to read the *credo* in the newspapers before it had been told of it and refused to become involved in a public debate. Instead, it quoted, with approval, the remark of the Chancellor (Lord Ashby) that 'Universities that have corporately dabbled in politics have lost the influence and liberties'.[44]

The incident crystallized a critical issue: just how should the University conduct itself in a society undergoing change? Sir Peter Froggatt reflected publicly on the question in 1977. He identified six possible roles for the University.[45] The first of these was that the University should take 'specific political stances

41 *Irish Times* 14 and 16 November 1971; *Belfast Telegraph*, 12 and 13 November 1971. 42 *THES*, 12 May 1972. Later that summer an external examiner in one subject refused to come further than Belfast airport and so the examiners' meeting had to be held there. 43 *Education Times*, 28 April 1973. 44 *Academic Council minutes, 1974–5*, 71–3; *Senate minutes, 1974*, 128–9. 45 Sir Peter Froggatt, 'The University as an instrument of social change: a dangerous or a desirable concept?' (Council of Queen's University and Schools, 1977).

or even direct action' by making a public stand on particular issues. But universities, he pointed out, have traditionally been custodians of the *status quo*, not agents of change. The Queen's colleges been had founded by Peel in 1845 to stabilise the Union, not to destroy it. But the crucial objection to Queen's throwing its corporate weight behind the reformation of society was that there was no agreed 'correct' position; to support one side was to enrage the other.

A less contentious role was that of the University engaging in social issues as 'a by-product of discharging normal university responsibilities'. The normal way into higher education was for school leavers to pass competitive examinations. 'Here the university can legitimately exercise an influence on society ... through its selection processes – for example by showing a preference, other things being equal, to persons of a certain social or occupational class, ethnic group or sex.' During the 1970s, 1980s and 1990s Queen's was busily engaged in widening access for men and women who had not had the opportunity of following the conventional route. But there were choices to be made when resources were limited. The eighteen-year-old school leavers with their three A-levels remained the major teaching responsibilities for the University.

A third form of social engagement flowed from the 'work of university professionals allied with other professionals'. There were two aspects to the relationship. Professional men and women (doctors, lawyers, architects, social workers, etc.) provided necessary services to the community. But they had also their professional networks. These networks interacted with the University, which provided the professional training. They also gave graduates an influence on the workings of society out of proportion to their numbers.

'The fourth means of university influence stem[s] from the nature of the university as a free and semi-autonomous community rather than as a formal corporate institution or an agency of the state apparatus.' This quasi-independent status confers benefits on all universities but also creates difficulties. Universities serve as havens 'for the dissenting, the unpopular, and the critical voice' where unpopular ideas can be discussed in an uninhibited fashion. In Northern Ireland, the nature of university autonomy was often not understood or, if understood, not appreciated The population of Northern Ireland, whose loyalties were to the crown, did not approve of youthful undergraduates, whose grants they paid from their taxes and who studied in a university paid for by Stormont, calling for the dismantling of the union.

There was a fifth form of influence, which the Vice-Chancellor described as 'academic triumphalism'. Put simply, 'the academic caste see themselves as essential to economic growth and prosperity.' With the growth in the number of students going to universities, so the influence of universities in society increased simply because there were more graduates in the community. At the time he believed the outbreak of student unrest in the late 1960s and the inflation of the early 1970s had soured judgements about the benefits of a university education and its contribution to economic growth. But he forecast that society would hear more of triumphalism in the future. He was right. Three decades later Queen's was faced with the challenge of educating more than 40 per cent of school leavers with only half the *per capita* income of twenty years before.

Finally universities become involved with society because their graduates are part of that society. This was particularly so in Northern Ireland where large numbers of Queen's graduates remained to live and work. Many of the leading local churchman and politicians were Queen's graduates, as were doctors, teachers, social workers, civil servants and business and women. Graduates were part of the structures of society and were in a position to influence their workings. It did not follow, though, that they were always good people or always right, or that the outcomes of their actions always added to the sum of human happiness. On the contrary they might be 'utterly and completely wrong; wrong on the grand scale.' But because of their education they possessed the training and proclivity to produce the answers. The composition the Northern Ireland Assembly following the Good Friday Agreement comprehensively illustrated the Vice-Chancellor's final point. Thirty-one of the 108 members held qualifications from Queen's, all in arts, social sciences, law, or medicine (none in the natural sciences or engineering). They included members of all the main parties ranging from the DUP to Sinn Féin.[46]

The University tried to stand above party politics and sectarian conflict. When revisions to the statutes were being considered in 1980 the Academic Council had the opportunity to agree to the removal of the prohibition on the teaching of theology in the University from public funds, a restriction that had existed since 1908. Those in favour argued that its removal would not undermine the non-denominational character of Queen's, but would recognize the study of religion as a respectable academic discipline. The counter argument was that in the circumstances of the time it was unwise to lift the restriction. As one speaker put it, 'it was the tragedy of Ireland that what was wise in 1908 was wise in 1980'. After a thoughtful debate the Academic Council agreed to allow the possibility of the teaching of theology in the future but not to do anything at the present.[47]

A decade later Queen's case to the University Funding Council for retaining scholastic philosophy as a 'minority subject' was not totally consistent with its stand against denominational teaching, but it was understandable in the context of the times.

> Queen's possesses the only department of Scholastic Philosophy in the United Kingdom. The presence of this subject at Queen's is a vital factor in the continued recruitment of intending Catholic priests from the diocese of Down and Connor. In addition, the continued presence of

46 Paul Bew, 'To serve them all our days?', *Vice-Chancellor's letter to graduates* (Belfast, 2000), 12–13. 47 *Academic Council minutes, 1980–1*, 66–9.

Scholastic Philosophy is an important sign to the Catholic community of higher education's commitment to its distinctive cultural interests and background. Its attenuation at Queen's would therefore, represent a major set-back to government policy in relation to Education for Mutual Understanding ...'[48]

As the Troubles continued many students came to use the Union only for everyday purposes such as having lunch or buying a drink. This left scope for those attracted by student politics. In other universities this took the form of demanding a role in running the institution, or protesting at remote outrages such as apartheid in South Africa. In Northern Ireland there were indignities closer to home. In October 1971, following the internment of several students the SRC declared it would continue to take a stance on political matters and 'mobilise' student opinion against violence and sectarianism. It would oppose actions that exacerbated the sectarian divide, safeguard the integrity of democratic processes and ensure the SRC would fairly represent student opinion.[49] These were highly laudable aims. The difficult one was the last, for there was no single 'student opinion'; there were many student opinions. A few weeks later the Union was thrown into turmoil by a meeting addressed by Tomás MacGiolla, the president of Sinn Féin, then an illegal organization in Northern Ireland. There followed an almost comic opera episode in which students barricaded the Union building so that MacGiolla could be smuggled out of the back to avoid being arrested by the RUC.[50]

In January 1974 the Republican Club (was it still an illegal organization?) accused the University of carrying out work for the Ministry of Defence, claiming this 'clearly demonstrates that the traditional concept of QUB as a political neutral institution of learning is an insidious and dangerous myth'.[51] A self-appointed 'Committee for Democracy in the University' claimed the policy of 'non-involvement' had 'led the University helping to preserve an unjust society in Northern Ireland.' The University responded by pointing to the many ways its staff contributed to the welfare of the community and affirming the freedom of 'members of staff of all grades and all persuasions to take part, as private citizens, in any political activity they wish, without involving the University as such.'[52]

Rhetorical condemnations of university authorities by radical students were common currency everywhere. Not so other incidents such as the murder of staff and students, one of whom was shot at random whilst leaving a church near the University. There was an atrocity in 1978 reported by the Vice-Chancellor in a paragraph unique in the official publications of any university in the United Kingdom.

48 *Academic Council minutes, 1990*, annex A after p. 36. 49 *Gown*, 12 October 1971. 50 *Gown*, 2 February 1971. 51 *Gown*, 29 January 1974. 52 *Academic Council minutes, 1973–4*, 71–2.

I would wish to mention one other episode whose nobility of response transcended the tragedy which inspired it. On Rag Day, 3 March last, a soldier and a civilian woman [security] searcher were murdered near the centre of Belfast by terrorists masquerading as students in rag day dress ... In dignified and silent protest most of the student body and many staff – some 7500 in all – walked in column to the centre of the town where the student union President spoke briefly, and then in silent procession walked back again, an action which attracted very wide admiration, sympathy and respect, and universal support: as stirring and moving an event as that which prompted it was sordid and squalid.[53]

In June 1980 a member of staff, Miriam Daly, a lecturer in economic history who was active in republican politics, was shot dead in her own home. One version of events was that she was killed by an army assassination squad; another that she was killed by a dissident republican group. In February the following year the IRA tried to kill the Lord Chief Justice when he came to the University to give a lecture; the bullet missed its target but wounded the Professor of Accounting who happened to be close by. In May there was an attempt to kill an RUC inspector who was sitting a law examination. There was a strong suspicion that there was a 'mole' in the Faculty of Law passing information about its affairs onto the IRA. Several years later a television programme in Dublin named a former lecturer whom it alleged was the person concerned.[54] In December 1983 Edgar Graham, a lecturer in law and a rising star in the Ulster Unionist Party, was gunned down in University Square.[55]

Throughout the 1980s and into the 1990s Queen's possessed almost a split personality. Academic life went on as usual and for the administration the pressing problems were how to cope with one financial squeeze after another, how to guess what the next switch in government educational policy might be, and how deal with the growing numbers of academic audits. Across University Road student politicians continued to play out the wider political battle. According to parts of the local press, the Union had become a nationalist preserve where a 'chill factor' operated to keep out Protestant students. The rising proportion of Roman Catholic students continued to worry many unionist politicians. Since the University did not keep the statistics of their numbers, there was plenty of scope for bandying about inflated figures. The flow of students from the Irish republic, attracted by free places for citizens of the European community, was seized upon as evidence that Protestant students were being squeezed out of their own university.[56] The appearance of signs both in Irish and in English in

53 *Academic Council minutes, 1977–8*, 182; *Senate minutes, 1978*, 45.   **54** *Irish Times*, 19, 20 April 1995.   **55** *Belfast Telegraph*, 2 and 27 March 1982, 7 December 1983. **56** Undergraduates in the UK at this time did not pay fees. Undergraduates from other countries within the European Community were treated in the same way. A headline in the *Belfast Telegraph* read, 'The student invasion from the Republic' (23 February 1987). See also the Union building added to the alleged sense of alienation. There was a tangible affront to Unionist susceptibilities, and indeed to students of no strong political opinions, in March 1988 when meeting was called in the Students' Union to protest at the killing by British soldiers in Gibraltar of Mairead Farrell, a student who had briefly interrupted her studies to take part in a bombing mission.[57] In October 1990 the *Sun* (more renowned for the colourfulness of its headlines than the accuracy of its reporting) claimed the Union was a recruiting ground for the IRA; the claim caused both outrage and alarm among students who feared that loyalist groups might seek to kill students.[58]

Charge and counter-charge simmered on. In September 1992 a student told the *Belfast News Letter* the Union stood only for 'vigorous sectarianism.' A few months later the Vice-Chancellor was forced to deny newspaper reports that he had described student societies as 'republican clubs'. Allegations swirled round the Union that a Protestant student had been disqualified from post of vice president of the Union because of her religion and that, generally, the Union was a den of republican intrigue.[59] At the end of 1994 the Union granted a much delayed life membership to a former student officer who had been convicted of terrorist offence, provoking the headline, 'terrorist row goes on at QUB'.[60] The elections for the Union President in February 1996, when the political temperature in the Province was lower than it had been for years, attracted headlines because two of the three candidates were children of prominent political figures, Bernadette Devlin (McAliskey) and John Taylor. That the third, non-political, candidate was elected was not news.[61]

DISCRIMINATION, THE NATIONAL ANTHEM, AND IRISH LANGUAGE SIGNS

At the end of the 1980s Queen's might have thought it had survived the Troubles, a little battered but firmly in business. It was a shock, therefore, to the find itself in 1989 accused of discrimination when appointing members of staff. For those with very long memories the charge should not have been a surprise. Many years before, in May 1912, the *Irish News* carried an account of a Home Rule debate in the Westminster House of Commons under the headline, 'QUB's sad record of discrimination raised in parliament'.

Belfast News Letter, 17 and 30 January 1992; *Irish News*, 20 January 1992.   **57** *Belfast Telegraph*, 10 March 1988.   **58** Reported in the *Belfast News Letter*, 13 October 1990, and the *Irish News*, 13 October 1990. See also the *Irish News*, 21 January 1991.   **59** *Belfast News Letter*, 22 September 1992, 9, 11, 16 March 1993; *Belfast Telegraph*, 8, 10, 12, 16 March 1993; *Irish News*, 9, 10, 12 March 1993.   **60** *Belfast News Letter*, 26 November 1994. The life membership was said to be for services to the Student's Union. Critics wondered why it had taken the Union several years to get round to awarding the honour.   **61** *THES*, 23 February 1996.

When Unionists talked of the universities of Ireland being Catholic in tone and spirit, they would find in Queen's University, Belfast, that out of the total salaries of £18,000, the only two Catholic officials were paid between them the magnificent sum of £300. The National University, with an overwhelming Catholic majority on the Senate, had not hesitated to appoint Protestant professors and Protestant officials, and had set an example to Queen's College, Belfast, which that College might well imitate![62]

But that was the past. Queen's was a non-denominational university, respectful of all shades of opinion and its door were open to all suitably qualified students regardless of religion. That only a quarter of them until the 1970s were Roman Catholics was because of the weaknesses of the Catholic schools and the relative poverty of the Roman Catholic population. The academic staff had been recruited according to qualifications and ability. Most of them had been men: whether Protestant, Catholic, or other, did not matter. Many of them had come from England. This, according to the author of the 'letter from Queen's', could lead to misunderstandings because they limited their social contacts to fellow Englishmen and were 'critical of Ulster, Ireland and the mores of the indigenous inhabitants.' They formed a 'colony of expatriates'.[63] At the end of 1989 a Nationalist politician claimed, 'there is an overwhelming, not just British ethos, but an English ethos in Queen's'.[64]

The occasion of the discrimination charges was the publication of the findings of an investigation into the religious (more strictly the denominational) composition of the workforce, begun in 1986 by the Fair Employment Agency. The University had not been seriously worried by the outcome. It had designated the Personnel Officer as its Equal Opportunities Officer and established an Equal Opportunities Group. In June 1988 it seconded a member of staff from the Department of Economics, with expertise in labour legislation and statistical methods, to the Personnel Office to monitor recruitment procedures and a few months later set up an Equal Opportunities Unit.[65]

When the FEA report was published the statistic that caught the eye was that only 16 per cent of the staff were Roman Catholics. This was less than half the proportion of Roman Catholics in the population. The *Irish News* echoed its predecessor seventy-seven years earlier with the headline, 'A sad tale of bigotry', followed by a feature under the stark title, 'Queen's Bigotry'. It increased the agony the following day by proclaiming a 'Cry of shame on Queen's over FEA report'.[66] The British and Irish newspapers were quick to join the chorus that Queen's discriminated against Roman Catholics.[67]

62 *Irish News*, 9 May 1990. This was part of a series recalling events that had occurred on 'this day' in earlier years.   63 'A letter from Queen's', *Belfast Telegraph*, 17 January 1964. 64 *Irish News*, 21 December 1989.   65 *Academic Council minutes, 1990*, annex B following p. 36.   66 *Irish News*, 20, 21 December 1989.   67 *Independent*, 21 December 1989; *Irish*

It was an uncomfortable time for the University. Protestations that nearly of a quarter of the staff were 'XNI' and therefore distorted the figures cut no ice. Neither did pointing out that the Roman Catholic proportion had already risen by three percentage points since 1986, to 19 per cent in 1989: it simply proved that Queen's had discriminated in the past and was frantically trying to catch up. The 'XNI' defence was a reasonable one when considering the academic staff. Twenty-seven per cent of academics in post in 1987 had received their school education outside Northern Ireland and so in terms of the act were neither Protestant nor Roman Catholic. When direct questioning was used later to discover denominational allegiance, several were unmasked as English or Irish Catholics. However, there were pronounced faculty differences. Close to 60 per cent of arts staff, for example, were XNI but only 14 per cent in medicine. These differences mirrored the origins of the staff discussed in an earlier chapter

The XNI argument could not explain the predominance of Protestants among the non-academic staff since only 5 per cent fell into the category. Between 70 and 75 per cent of the administrative, technical, clerical and miscellaneous staff were Protestants. There were several possible explanations. One was that the proportions reflected the pattern in the localities from which the workforce was recruited; but a detailed analysis of recruitment areas did not support this explanation. A second possibility was that Roman Catholics did not apply for jobs in the University. If so, it raised the question why such an attitude existed. A third possibility was that Roman Catholics were less well qualified for posts in Queen's than their Protestant counterparts This might have been the case for the more senior administrative positions, but it could not explain the imbalance in the clerical and manual grades. There remained the possibility that Queen's had discriminated, directly or indirectly, intentionally or unintentionally when making appointments. Discrimination was a practice deeply engrained in Ulster society – it was the reason for the fair employment legislation of 1976 and 1989 – and Queen's was part of that society.

The University responded to the FEA report by tightening up its employment procedures. In January 1992 it published an 'Equal Opportunities Code of Practice'. But the hostile publicity hung like a bad smell, particularly as there were several cases of alleged discrimination coming before the Fair Employment Tribunal. One in particular during the spring of 1992 created serious difficulties for the University for the next three years. Two years earlier a member of the Bursar's department had applied for a more senior position in the same department but was unsuccessful. He complained to the Fair Employment Tribunal he had been discriminated against because he was a Roman Catholic. The Personnel and Equal Opportunities officer told the Tribunal that, in his opinion, proper procedures had not been followed. He said he had warned the Vice-Chancellor who had not acted on the warning. Fearing that the Tribunal

Times, 21 December 1989; *THES*, 29 December 1989.

would call the Vice-Chancellor to give his version of events, the University withdrew from the case and paid compensation to the claimant for the distress caused, although it denied any discrimination had occurred.

The headline writers were kept busy. 'Queen's chief did nothing in bias case, tribunal told', was one of less sensational statements.[68] There was a continual flow of articles in the local and national press discussing discrimination by the University. A self-appointed body in Belfast calling itself 'Equality' circularised universities in Britain and Ireland calling for a boycott of Queen's because of its 'culture of discrimination' against Roman Catholics and the Vice-Chancellor was forced to contact his fellow Vice-Chancellors setting out the University's case. The same organization also tried to persuade local firms with international links (Bombardier and Du Pont) to withdraw their research funding. The MP for West Belfast, in an echo of 1912, raised the question of discrimination in Queen's in the House of Commons. In America the Irish National Caucus took up cudgels against the University and Congressman Joe Kennedy decided it was a matter for Congress.[69]

The Senate meeting in June was the first following the collapse of the tribunal case. It was a painful occasion. One senator described the debacle as 'potentially the gravest matter to be discussed by this Senate in the University's distinguished history.' The handling of the case at the tribunal, particularly the decision to contest it in the first place, revealed a serious breakdown of management and undermined much of the good work that had been done since the publication of the fair employment report in 1989.[70]

To make matters more difficult the Senate was divided. There was a continual leaking of Senate papers (who by was never established) to the newspapers that did nothing to increase public confidence in the University. The Vice-Chancellor explained that in 1990, following the report of the Fair Employment Agency, he had engaged consultants to examine the University's employment procedures and he believed they complied with legislation and code of practice. But 'recent events had led him to realise that confidence in the operation of the system was not as high as it should be, especially in relation to the practical application of arrangements.' He had therefore commissioned Employment Equality Services (EES), to conduct a review of its procedures and practices relating to equality of opportunity and fair employment. EES was to report to an *ad hoc* committee composed of six members of Senate. He had also set aside £200,000 to cover legal and other expenses. The Senate endorsed these actions after a long and anguished debate.

68 *Irish News*, 22 May 1992. 69 *Academic Council minutes, 1992*, 121–3; *Senate minutes, 1992*, 310–3, *Belfast News Letter*, 24 June 1992; *Irish News*, 20 and 23 June 1992, 23 September 1992; *THES*, 10 July 1992. 70 *Senate minutes, 1992*, 258–62. The published minutes give only a bare summary of the debate. A member of the Senate has given me the typescript of his comments. I also have my own recollections of the proceedings. I have followed the convention of the Senate of not identifying the speakers except where the Vice-Chancellor or other officers made statements as University officials.

The EES report was ready in February 1993.[71] Parts of it were confidential (most of these were leaked to the press) but the published sections were sufficiently critical to be highly embarrassing. They did not say explicitly that the University discriminated against Roman Catholics but the report made ninety-three recommendations for changes in procedures, leaving little doubt that the chances of unintentional discrimination had been high. There followed another uncomfortable debate, at the end of which the Pro-Chancellor (Mr John McGuckian) and Vice-Chancellor held a press conference where the former announced the University accepted the report in total, adding 'it is absolutely the case that the position at Queen's reflected Northern Ireland as a whole and there was discrimination against Catholics.'[72] Although the interview was badly reported in a television programme later that evening, the admission did something to dispel an impression created some months earlier when a hostile journalist manoeuvred the Vice-Chancellor into saying 'the University concedes nothing. Discrimination in the legal sense means different things.'[73] Twelve academic members of staff with expertise in employment matters wrote to newspapers pointing out the University's equal opportunity policies were a model for other universities.[74]

There remained the task of implementing the ninety-three recommendations. They ranged from including statements in relevant University documents aspiring to equality of opportunity, to detailed procedures relating to recruitment, appointments, promotions, appraisal, staff training, discretionary pay, discipline, and the roles of the Personnel Office and the Equal Opportunities Group. Even with good will their implementation took many months. They placed time-consuming burdens on heads of departments involved in making appointments and prevented practices that would be normal in most universities, such as phoning an academic colleague to find out if he or she knew of anybody suitable. The EES report was a huge intrusion into the autonomy of a self-governing institution.

Two aspects of the report created difficulties in another direction. The first was its suggestion (not a recommendation) that Queen's should think again about having a Registrar. As we saw in an earlier chapter this was a question that divided the Academic Council and Senate for years and was not resolved until Sir George Bain assumed office in 1998. The other was recommendation sixty-eight, which read:

> The University, in the context of fulfilling its obligations to promote a
> neutral working environment, should consult widely and sensitively on

71 Employment Equality Services, *Review of the structures, procedures and practices of the Queen's University of Belfast as they relate to the provision for and application of the equality of opportunity and fair participation in employment* (February 1993).   72 *THES*, 26 February 1993.   73 *Irish News*, 2 July 1992.   74 *Irish News*, 20 April 1993; *Belfast Telegraph*, 8 April 1993; *THES*, 2 and 16 April 93; *Irish Times*, 7 April 1993; *Senate minutes, 1993*, 124–6.

the appropriateness [of] playing of the National Anthem at graduation ceremonies, the RUC band playing at graduation ceremonies and the use of Irish language signs in the Students' Union.

The University appointed a group to advise on these matters, chaired by a Pro-Vice-Chancellor and composed of representatives of the Senate and the academic, administrative, secretarial and technical staff. It completed its business in November and the Senate considered its report in December.[75] The group made three main recommendations. The first was that the National Anthem should not be played at normal graduation ceremonies; graduations were domestic occasions and the National Anthem was unnecessary. Slightly illogically, it suggested playing the anthem of the European Union ('Ode To Joy') instead. Secondly, the band of the RUC should be only one of several bands playing at the garden parties. This had already become the case because the number of parties had increased to five in a week, but the recommendation was widely interpreted as a 'ban' on the RUC. The third recommendation was that the Irish language signs (more strictly, the bi-lingual signs) in the Students' Union should be 'de-politicised'. They should be recognized as cultural symbols and not as badges of political identity.

The recommendations provoked yet another protracted debate in Senate, which was now spending so much time putting the discrimination house in order it had little time for the financial or academic health of the University. Many members of the Senate were unhappy about letting the National Anthem go. The report pointed out a growing minority of students and their relatives were not happy to stand for the National Anthem at graduations and for some years handfuls of graduating students had remained seated when it was played. As a gesture of good will it should be dropped. A respectable defence of the National Anthem was that the University had been established by royal charter and was funded from the United Kingdom exchequer. Queen's should therefore acknowledge its origins on ceremonial occasions. An objection, more often articulated outside the University, was that Queen's was caving in to the pressure of a nationalist minority with a republican agenda. The presence of the RUC band at the garden parties provoked similar arguments.

The display of Irish language signs in the Students' Union was a tricky one for the University. The Union was a quasi-autonomous body and the University was reluctant to interfere in its affairs. Furthermore, Irish was a minority language recognized by the European Community and it would be strange for an institution of higher learning to ban its use. On the other hand, the hope of the advisory group that the bi-lingual signs would be accepted as symbols of cultural diversity was touchingly optimistic. To its sternest critics it looked as

---

75 *Senate minutes, 1994*, 552–66. 'Final report of the special advisory group for the promotion of a neutral working and social environment.'

though the University was scorning unionists by 'banning' the National Anthem and the RUC and pandering to nationalists by keeping the Irish language signs.

The Senate accepted the report of the advisory group with some misgiving, with two votes against and two abstentions.[76] The public outcry then began. By an unfortunate stroke of timing the report came to the Senate at the same time as the report of the honorary degrees' committee, which recommended an honorary doctorate for Mr James Molyneaux, the leader of the Ulster Unionist Party. The business of the committee was supposed to be strictly confidential until offers had been accepted (the refusals were never published). Nevertheless, it soon became public that Mr Molyneaux had refused the degree because of the National Anthem decision. His action further fuelled the sense of indignation that Queen's had betrayed its birthright. By the time of the next meeting of Senate in February 1995 the University had received letters of objection from five borough or county councils, thirteen individual councillors and members of parliament, eight organizations such as Oranges lodges, and 143 individuals.[77] These were in addition to the hundreds of letters to the Belfast and provincial newspapers and to individual members of the University.

Queen's published a justification of its position in a letter to the three Belfast newspapers on 24 January 1995, more than month after they had been announced. Although welcomed by its supporters, the letter was criticised for being late and not signed by the Vice-Chancellor but by the senior Pro-Vice-Chancellor. The University's opponents dismissed it with various degrees of contempt, one columnist in the *Belfast News Letter* describing it as 'claptrap cloaking educated treason.'[78] There had been a protracted discussion behind the scenes about whether the University should respond publicly at all and, if so, in what way. The *Irish News* had been sympathetic to the University throughout. The *Belfast Telegraph* had published a couple of supportive editorials but its letters' columns were almost uniformly hostile. The *Belfast News Letter* was implacably hostile. Local television coverage had been damaging. It was decided that Queen's could not remain silent but should use a Pro-Vice-Chancellor to speak for the University.

The Senate meeting in February stuck by its decisions and it did so again in April. It then had another clutch of protesting letters to deal with, as well as a resolution from Convocation condemning 'the decision of the Senate of the university on 20 December 1994 to ban the playing of the National Anthem at graduation ceremonies and call[ing] on the Senate to review that decision immediately.'[79] The resolution had been passed at an emergency meeting on 5 April. The newspapers reported an attendance of between 1200 and 2000. The official

76 *Senate minutes, 1994*, 449–503.   **77** *Senate minutes, 1995*, 65–75. There were twenty letters of support.   **78** *Belfast Telegraph*, 24 January 1995; *Belfast News Letter*, 24 and 30 January 1995; *Irish News*, 25 January 1995.   **79** *Senate minutes, 1995*, 142.

figure was 1094. Whatever the figure, it was the largest attendance in the history of Convocation and most of those present opposed what had been done. Queen's had made many of its graduates extremely angry.

As the graduation season became closer the local newspapers forecast there would be protests ranging from community singing of the Anthem, to massed picketing of the Whitla Hall. In the event the protests were restrained. At one ceremony two graduands used a small tape recorder to play the National Anthem and several graduating students handed letters of protest to the Chancellor as they crossed the platform. There was also some lobbying outside the Whitla Hall.[80] During the summer some of the heat went out of the controversy and when the new academic year started the atmosphere was less tense. Both the UUP and the DUP returned to the anthem controversy at their autumn conferences.[81] There were threats of more protests at the winter graduations and again in the summer of 1996, but nothing of significance occurred.

CONCLUSION: INTO THE LIGHT

During the protracted furore a newspaper letter writer asked why there should be such a fuss about anthems, flags and signs. Most members of the academic staff, busy with teaching and research and beset by quality audits, took the same attitude. But the National Anthem, the RUC band, and the use of Irish in the Union building (and on Student Union notepaper) were important because of what they represented. The tensions within Northern Ireland since 1920 had intensified and nationalist aspirations threatened the existence of the state. The University found itself caught between opposing forces. As Sir Peter Froggatt had pointed out two decades earlier, universities are more usually the targets of changes in society than they are instruments of those changes. As Queen's was buffeted by the events outside, the National Anthem, the RUC band, and the Irish language became the weapons in a wider conflict. The University had been faced by the worst public crisis in its history

Several events helped to heal the wounds. The 150th anniversary celebrations shifted the focus to decades of real achievement. The Belfast City Council, which earlier had sent three letters of protest to Queen's, held a dinner in the University's honour. People began to get used to graduations without an anthem (the 'Ode To Joy' never had a note played) and the garden parties were made merry by the cheerful music of youth bands and jazz bands. In February 1995 the President of the Students' Union told the Senate the bi-lingual signs policy

---

80 One of the protesters was Ian Paisley Jnr who was graduating with a master's degree in political science. A newspaper reported he had disrupted the ceremony, but he claimed correctly that his protest had been dignified. See *Irish News*, 3 July 1995; *Belfast News Letter*, 5, 8, 21 July 1995; *Belfast Telegraph*, 7 July 1995; *Irish Times*, 4 July 1995. 81 *Belfast News Letter*, 9 October 1995; *Belfast Telegraph*, 25 November 1995.

had 'lapsed' (nobody noticed at the time).[82] The opening of Queen's at Armagh in 1995, with the full support of the local council, was an earnest of University efforts to reach out to the whole community.

There were other reasons for the easing of the tensions. In spite of a number of employment cases still before the Fair Employment Tribunal, there was a growing appreciation that Queen's was tackling the discrimination issue effectively. More generally, during the 1990s some of the passion was going out of community politics. They were being conducted once more by argument and debate rather than by bombs and bullets. As political life became more normal Queen's was able to revert to being a normal university attending to what it was set up to do: advancing and disseminating knowledge through teaching and research.

82 *Senate minutes, 1995*, 6–12.

11

Conclusion

The historian of a university can choose from among several approaches. He or she can organize the discussion within the periods of office of successive Vice-Chancellors. This was the method followed by Moody and Beckett in their history of the first century of Queen's, although it was necessary for them also to deal with the foundations of the three Queen's colleges in 1845, the transition to the Royal University in 1879–80, the emergence of an independent Queen's in 1908–9 and the consequences for the University of Partition.

The attraction of this method is it provides the historian with a convenient explanatory tool. Vice-Chancellors become the cause of the changes occurring during their tenure of office. But there is a problem with this line of attack. It carries the risk of exaggerating the power of Vice-Chancellors. This is not to argue that they are unimportant. On the contrary, they have the vital task of guiding their institutions through the turbulence of the times. But they cannot do it by themselves. They need the assistance of managers and administrators and their academic colleagues and they are constrained by requirements of government policy and the health of the balance sheet.

A second approach is to focus on the scholarly activities of lecturers and students. After all, universities are communities of scholars and teaching and learning are the reasons for their existence. The difficulty with this method is that there is too much scholarship, too many lecturers, and far too many students, for a single writer to deal with. Possibly the task might be simplified by leaving the students out of the story and concentrating only on the most prominent of the staff. But this runs the risk of turning history into hagiography. The story of a university should be more than an account of the achievements of a few bright stars and it is incomplete if it leaves students out of the picture. As Newman suggested a century and a half ago, the achievements of universities are greater than the sum of the contributions of a few great scholars.

There remains a third approach. In the foreword to the centenary history of the University of Dundee, its Vice-Chancellor wrote, 'this book is not about institutional matters because universities, more than other organizations, reflect the ideas of, aspirations and attitudes of individuals. They are not even organized organizations but, as I sometimes thought in the midst of a Senate debate, a collection of special interests joined by a common telephone number'.[1]

---

1 D. Southgate, *University education in Dundee: a centenary history* (Edinburgh, 1982), iv (foreword by the Principal and Vice-Chancellor).

This applies to Queen's as much as to Dundee. But unorganized organizations exist to serve society. Modern universities are expected to contribute to the wealth and well being of society and to stand as guardians of the liberal values that underpin society. I have tried therefore to write a social history of Queen's. The approach has pitfalls by playing down the contributions and eccentricities of individuals within its walls. On the other hand, such details are often of interest only to the cognoscenti. The social setting is of wide interest, especially in Northern Ireland where the relationship with Queen's has been intense.

We have identified five major developments in the history of Queen's during the second half of the twentieth century. The first was the University became ten-times bigger. The growth changed both the physical appearance and way the University was run. This led onto the second change. Queen's became managerially and administratively a more complex organization. What Sir David Keir once described as the managerial and bureaucratic devices multiplied and the academics became less in control of their own activities. It took a long time for them to admit that the University needed to modernize its managerial arrangements. The third development was that the government became much more intrusive in the affairs of the University. It did this by the enunciation of policies and, even more by changes in the scale and methods of finance. It is an exaggeration to say that universities became nationalized during the 1980s, but it sometimes felt like it. A symbol of the change was the demise of the UGC that had been a buffer between the state and the universities since 1919.

The remaining two developments were at the heart of the University. Queen's became an international university. Before 1945 it had contained a few scholars of international standing, but for most of them their reputations did not extend much beyond the Province. The international links were greatly strengthened after the war. Sir Eric Ashby went out of his way to recruit good young scholars and the trend continued thereafter, notwithstanding the dispiriting effects of the Troubles. Queen's scholars travelled internationally as visiting lecturers and professors, their articles were published in journals of international repute and their books were read and reviewed world-wide. In return, scholars from overseas came to Queen's for periods of study. The student population was much less cosmopolitan but a considerable proportion of them found employment outside Northern Ireland after graduation and in this way, too, Queen's was more than a university for its region.

Finally there was the development that gives the story of Queen's its unique characteristic. Because its history was so entangled with that of the state of Northern Ireland, Queen's was particularly affected by the political upheavals that occurred in the Province between the 1960s and the 1990s The University had to adjust to a community that was becoming transformed socially and politically. The transformation was painful and sometime violent. Queen's was for several decades a university working in troubled times.

Appendices

Appendix 1.1: Senior officers of the University

Chancellors

1923–49	The Seventh Marquess of Londonderry	1970–83	Lord Ashby of Brandon
		1984–91	Sir Rowland Wright
1949–63	Field Marshall the Viscount Alanbrooke	1992–8	Sir David Orr
		1999–	Senator George Mitchell
1963–70	Sir Tyrone Guthrie		

Vice-Chancellors

(The names are given according to their titles when they left office.)

1939–49	Sir David Keir	1976–86	Sir Peter Froggatt
1950–1959	Sir Eric Ashby	1976–87	Sir Gordon Beveridge
1959–66	Dr Michael Grant	1998–2004	Professor Sir George Bain
1966–76	Sir Arthur Vick		

Pro-Vice-Chancellors

1949–50	Professor F.H. Newark	1984–8	Professor I.C. Roddie
1965–6	Professor A. Williams	1987–92	Professor J.F. Fulton
1967–74	Professor A. Williams	1988–90	Professor R. Wallis
1967–71	Professor Sir John Biggart	1989–91	Professor G.P. Blair
1971–4	Professor R.D.C. Black	1990–5	Professor L.A. Clarkson
1974–5	Professor G. Owen	1992–3	Professor G.P. Blair
1975–9	Professor A.E. Astin	1994–7	Professor Mary P. McAleese
1978–82	Professor B. Crossland	1995–2001	Professor R.J. Cormack
1979–83	Professor. J. Braidwood	1997–8	Professor L.A. Clarkson
1982–86	Professor W. Kirk	1998–2002	Professor M. Andrew
1983–7	Professor C. Campbell	1998–2001	Professor B.W. Hogg

Vice-Presidents

1962–4	Professor C. Kemball	1965–6	Professor E.A. Cheeseman
1964–6	Professor A.V. Stephens		

Secretaries of the Academic Council

(Full-time from 1966)

1947–65	Professor F.H. Newark	1978–84	A.H. Graham
1965–6	Professor A. Williams	1985–97	Dr G. Baird
1966–78	D.G. Neill		

Secretaries of the University

1938–48	R.H. Hunter	1977–85	R.G. Topping
1948–77	G.R. Cowie		

Administrative secretary

1985–98	D.H. Wilson

Full-time registrars

1985–7	F. Smyth	2000–	J.P.J. O'Kane
1998–9	J. Town		

Bursars (later directors of finance)

1948–78	G.D. Burland	1985–93	D.N. Gass
1978–85	R.J. Brown	1993–1999	J.P.J. O'Kane

Librarians

1945–61	J.J. Graneek	1975–90	A. Blamire
1961–72	P. Harvard-Williams	1990–	N.J. Russell (later Director of Information)
1972–5	H.J.F. Heaney		

Appendix 1.2. Full-time academic staff by faculty (teaching and research)

Year ending December	Arts	Medicine and dentistry/ Health sciences	Applied science/ engineering	Law	Economics and social sciences	Science	Agriculture and food science	Education and extra-mural studies	TOTAL
1945	na	na	na	na	na	na	na	na	127
1946	na	na	na	na	na	na	na	na	154
1947	na	na	na	na	na	na	na	na	163
1948	31	46	?	4	8	49	?	9	204
1949	na	na	na	na	na	na	na	na	217
1950	na	na	na	na	na	na	na	na	197
1951	38	54	9	6	12	53	35	12	219
1952	44	87	?	6	11	58	?	11	246
1953	41	65	8	8	18	69	39	12	260
1954	48	69	11	7	20	76	39	11	281
1955	49	72	17	8	18	84	38	11	297
1956	49	76	23	7	18	80	38	11	302
1957	52	73	24	8	18	84	38	11	308
1958	53	78	25	7	12	83	37	12	307
1959	58	78	33	9	21	101	37	12	349
1960	62	83	42	9	27	111	37	12	383
1961	69	89	47	11	25	112	39	12	404
1962	69	86	52	16	27	125	44	13	432
1963	81	123	53	15	28	117	44	11	472
1964	80	119	52	14	28	119	48	14	474
1965	87	102	67	16	36	142	49	13	512
1966	88	138	79	21	38	144	36	18	562
1967	93	158	93	22	37	158	35	20	616
1968	111	151	91	21	42	141	36	22	615
1969	116	152	98	24	39	181	42	21	652
1970	124	141	93	23	54	179	42	25	656
1971	125	153	103	22	54	195	41	27	693
1972	124	149	106	19	45	199	47	12	701
1973	143	143	103	20	55	210	54	14	742
1974	147	149	84	20	55	202	53	14	724
1975	147	163	106	22	53	233	59	15	798
1976	124	107	106	25	62	238	58	30	750
1977	128	109	109	28	63	230	57	32	756

Appendix 1.2. Full-time academic staff by faculty (teaching and research) (continued)

Year ending December	Arts	Medicine and dentistry	Applied science/ engineering	Law	Economics and social sciences	Science	Agriculture and food science	Education and extra-mural studies	TOTAL
1978	137	125	110	30	65	241	62	35	805
1979	137	132	112	32	69	233	67	33	815
1980	140	143	116	36	70	234	58	33	830
1981	140	143	116	36	78	238	62	35	848
1982	136	143	124	35	82	229	63	35	848
1983	133	139	122	37	80	231	66	34	846
1984	133	151	151	35	89	276	74	32	948
1985	137	170	151	35	87	281	77	35	958
1986	123	175	149	40	86	274	73	31	962
1987	130	175	150	43	88	255	75	31	922
1988	123	170	143	37	83	254	84	31	913
1989	117	176	130	36	78	261	95	33	941
1990	119	180	134	39	74	280	101	35	970
1991	118	173	141	48	83	291	97	35	994
1992	119	185	147	38	90	283	111	39	1021
1993	133	189	152	43	92	275	116	38	1043
1994	140	226	157	37*	223	365	120**	40*	1205
1995	138	242	251		234	400			1261
1996	135	226	247		214	413			1229
1997	130	350	241		222	436			1386
1998	119	349	248		230	409			1353
1999	155	390	246		253	448			1521
2000	183	435	275		259	490			1643
			276						

* With LSES
** With Science

Notes

1 Totals between 1945 and 1948 have been estimated from the annual calendars.
2 Totals between 1949 and 1963 have been taken from the Lockwood report.
3 Totals and faculty distributions between 1969 and 2000 have been taken from the annual Vice Chancellor's reports.
4 Faculty distributions for 1948 and 1952 have been taken from the 1952 submission to the UGC.
5 The remaining faculty distributions before 1969 have been estimated fom the annual calendars.

Appendix 1.3: Annual full-time lecturing appointments (excludes research staff)

Year	Full-time lecturing appointments	Male	Female	Male	Female
1945	27	27	0	100.0	0.0
1946	30	29	1	96.7	3.3
1947	12	11	1	91.7	8.3
1948	17	13	4	76.5	23.5
1949	8	7	1	87.5	12.5
1950	3	3	0	100.0	0.0
1951	30	28	2	93.3	6.7
1952	11	11	0	100.0	0.0
1953	24	24	0	100.0	0.0
1954	24	23	1	95.8	4.2
1955	27	25	2	92.6	7.4
1956	11	11	0	100.0	0.0
1957	18	18	0	100.0	0.0
1958	32	31	1	96.9	3.1
1959	37	35	2	94.6	5.4
1960	29	26	3	89.7	10.3
1961	27	26	1	96.3	3.7
1962	32	32	0	100.0	0.0
1963	33	33	0	100.0	0.0
1964	51	49	2	96.1	3.9
1965	53	50	3	94.3	5.7
1966	78	68	10	87.2	12.8
1967	58	55	3	94.8	5.2
1968	85	79	6	92.9	7.1
1969	55	51	4	92.7	7.3
1970	64	59	5	92.2	7.8
1971	90	82	8	91.1	8.9
1972	96	88	8	91.7	8.3
1973	91	84	7	92.3	7.7
1974	71	51	20	71.8	28.2
1975	54	51	3	94.4	5.6
1976	55	46	9	83.6	16.4
1977	44	35	9	79.5	20.5
1978	53	44	9	83.0	17.0
1979	51	42	9	82.4	17.6
1980	55	54	1	98.2	1.8
1981	55	47	8	85.5	14.5
1982	23	20	3	87.0	13.0
1983	28	24	4	85.7	14.3
1984	61	52	9	85.2	14.8
1985	43	37	6	86.0	14.0
1986	16	15	1	93.8	6.3
1987	14	14	0	100.0	0.0
1988	20	14	6	70.0	30.0
1989	44	34	10	77.3	22.7
1990	46	36	10	78.3	21.7
1991	51	40	11	78.4	21.6

Year	Full-time lecturing appointments	Male	Female	Male	Female
1992	55	42	13	76.4	23.6
1993	56	42	14	75.0	25.0
1994	31	23	8	74.2	25.8
1995	61	43	18	70.5	29.5
1996	23	20	3	87.0	13.0
1997	19	14	5	73.7	26.3
1998	42	32	10	76.2	23.8
1999	84	65	19	77.4	22.6
2000	48	32	16	66.7	33.3

Appendix 2.1: Student numbers (pre-1997 faculties)

Year ending July	Arts	Education (excludes college students)	Science	Applied science/ Engineering	Medicine and Dentistry/ Health sciences	Law	Economics and social sciences	Theology	Agriculture Food Science	General studies	Academic general	TOTAL
1945	476	24	228	423	699	59	175	19	59	0	0	2162
1946	470	38	225	435	729	81	176	16	56	0	0	2226
1947	473	25	274	543	818	96	179	15	70	0	0	2493
1948	489	32	341	562	768	101	186	14	71	0	0	2564
1949	531	63	355	621	779	106	205	19	81	0	0	2760
1950	583	69	375	578	745	98	198	14	81	0	0	2741
1951	604	56	365	533	698	87	182	9	67	0	0	2601
1952	651	60	382	511	710	85	189	30	68	0	0	2686
1953	650	80	384	472	703	93	181	33	59	0	0	2655
1954	661	81	395	446	667	89	162	10	59	0	0	2570
1955	669	95	405	441	626	82	180	29	63	0	0	2590
1956	674	96	426	447	586	90	218	39	54	0	0	2630
1957	704	83	447	469	564	83	244	24	60	0	0	2678
1958	752	86	498	506	572	85	296	21	62	0	0	2878
1959	833	85	612	559	590	91	345	28	71	0	0	3214
1960	951	84	697	646	614	94	370	32	82	0	0	3570
1961	1010	109	781	682	645	105	402	45	92	0	0	3871
1962	1165	109	881	712	643	128	406	59	89	0	0	4192
1963	1215	140	930	753	658	138	416	23	103	0	0	4376
1964	1283	192	1011	806	692	154	444	13	122	0	0	4717
1965	1380	218	997	842	705	188	430	30	119	0	0	4909
1966	1554	222	1052	981	677	212	499	38	120	0	0	5355
1967	1697	253	1101	1119	787	253	620	43	122	0	0	5995
1968	1789	292	1191	1225	903	303	637	31	136	0	0	6507
1969	1820	286	1530	1087	820	307	631	50	158	0	0	6689
1970	1972	270	1606	1055	764	313	620	72	164	0	0	6836
1971	2018	263	1456	1054	760	283	622	75	172	0	0	6703
1972	1911	328	1587	1034	784	318	633	110	190	0	0	6895
1973	1889	317	1440	943	820	346	600	94	179	0	0	6628
1974	1746	349	1316	883	887	355	580	101	168	0	0	6385
1975	1798	367	1193	813	931	388	585	99	162	0	0	6336

Appendix 2.1: Student numbers (pre-1997 faculties) (continued)

Year ending July	Arts	Education (excludes college students)	Science	Applied science Engineering	Medicine and Dentistry/ Health sciences	Law	Economics and social sciences	Theology	Agriculture Food Science	General studies	Academic general	Total
1976	1880	416	1225	805	989	414	634	90	181	0	0	6634
1977	1785	425	1285	819	1010	397	689	94	176	0	0	6680
1978	1757	398	1247	801	958	469	725	112	184	0	0	6741
1979	1766	312	1317	911	917	456	756	112	199	0	0	6746
1980	1790	400	1390	947	907	486	798	113	222	0	0	7053
1981	1765	344	1462	1025	949	484	830	120	229	0	0	7208
1982	1798	313	1544	1046	942	495	865	124	237	0	0	7364
1983	1818	342	1539	1187	932	499	898	121	230	0	0	7566
1984	1863	353	1625	1194	900	543	876	139	224	124	0	7841
1985	1897	381	1733	1242	921	593	899	129	242	178	0	8215
1986	1881	397	1854	1307	940	626	919	135	237	257	0	8553
1987	1872	384	1929	1392	939	624	998	172	256	305	0	8871
1988	1943	447	1945	1382	969	634	1053	182	257	390	0	9202
1989	2073	397	1989	1377	996	665	1008	159	251	455	0	9370
1990	2019	411	2069	1373	1059	734	1082	135	301	484	0	9667
1991	2166	610	2249	1551	1115	793	1179	125	327	575	0	10,690
1992	2283	829	2468	1698	1233	837	1233	162	362	647	0	11,752
1993	2426	855	2652	1791	1290	902	1305	175	354	753	0	12,503
1994	2595	892	2914	1970	1373	954	1361	189	356	801	0	13,405
1995	2608	826	2958	1945	1448	996	1652	204	367	816	0	13,820
1996	2753	808	3153	2010	1502	993	1719	208	381	898	0	14,425
1997	2952	*	3918	2227	1658	*	4544	**	***	0	144	15,443
1998	2590	*	3512	2263	4019	*	5557	**	***	0	248	18,189
1999	2520	*	3709	2572	4751	*	5322	**	***	*	13	18,887
2000	2148	*	3408	2749	4212	*	5655	**	***	*	121	18,293

* With LSES
** With Arts
*** With Science

Appendix 2.2: Percentage distribution of students (pre-1997 faculties)

Year ending July	Arts	Education (excludes college students)	Science	Applied science/ Engineering	Medicine and Dentistry/ Health sciences	Law	Economics and social sciences	Theology	Agriculture Food Science	General studies	Academic general	Total
1945	22.0	1.1	10.5	19.6	32.3	2.7	8.1	0.9	2.7	0.0	0.0	100.0
1946	21.1	1.7	10.1	19.5	32.7	3.6	7.9	0.7	2.5	0.0	0.0	100.0
1947	19.0	1.0	11.0	21.8	32.8	3.9	7.2	0.6	2.8	0.0	0.0	100.0
1948	19.1	1.2	13.3	21.9	30.0	3.9	7.3	0.5	2.8	0.0	0.0	100.0
1949	19.2	2.3	12.9	22.5	28.2	3.8	7.4	0.7	2.9	0.0	0.0	100.0
1950	21.3	2.5	13.7	21.1	27.2	3.6	7.2	0.5	3.0	0.0	0.0	100.0
1951	23.2	2.2	14.0	20.5	26.8	3.3	7.0	0.3	2.6	0.0	0.0	100.0
1952	24.2	2.2	14.2	19.0	26.4	3.2	7.0	1.1	2.5	0.0	0.0	100.0
1953	24.5	3.0	14.5	17.8	26.5	3.5	6.8	1.2	2.2	0.0	0.0	100.0
1954	25.7	3.2	15.4	17.4	26.0	3.5	6.3	0.4	2.3	0.0	0.0	100.0
1955	25.8	3.7	15.6	17.0	24.2	3.2	6.9	1.1	2.4	0.0	0.0	100.0
1956	25.6	3.7	16.2	17.0	22.3	3.4	8.3	1.5	2.1	0.0	0.0	100.0
1957	26.3	3.1	16.7	17.5	21.1	3.1	9.1	0.9	2.2	0.0	0.0	100.0
1958	26.1	3.0	17.3	17.6	19.9	3.0	10.3	0.7	2.2	0.0	0.0	100.0
1959	25.9	2.6	19.0	17.4	18.4	2.8	10.7	0.9	2.2	0.0	0.0	100.0
1960	26.6	2.4	19.5	18.1	17.2	2.6	10.4	0.9	2.3	0.0	0.0	100.0
1961	26.1	2.8	20.2	17.6	16.7	2.7	10.4	1.2	2.4	0.0	0.0	100.0
1962	27.8	2.6	21.0	17.0	15.3	3.1	9.7	1.4	2.1	0.0	0.0	100.0
1963	27.8	3.2	21.3	17.2	15.0	3.2	9.5	0.5	2.4	0.0	0.0	100.0
1964	27.2	4.1	21.4	17.1	14.7	3.3	9.4	0.3	2.6	0.0	0.0	100.0
1965	28.1	4.4	20.3	17.2	14.4	3.8	8.8	0.6	2.4	0.0	0.0	100.0
1966	29.0	4.1	19.6	18.3	12.6	4.0	9.3	0.7	2.2	0.0	0.0	100.0
1967	28.3	4.2	18.4	18.7	13.1	4.2	9.3	0.7	2.0	0.0	0.0	100.0
1968	27.5	4.5	18.3	18.8	13.9	4.7	9.8	0.5	2.1	0.0	0.0	100.0
1969	27.2	4.3	22.9	16.3	12.3	4.6	9.4	0.7	2.4	0.0	0.0	100.0
1970	28.8	3.9	23.5	15.4	11.2	4.6	9.1	1.1	2.4	0.0	0.0	100.0
1971	30.1	3.9	21.7	15.7	11.3	4.2	9.3	1.1	2.6	0.0	0.0	100.0
1972	27.7	4.8	23.0	15.0	11.4	4.6	9.2	1.6	2.8	0.0	0.0	100.0
1973	28.5	4.8	21.7	14.2	12.4	5.2	9.1	1.4	2.7	0.0	0.0	100.0
1974	27.3	5.5	20.6	13.8	13.9	5.6	9.1	1.6	2.6	0.0	0.0	100.0
1975	28.4	5.8	18.8	12.8	14.7	6.1	9.2	1.6	2.6	0.0	0.0	100.0

Appendix 2.2: Percentage distribution of students (pre-1997 faculties) (continued)

Year ending July	Arts	Education (excludes college students)	Science	Applied science/ Engineering	Medicine and Dentistry/ Health sciences	Law	Economics and social sciences	Theology	Agriculture Food Science	General studies	Academic general	Total
1976	28.3	6.3	18.5	12.1	14.9	6.2	9.6	1.4	2.7	0.0	0.0	100.0
1977	26.7	6.4	19.2	12.3	15.1	5.9	10.3	1.4	2.6	0.0	0.0	100.0
1978	26.1	5.9	18.5	13.2	14.2	7.0	10.8	1.7	2.7	0.0	0.0	100.0
1979	26.2	4.6	19.5	13.5	13.6	6.8	11.2	1.7	2.9	0.0	0.0	100.0
1980	25.4	5.7	19.7	13.4	12.9	6.9	11.3	1.6	3.1	0.0	0.0	100.0
1981	24.5	4.8	20.3	14.2	13.2	6.9	11.5	1.6	3.2	0.0	0.0	100.0
1982	24.4	4.3	21.0	14.2	12.8	6.7	11.7	1.7	3.2	0.0	0.0	100.0
1983	24.0	4.3	20.3	15.7	12.3	6.6	11.9	1.7	3.0	0.0	0.0	100.0
1984	23.8	4.5	20.7	15.2	11.5	6.9	11.2	1.6	3.0	0.0	0.0	100.0
1985	23.1	4.6	21.1	15.1	11.2	7.2	10.9	1.8	2.9	1.6	0.0	100.0
1986	22.0	4.6	21.7	15.3	11.0	7.3	10.7	1.6	2.8	2.2	0.0	100.0
1987	21.1	4.3	21.7	15.7	10.6	7.0	11.3	1.9	2.9	3.4	0.0	100.0
1988	21.1	4.9	21.1	15.0	10.5	6.9	11.4	2.0	2.8	4.2	0.0	100.0
1989	22.1	4.2	21.2	14.7	10.6	7.1	10.8	1.7	2.7	4.9	0.0	100.0
1990	20.9	4.3	21.4	14.2	11.0	7.6	11.2	1.4	3.1	5.0	0.0	100.0
1991	20.3	5.7	21.0	14.5	10.4	7.4	11.0	1.2	3.1	5.4	0.0	100.0
1992	19.4	7.1	21.0	14.4	10.5	7.1	10.5	1.4	3.1	5.5	0.0	100.0
1993	19.4	6.8	21.2	14.3	10.3	7.2	10.4	1.4	2.8	6.0	0.0	100.0
1994	19.4	6.7	21.7	14.7	10.2	7.1	10.2	1.4	2.7	6.0	0.0	100.0
1995	18.9	6.7	21.4	14.1	10.5	7.2	12.0	1.5	2.7	6.0	0.0	100.0
1996	19.1	6.0	21.9	13.9	10.4	6.9	11.9	1.4	2.6	5.9	0.0	100.0
1997	19.1	5.6	25.4	14.4	10.7	*	29.4	**	***	6.2	0.9	100.0
1998	14.2	*	19.3	12.4	22.1	*	30.6	**	***	*	1.4	100.0
1999	13.3	*	19.6	13.6	25.2	*	28.2	**	***	*	0.1	100.0
2000	11.7	*	18.6	15.0	23.0	*	30.9	**	***	*	0.7	100.0

* With LSES
** With Arts
*** With Science

Appendix 2.3: Totals of male and female students (post-1996 faculties)

Year	Humanities Male	Humanities Female	Science, agriculture Male	Science, agriculture Female	LSES Male	LSES Female	Engineering Male	Engineering Female	Health sciences Male	Health sciences Female	Academic general Male	Academic general Female	Total male	Total female	Total
1945	253	243	234	53	178	38	406	17	543	156	0	0	1614	507	2121
1946	236	250	209	72	221	74	428	7	575	154	0	0	1669	557	2226
1947	260	230	282	82	238	64	531	12	662	156	0	0	1973	544	2517
1948	283	220	326	86	254	65	554	8	623	145	0	0	2040	524	2564
1949	315	237	349	87	288	88	608	10	616	164	0	0	2176	586	2762
1950	336	261	381	75	267	88	566	12	593	152	0	0	2143	588	2731
1951	311	302	355	77	239	87	526	7	570	128	0	0	2001	601	2602
1952	354	327	373	77	238	96	503	8	574	136	0	0	2042	644	2686
1953	361	316	365	73	248	55	465	6	562	130	0	0	2001	580	2581
1954	329	349	372	82	247	85	499	6	537	130	0	0	1984	652	2636
1955	350	348	389	79	272	85	435	6	493	133	0	0	1939	651	2590
1956	332	366	398	82	304	98	443	4	472	114	0	0	1949	664	2613
1957	371	356	429	78	327	82	466	3	449	115	0	0	2042	634	2676
1958	415	363	476	84	382	85	499	7	463	109	0	0	2235	648	2883
1959	457	404	577	106	448	73	550	9	479	111	0	0	2511	703	3214
1960	535	448	664	114	476	72	632	14	499	115	0	0	2806	763	3569
1961	553	502	730	143	526	90	666	16	503	142	0	0	2978	893	3871
1962	664	608	795	175	543	100	688	24	497	146	0	0	3187	1053	4240
1963	649	589	847	186	593	101	726	27	506	152	0	0	3321	1055	4376
1964	670	627	924	197	662	128	777	29	524	168	0	0	3557	1149	4706
1965	751	641	927	189	680	155	811	31	539	166	0	0	3708	1182	4890
1966	845	756	964	208	764	175	945	37	510	167	0	0	4028	1343	5371
1967	904	835	1010	213	925	201	1080	40	599	188	0	0	4518	1477	5995
1968	878	942	1073	254	1007	225	1175	50	689	214	0	0	4822	1685	6507
1969	915	955	1331	357	1004	260	1066	21	679	232	0	0	4995	1825	6820
1970	1027	1017	1383	387	951	252	1031	24	553	211	0	0	4945	1891	6836
1971	1041	1052	1267	361	889	279	1028	26	526	234	0	0	4751	1952	6703
1972	1029	992	1382	395	941	338	1007	27	537	247	0	0	4896	1999	6895
1973	973	1010	1255	364	901	362	918	25	550	270	0	0	4597	2031	6628
1974	847	1000	1115	369	851	433	857	26	602	284	0	0	4272	2112	6384
1975	849	1048	1013	342	926	414	784	29	625	306	0	0	4197	2139	6336
1976	859	1111	1039	367	1016	448	773	32	667	322	0	0	4354	2280	6634
1977	792	1087	1032	429	1040	471	783	36	686	324	0	0	4333	2347	6680

Appendix 2.3: Totals of male and female students (post-1996 faculties) (continued)

Year	Humanities		Science, agriculture		LSES		Engineering		Health sciences		Academic general		Total male	Total female	Total
	Male	Female	Male	Female	Male	Female	Male	Female	Male	Female	Male	Female			
1978	837	1061	976	455	1071	505	847	44	645	313	0	0	4376	2378	6754
1979	837	1041	1028	488	1038	486	861	50	614	303	0	0	4378	2368	6746
1980	826	1077	1073	539	1107	577	886	61	606	301	0	0	4498	2555	7053
1981	835	1050	1120	571	1065	593	964	61	634	315	0	0	4618	2590	7208
1982	839	1083	1163	618	1038	635	975	71	620	322	0	0	4635	2729	7364
1983	797	1142	1102	667	1047	672	1105	82	597	335	0	0	4648	2898	7546
1984	801	1201	1124	725	1087	809	1103	91	561	339	0	0	4676	3165	7841
1985	788	1238	1162	813	1148	903	1138	104	570	351	0	0	4806	3409	8215
1986	822	1194	1211	880	1188	1011	1176	131	563	377	0	0	4960	3593	8553
1987	853	1191	1242	943	1262	1049	1208	184	550	389	0	0	5115	3756	8871
1988	901	1224	1258	944	1309	1215	1185	197	577	392	0	0	5230	3972	9202
1989	973	1259	1301	939	1300	1256	1179	198	573	423	0	0	5326	4075	9401
1990	928	1226	1368	1002	1322	1389	1163	212	605	454	0	0	5386	4283	9669
1991	973	1318	1500	1076	1463	1609	1228	254	611	504	0	0	5775	4761	10,536
1992	1036	1409	1647	1183	1604	1942	1436	262	659	574	0	0	6382	5370	11,752
1993	1001	1562	1758	1248	1682	2133	1428	302	673	617	0	0	6542	5862	12,404
1994	1104	1680	1918	1384	1697	1813	1637	333	691	682	0	0	7047	5892	12,939
1995	1110	1702	1953	1372	1805	1961	1595	350	683	765	0	0	7146	6150	13,296
1996	1183	1778	2010	1534	1795	2626	1624	386	682	820	0	0	7294	7144	14,438
1997	1160	1792	2087	1831	1731	2813	1788	439	650	1008	64	80	7480	7963	15,443
1998	1036	1554	1667	1845	2223	3334	1789	474	847	3172	118	130	7680	10,509	18,189
1999	986	1534	1680	2029	2032	3290	2018	554	935	3816	8	5	7659	11,228	18,887
2000	831	1317	1489	1919	2262	3393	2111	638	865	3347	46	75	7604	10,689	18,293

Appendix 2.4: Percentage distribution of male and female students (post-1996 faculties)

Year	Humanities Male	Humanities Female	Science, agriculture Male	Science, agriculture Female	LSES Male	LSES Female	Engineering Male	Engineering Female	Health sciences Male	Health sciences Female	Academic general Male	Academic general Female	Total male	Total female
1945	51.0	49.0	81.5	18.5	82.4	17.6	96.0	4.0	77.7	22.3	0	0	76.1	23.9
1946	48.6	51.4	74.4	25.6	74.9	25.1	98.4	1.6	78.9	21.1	0	0	75.0	25.0
1947	53.1	46.9	77.5	22.5	78.8	21.2	97.8	2.2	80.9	19.1	0	0	78.4	21.6
1948	56.3	43.7	79.1	20.9	79.6	20.4	98.6	1.4	81.1	18.9	0	0	79.6	20.4
1949	57.1	42.9	80.0	20.0	76.6	23.4	98.4	1.6	79.0	21.0	0	0	78.8	21.2
1950	56.3	43.7	83.6	16.4	75.2	24.8	97.9	2.1	79.6	20.4	0	0	78.5	21.5
1951	50.7	49.3	82.2	17.8	73.3	26.7	98.7	1.3	81.7	18.3	0	0	76.9	23.1
1952	52.0	48.0	82.9	17.1	71.3	28.7	98.4	1.6	80.8	19.2	0	0	76.0	24.0
1953	53.3	46.7	83.3	16.7	81.8	18.2	98.7	1.3	81.2	18.8	0	0	77.5	22.5
1954	48.5	51.5	81.9	18.1	74.4	25.6	98.8	1.2	80.5	19.5	0	0	75.3	24.7
1955	50.1	49.9	83.1	16.9	76.2	23.8	98.6	1.4	78.8	21.2	0	0	74.9	25.1
1956	47.6	52.4	82.9	17.1	75.6	24.4	99.1	0.9	80.5	19.5	0	0	74.6	25.4
1957	51.0	49.0	84.6	15.4	80.0	20.0	99.4	0.6	79.6	20.4	0	0	76.3	23.7
1958	53.3	46.7	85.0	15.0	81.8	18.2	98.6	1.4	80.9	19.1	0	0	77.5	22.5
1959	53.1	46.9	84.5	15.5	86.0	14.0	98.4	1.6	81.2	18.8	0	0	78.1	21.9
1960	54.4	45.6	85.3	14.7	86.9	13.1	97.8	2.2	81.3	18.7	0	0	78.6	21.4
1961	52.4	47.6	83.6	16.4	85.4	14.6	97.7	2.3	78.0	22.0	0	0	76.9	23.1
1962	52.2	47.8	82.0	18.0	84.4	15.6	96.6	3.4	77.3	22.7	0	0	75.2	24.8
1963	52.4	47.6	82.0	18.0	85.4	14.6	96.4	3.6	76.9	23.1	0	0	75.9	24.1
1964	51.7	48.3	82.4	17.6	83.8	16.2	96.4	3.6	75.7	24.3	0	0	75.6	24.4
1965	54.0	46.0	83.1	16.9	81.4	18.6	96.3	3.7	76.5	23.5	0	0	75.8	24.2
1966	52.8	47.2	82.3	17.7	81.4	18.6	96.2	3.8	75.3	24.7	0	0	75.0	25.0
1967	52.0	48.0	82.6	17.4	82.1	17.9	96.4	3.6	76.1	23.9	0	0	75.4	24.6
1968	48.2	51.8	80.9	19.1	81.7	18.3	95.9	4.1	76.3	23.7	0	0	74.1	25.9
1969	48.9	51.1	78.9	21.1	79.4	20.6	98.1	1.9	74.5	25.5	0	0	73.2	26.8
1970	50.2	49.8	78.1	21.9	79.1	20.9	97.7	2.3	72.4	27.6	0	0	72.3	27.7
1971	49.7	50.3	77.8	22.2	76.1	23.9	97.5	2.5	69.2	30.8	0	0	70.9	29.1
1972	50.9	49.1	77.8	22.2	73.6	26.4	97.4	2.6	68.5	31.5	0	0	71.0	29.0
1973	49.1	50.9	77.5	22.5	71.3	28.7	97.3	2.7	67.1	32.9	0	0	69.4	30.6
1974	45.9	54.1	75.1	24.9	66.3	33.7	97.1	2.9	67.9	32.1	0	0	66.9	33.1
1975	44.8	55.2	74.8	25.2	69.1	30.9	96.4	3.6	67.1	32.9	0	0	66.2	33.8
1976	43.6	56.4	73.9	26.1	69.4	30.6	96.0	4.0	67.4	32.6	0	0	65.6	34.4
1977	42.2	57.8	70.6	29.4	68.8	31.2	95.6	4.4	67.9	32.1	0	0	64.9	35.1

2.4: Percentage distribution of male and female students (post-1996 faculties) (continued)

Year	Humanities		Science, agriculture		LSES		Engineering		Health sciences		Academic general		Total	
	Male	Female	Male	Female	Male	Female	Male	Female	Male	Female	Male	Female	male	female
1978	44.1	55.9	68.2	31.8	68.0	32.0	95.1	4.9	67.3	32.7	0.0	0.0	64.8	35.2
1979	44.6	55.4	67.8	32.2	68.1	31.9	94.5	5.5	67.0	33.0	0.0	0.0	64.9	35.1
1980	43.4	56.6	66.6	33.4	65.7	34.3	93.6	6.4	66.8	33.2	0.0	0.0	63.8	36.2
1981	44.3	55.7	66.2	33.8	64.2	35.8	94.0	6.0	66.8	33.2	0.0	0.0	64.1	35.9
1982	43.7	56.3	65.3	34.7	62.0	38.0	93.2	6.8	65.8	34.2	0.0	0.0	62.9	37.1
1983	41.1	58.9	62.3	37.7	60.9	39.1	93.1	6.9	64.1	35.9	0.0	0.0	61.6	38.4
1984	40.0	60.0	60.8	39.2	57.3	42.7	92.4	7.6	62.3	37.7	0.0	0.0	59.6	40.4
1985	38.9	61.1	58.8	41.2	56.0	44.0	91.6	8.4	61.9	38.1	0.0	0.0	58.5	41.5
1986	40.8	59.2	57.9	42.1	54.0	46.0	90.0	10.0	59.9	40.1	0.0	0.0	58.0	42.0
1987	41.7	58.3	56.8	43.2	54.6	45.4	86.8	13.2	58.6	41.4	0.0	0.0	57.7	42.3
1988	42.4	57.6	57.1	42.9	51.9	48.1	85.7	14.3	59.5	40.5	0.0	0.0	56.8	43.2
1989	43.6	56.4	58.1	41.9	50.9	49.1	85.6	14.4	57.5	42.5	0.0	0.0	56.7	43.3
1990	43.1	56.9	57.7	42.3	48.8	51.2	84.6	15.4	57.1	42.9	0.0	0.0	55.7	44.3
1991	42.5	57.5	58.2	41.8	47.6	52.4	82.9	17.1	54.8	45.2	0.0	0.0	54.8	45.2
1992	42.4	57.6	58.5	41.5	45.2	54.8	82.5	17.5	53.4	46.6	0.0	0.0	54.3	45.7
1993	39.1	60.9	58.1	41.9	44.1	55.9	83.1	16.9	52.4	47.6	0.0	0.0	52.7	47.3
1994	39.7	60.3	58.7	41.3	48.3	51.7	82.0	18.0	50.3	49.7	0.0	0.0	54.5	45.5
1995	39.5	60.5	58.1	41.9	47.9	52.1	80.8	19.2	47.2	52.8	0.0	0.0	53.7	46.3
1996	40.0	60.0	56.7	43.3	40.6	59.4	80.8	19.2	45.4	54.6	0.0	0.0	50.5	49.5
1997	40.0	60.0	53.3	46.7	38.1	61.9	80.3	19.7	39.2	60.8	44.4	55.6	48.4	51.6
1998	39.3	60.7	47.5	52.5	39.1	60.9	79.1	20.9	21.1	78.9	47.6	52.4	42.2	57.8
1999	38.9	61.1	45.6	54.4	40.3	59.7	78.0	22.0	20.5	79.5	61.5	38.5	40.6	59.4
2000	38.7	61.3	43.7	56.3	37.9	62.1	76.8	23.2	20.5	79.5	38.0	62.0	41.6	58.4

Appendix 2.5: Full-time, part-time, and postgraudate students

Year ending July	Full-time students	Part-time students	Total students	Postgraduate students	Full-time students as per cent of total	Part-time students as per cent of total	Postgraduate students as a percent of total
1945	na	na	2121	na	na	na	na
1946	na	na	2226	na	na	na	na
1947	na	na	2517	na	na	na	na
1948	na	na	2564	na	na	na	na
1949	na	na	2762	na	na	na	na
1950	na	na	2741	na	na	na	na
1951	na	na	2601	na	na	na	na
1952	2276	410	2686	200	84.7	15.3	7.4
1953	2211	434	2645	108	83.6	16.4	4.1
1954	2182	395	2577	153	84.7	15.3	5.9
1955	2132	458	2590	40	82.3	17.7	1.5
1956	2171	459	2630	158	82.5	17.5	6.0
1957	2245	431	2676	na	83.9	16.1	na
1958	2409	470	2879	na	83.7	16.3	na
1959	2691	523	3214	na	83.7	16.3	na
1960	3001	569	3570	na	84.1	15.9	na
1961	3319	552	3871	na	85.7	14.3	na
1962	3751	488	4239	na	88.5	11.5	na
1963	3841	535	4376	na	87.8	12.2	na
1964	4135	573	4708	na	87.8	12.2	na
1965	4296	612	4908	na	87.5	12.5	na
1966	4701	670	5371	na	87.5	12.5	na
1967	5056	939	5995	na	84.3	15.7	na
1968	5523	846	6369	na	86.7	13.3	na
1969	6115	1071	7186	na	85.1	14.9	na
1970	5964	872	6836	1136	87.2	12.8	16.6
1971	6046	808	6854	1093	88.2	11.8	15.9
1972	5998	897	6985	1220	85.9	12.8	17.5
1973	5822	806	6628	1172	87.8	12.2	17.7
1974	5530	855	6385	1220	86.6	13.4	19.1
1975	5471	865	6336	1214	86.3	13.7	19.2
1976	5708	926	6634	1344	86.0	14.0	20.3
1977	5754	926	6680	1281	86.1	13.9	19.2
1978	5816	925	6741	1295	86.3	13.7	19.2
1979	5816	930	6746	1302	86.2	13.8	19.3
1980	6105	948	7053	1454	86.6	13.4	20.6
1981	6248	960	7208	1462	86.7	13.3	20.3
1982	6376	988	7364	1477	86.6	13.4	20.1
1983	6561	1005	7566	1499	86.7	13.3	19.8
1984	6645	1196	7841	1494	84.7	15.3	19.1
1985	6936	1279	8215	1639	84.4	15.6	20.0
1986	7164	1389	8553	1652	83.8	16.2	19.3
1987	7360	1511	8871	1724	83.0	17.0	19.4
1988	7537	1665	9202	1875	81.9	18.1	20.4
1989	7683	1687	9370	1828	82.0	18.0	19.5
1990	7876	1800	9676	2055	81.4	18.6	21.2
1991	8475	2215	10,690	2504	79.3	20.7	23.4
1992	9259	2493	11,752	2935	78.8	21.2	25.0
1993	9850	2653	12,503	3061	78.8	21.2	24.5
1994	10,565	2819	13,384	3355	78.9	21.1	25.1
1995	10,922	2898	13,820	3235	79.0	21.0	23.4
1996	11,444	2981	14,425	3473	79.3	20.7	24.1

Year ending July	Full-time students	Part-time students	Total students	Postgraduate students	Full-time students as per cent of total	Part-time students as per cent of total	Postgraduate students as a percent of total
1997	12,656	2787	15,443	4621	82.0	18.0	29.9
1998	13,038	3848	16,886	3781	77.2	22.8	22.4
1999	12,716	3696	16,412	3686	77.5	22.5	22.5
2000	12,838	3297	16,135	3917	79.6	20.4	24.3

Apppendix 3.1: Sources of income (£s)

Year ending July	Government grants	Academic fees and support grants	Research grants and contracts	Other operating income	Endowments, income and interest receivable	Total
1945	84,974	45,974	–	10,236	7811	148,995
1946	140,305	45,923	–	11,462	5889	203,579
1947	156,751	55,964	–	14,381	6878	233,974
1948	154,522	61,591	–	15,800	5912	237,825
1949	214,657	63,966	–	23,540	10,078	312,241
1950	244,881	64,887	–	24,908	13,133	347,809
1951	257,570	67,401	–	23,256	16,567	364,794
1952	271,987	81,702	–	23,400	19,590	396,679
1953	304,757	80,138	–	22,771	17,211	424,877
1954	362,797	84,331	–	23,808	18,333	489,269
1955	422,795	83,872	–	29,231	17,462	553,360
1956	462,949	85,401	–	38,680	23,311	610,341
1957	496,825	88,765	–	42,960	19,632	648,182
1958	591,680	125,204	–	50,592	16,292	783,768
1959	656,810	141,710	–	54,423	22,527	875,470
1960	751,406	157,696	–	52,812	25,829	987,743
1961	946,915	171,304	–	59,007	20,002	1,197,228
1962	1,018,115	194,289	–	66,562	37,817	1,316,783
1963	1,133,072	199,306	–	60,963	30,350	1,423,691
1964	1,442,788	209,590	–	68,158	31,608	1,752,144
1965	1,844,558	253,457	–	69,699	31,467	2,199,181
1966	2,079,315	289,196	–	78,147	44,262	2,490,920
1967	2,500,435	327,127	257,822	92,798	55,966	3,234,148
1968	2,824,818	352,949	318,500	73,404	71,661	3,641,332
1969	3,011,365	374,868	377,404	123,108	82,909	3,969,654
1970	3,516,646	395,719	503,656	139,693	72,787	4,628,501
1971	4,306,022	403,692	515,496	149,091	47,673	5,421,974
1972	4,949,972	412,338	597,819	177,596	59,181	6,196,906
1973	6,062,963	420,571	596,057	176,540	73,420	7,329,551
1974	7,565,252	499,210	603,295	195,596	141,592	9,004,945
1975	9,431,907	565,309	765,916	349,037	187,913	11,300,082
1976	11,564,669	1,094,216	967,478	430,455	222,714	14,279,532
1977	13,096,613	1,400,578	1,011,865	453,665	302,901	16,265,622
1978	12,097,591	3,492,755	1,148,929	880,474	274,030	17,893,779
1979	13,809,208	3,761,663	1,405,254	466,948	579,623	20,022,696
1980	17,557,215	4,222,242	2,159,040	902,267	755,373	25,596,137

1981	23,110,303	5,418,536	2,459,279	963,282	787,830	32,739,230
1982	24,047,500	6,319,346	2,552,706	1,574,856	1,059,393	35,553,801
1983	28,060,499	4,178,840	3,033,464	1,513,961	972,667	37,759,431
1984	29,903,178	4,396,961	3,670,327	2,240,151	819,053	41,029,670
1985	31,082,631	4,819,056	3,810,386	2,410,096	911,294	43,033,463
1986	34,761,995	5,253,679	4,337,512	3,670,449	541,848	48,565,483
1987	34,854,669	5,695,328	4,691,102	4,582,964	1,381,190	51,205,253
1988	37,371,000	6,199,000	5,795,000	4,876,000	1,155,000	55,396,000
1989	39,636,000	7,437,000	7,095,000	9,816,000	2,838,000	66,822,000
1990	43,011,000	8,438,000	8,185,000	14,922,000	3,220,000	77,776,000
1991	41,048,000	17,082,000	10,659,000	18,509,000	3,457,000	90,755,000
1992	38,147,000	24,519,000	12,472,000	19,825,000	3,879,000	98,842,000
1993	40,530,000	27,198,000	15,478,000	21,110,000	4,120,000	108,436,000
1994	46,942,000	26,728,000	15,795,000	23,597,000	2,015,000	115,077,000
1995	57,028,000	19,415,000	16,767,000	21,814,000	2,238,000	117,262,000
1996	59,596,000	20,424,000	17,147,000	21,796,000	2,606,000	121,569,000
1997	58,304,000	21,143,000	19,319,000	23,256,000	2,452,000	124,474,000
1998	57,931,000	28,268,000	20,258,000	23,572,000	3,332,000	133,361,000
1999	60,455,000	26,174,000	20,551,000	24,866,000	3,289,000	135,335,000

Notes:
The figures are taken from the annual financial statements, using the categories employed in 1999.
1 Government grants: recurrent; specific; deferred capital
2 Fees: student fees; short course fees; etc.
3 Research grants: research councils and charities; other.
4 Other operating income: payments for services; residences; catering, joint-appointment salaries, sale of property; etc.
5 Endowments etc: general and specific endowments; interest on investments.

Appendix 3.2: Sources of income (per cent)

Year ending July	Government grants	Academic fees and support grants	Research grants and contracts	Other operating income	Endowments, income and interest receivable	Total
1945	57.0	30.9	0.0	6.9	5.2	100.0
1946	68.9	22.6	0.0	5.6	2.9	100.0
1947	67.0	23.9	0.0	6.1	2.9	100.0
1948	65.0	25.9	0.0	6.6	2.5	100.0
1949	68.7	20.5	0.0	7.5	3.2	100.0
1950	70.4	18.7	0.0	7.2	3.8	100.0
1951	70.6	18.5	0.0	6.4	4.5	100.0
1952	68.6	20.6	0.0	5.9	4.9	100.0
1953	71.7	18.9	0.0	5.4	4.1	100.0
1954	74.2	17.2	0.0	4.9	3.7	100.0
1955	76.4	15.2	0.0	5.3	3.2	100.0
1956	75.9	14.0	0.0	6.3	3.8	100.0
1957	76.6	13.7	0.0	6.6	3.0	100.0
1958	75.5	16.0	0.0	6.5	2.1	100.0
1959	75.0	16.2	0.0	6.2	2.6	100.0
1960	76.1	16.0	0.0	5.3	2.6	100.0
1961	79.1	14.3	0.0	4.9	1.7	100.0
1962	77.3	14.8	0.0	5.1	2.9	100.0

Year ending July	Government grants	Academic fees and support grants	Research grants and contracts	Other operating income	Endowments, income and interest receivable	Total
1963	79.6	14.0	0.0	4.3	2.1	100.0
1964	82.3	12.0	0.0	3.9	1.8	100.0
1965	83.9	11.5	0.0	3.2	1.4	100.0
1966	83.5	11.6	0.0	3.1	1.8	100.0
1967	77.3	10.1	8.0	2.9	1.7	100.0
1968	77.6	9.7	8.7	2.0	2.0	100.0
1969	75.9	9.4	9.5	3.1	2.1	100.0
1970	76.0	8.5	10.9	3.0	1.6	100.0
1971	79.4	7.4	9.5	2.7	0.9	100.0
1972	79.9	6.7	9.6	2.9	1.0	100.0
1973	82.7	5.7	8.1	2.4	1.0	100.0
1974	84.0	5.5	6.7	2.2	1.6	100.0
1975	83.5	5.0	6.8	3.1	1.7	100.0
1976	81.0	7.7	6.8	3.0	1.6	100.0
1977	80.5	8.6	6.2	2.8	1.9	100.0
1978	67.6	19.5	6.4	4.9	1.5	100.0
1979	69.0	18.8	7.0	2.3	2.9	100.0
1980	68.6	16.5	8.4	3.5	3.0	100.0
1981	70.6	16.6	7.5	2.9	2.4	100.0
1982	67.6	17.8	7.2	4.4	3.0	100.0
1983	74.3	11.1	8.0	4.0	2.6	100.0
1984	72.9	10.7	8.9	5.5	2.0	100.0
1985	72.2	11.2	8.9	5.6	2.1	100.0
1986	71.6	10.8	8.9	7.6	1.1	100.0
1987	68.1	11.1	9.2	9.0	2.7	100.0
1988	67.5	11.2	10.5	8.8	2.1	100.0
1989	59.3	11.1	10.6	14.7	4.2	100.0
1990	55.3	10.8	10.5	19.2	4.1	100.0
1991	45.2	18.8	11.7	20.4	3.8	100.0
1992	38.6	24.8	12.6	20.1	3.9	100.0
1993	37.4	25.1	14.3	19.5	3.8	100.0
1994	40.8	23.2	13.7	20.5	1.8	100.0
1995	48.6	16.6	14.3	18.6	1.9	100.0
1996	49.0	16.8	14.1	17.9	2.1	100.0
1997	46.8	17.0	15.5	18.7	2.0	100.0
1998	43.4	21.2	15.2	17.7	2.5	100.0
1999	44.7	19.3	15.2	18.4	2.4	100.0

Notes:

The figures are taken from the annual financial statements, using the categories employed in 1999.

1 Government grants: recurrent; specific; deferred capital.
2 Fees: student fees; short course fees; etc.
3 Research grants: research councils and charities; other.
4 Other operating income: payments for services; residences; catering, joint-appointment salaries, sale of property; etc.
5 Endowments etc.: general and specific endowments; interest on investments.

Bibliography

RECORDS OF THE CENTRAL ADMINISTRATION

Academic Board minutes
Academic Council minutes
Annual financial statements
Building Committee minutes
Estates Committee minutes
Senate minutes
Standing Committee minutes
Vice-Chancellor's reports (published as appendices to the *Senate minutes* until
    1987; thereafter separately)

OTHER UNIVERSITY PUBLICATION AND PAPERS

A fresher's guide to Queen's (no date), QUB archives P/870
Paul Bew, 'To serve them all our days?', *Vice-Chancellor's letter to graduates*
    (2000), 12–13
Butler working party. One box of uncatalogued papers, QUB archives
Calendars 1945/6–1999/2000
Catalogues of the art exhibitions and press coverage, 1956–1977. Uncatalogued
    papers, QUB archives
Chilver report. Seven boxes of uncatalogued papers, QUB archives
Correspondence relating to the publication of H.A. Cronne (ed.), *Essays in
    British and Irish history: in honour of James Eadie Todd* (London, 1949).
    Uncatalogued papers, QUB archives
Employment Equality Services, *Review of the structures, procedures and practices
    of the Queen's University of Belfast as they relate to the provision for and appli-
    cation of the equality of opportunity and fair participation in employment*
    (February 1993)
Estates master plan, 2001
Fifth report on equal opportunities (May 2001)
Michael Forster, *An audit of academic performance: a study of the prediction of aca-
    demic success in the Queen's University of Belfast* (1959)
Peter Froggatt, 'The University as an instrument of social change: a dangerous
    or a desirable concept?' (Council of Queen's University and Schools, 1977)

File of miscellaneous letters, uncatalogued QUB archives
Memorandum to the UGC 1952
On being a student (1964), QUB archives P/870
Personnel department, 'Gender report, third draft' (May 1994)
QUB, *Centenary celebrations held 25th–30th September 1949*
QUB, *Submission to the Lockwood committee on university and higher technical education in Northern Ireland* (March 1964), QUB archives E/7/9
QUB, Women's Forum, *Report on gender imbalance at Queen's* (May, 2000)
Ethne McLaughlin and Janet Trewsdale, *Gender equality at Queen's: a policy paper prepared for the Vice-Chancellor* (April 2000)
Report of the Strategic Review Group (1997)
Michael Shattock and David Holmes, *The governance, management and administration of the University* (January 1998)
Staff Training & Development Unit, *Training and development opportunities for all university staff, 1999–2000* (1999)
The Queen's University of Belfast Foundation, honorary graduation ceremony and gala concert, Thursday 24th May 2001: programme (2001)

OTHER PAPERS

AUT (Belfast), 'Evidence submitted to the chairman and members of the Lockwood committee on university and higher technical education in Northern Ireland (March 1964), QUB archives E/7/8.
AUT, *Report and recommendations to the Chilver review group concerning the two universities in Northern Ireland* (Belfast, June 1979), QUB archives E/7/15
QUB, *The annual record of the Queen's University Association* (Belfast, published annually)
QUB Labour group, 'Submission to the Lockwood committee on higher education in Northern Ireland' (1964), QUB archives E/7/11
Peter Harvard-Williams, 'Memorandum on legal deposit library for Northern Ireland' (May, 1964), QUB archives, E/7/10

GOVERNMENT PUBLICATIONS
(in chronological order)

Report of the Committee on Higher Education [Robbins report] (London, 1963)
Report of an interdepartmental committee on the demand for agricultural graduates [Bosanquet report] (London, 1964)
The Government of Northern Ireland, *Higher education in Northern Ireland [Lockwood report]* (Belfast, 1965)

DENI, *The future structure of teacher education in Northern Ireland: an interim report of the higher education review group for Northern Ireland* (Belfast, 1980)
DENI, *Report of the Higher Education Review Group for Northern Ireland* [*Chilver report*] (Belfast, 1982)
DENI, *Higher education in Northern Ireland: the future structure* (Belfast, 1982)
Advisory Board of the Research Councils, *Report of a joint working party on the support of university scientific research* (London, 1982)
UGC, *Northern Ireland working party, first report* (Belfast, 1984)
UGC, *A strategy for higher education into the 1990s* (London, 1984)
CVCP, *Report of the steering committee for efficiency studies in universities* [*Jarratt report*] (London, 1985)
Working Party on Research Selectivity, *Final report to the Department of Education for Northern Ireland, The Queen's University of Belfast and the University of Ulster* [*Butler report*] (Belfast, 1987)
Review of the University Grants Committee [*Croham report*] (London, 1987)
The National Committee of Inquiry into Higher Education, *Higher education in the learning society* [*Dearing report*] (London, 1997)

STUDENT PUBLICATIONS

Lynda Egerton, 'Social and economic discrimination against women in Northern Ireland'. Typescript produced by the Welfare Committee of the Students' Union (*c.*1975). QUB archive, P/879.
Gown (1955–), QUB archives F/876.
National Union of Students, *Memorandum to the committee on higher education in Northern Ireland* (Belfast, 1964), QUB archives E/7/12
Qubis (1949–55), QUB archives P/876.
Q: A literary magazine, QUB archives P/876
SRC, *Staff-student committees and the position in Queen's* (1945), QUB archive P/871
SRC, *Memorandum to the committee on higher education* (Belfast, February 1964), QUB archives E/7/13.
SRC, *Memoranda to the committee on higher education* (Belfast, June 1964), QUB archives E/7/14
SRCSU, Constitution and laws, 1965, 1968, QUB archives P/871
SRCSU, A memorandum from the executive of the SRCSU on student representation, QUB archives, P/879
SRC, 'Student opinion on aspects of University education', 1968. QUB archives, P/871
SRCULAR, (1970?), QUB archives P/871
Students' Union Society books, 1951, 1953–4. QUB archives P/872, P/879
Ulster students' songbook, QUB archives, P/879

INTERVIEWS AND REMINISCENCES

(Those marked M were taped interviews conducted by Mr Alf McCreary and which he kindly made available to me.)

Sir Eric Ashby (Lord Ashby of Brandon) (1990) (M)
Professor Sir David Bates (February 1992) (M)
Sir Gordon Beveridge (1999)
Mr George Cowie (1991) (M)
Professor Sir Bernard Crossland (1990) (M)
Professor Sir Bernard Crossland, 'Interview', *University of Nottingham Magazine*, 15 (autumn 2002), 12
Mrs Florence Emeleus, (March 1992) (M)
Mrs G. Evans, Typed reminiscences of Professor Estyn Evans
Sir Peter Froggatt (1999)
Professor H. Godin', address to QUB Association of Women Graduates, March 1983) (M)
Dr Robin Harland, unpublished history of the University Health Service (2000)
Dr R. B. Henderson, a member of the Lockwood committee (October 2002)
Dr Eammon Hughes, typescript memoir of Seamus Heaney (2000)
President Mary McAleese (1999)
Professor Robin Shanks (1999)

BOOKS AND ARTICLES

R.D. Anderson, *Universities and elites in Britain since 1800* (London, 1992)
Anon. *The book of the fete: Queen's College Belfast* (Belfast, 1907)
Eric Ashby, *Adapting universities to a technological age* (London, 1974)
AUT, *Efficiency gains or quality losses?* (London, 1996)
AUT, *Higher education in the UK: mapping the future* (London, 1997)
Sir Michael Bett, *Independent review of higher education pay and conditions* (London, 1999)
Eileen Black, *A sesquicentennial celebration: art from the Queen's University Collection* (Ulster Museum 1995)
R.D.C. Black, 'E.R.R. Green 1920–82', *Irish Economic and Social History*, 8 (1981), 5–7
John Boyd, *Out of my class* (Belfast, 1985)
John Boyd, *The middle of my journey* (Belfast, 1990)
C.E.B. Brett, *The buildings of Belfast 1700–1914* (Belfast, revised edn 1985)
John Bridges, *Belfast Medical Students Association* (Belfast, no date)
J.S. Brubacher, *On the philosophy of higher education* (London, 1978)
R.H. Buchanan, 'Obituary: Emyr Estyn Evans, 1905–1989', *Ulster Folklife*, 26 (1990), 1–3

Anon. *The book of the fete: Queen's College Belfast* (Belfast, 1907)

Patrick Buckland, *A history of Northern Ireland* (Dublin, 1981)

T.M. Charlton, *Professor emeritus* (published privately, 1991)

Richard Clarke, 'Giants in Ulster medicine', *Northern Ireland Medicine Today* (February 2000), 5

D.C. Coleman, 'Gentlemen and players', *Economic History Review*, 2nd series, 36 (1973), 92–116

F.M. Cornford, *Microcosmographia, being a guide for the young academic politician* (Cambridge, 1908)

D. Felicitas Corrigan, *Helen Waddell: a biography* (London, 1986)

H.A. Cronne (ed.), *Essays in British and Irish history: in honour of James Eadie Todd* (London, 1949)

M.J. Davidson and, C.L. Cooper, *Shattering the glass ceiling: the woman manager* (London, 1992)

Norma Dawson, Desmond Greer and Peter Ingram (eds), *One hundred and fifty years of Irish law* (Belfast and Dublin, 1996)

Bernadette Devlin, *Price of my soul* (London, 1969)

Disturbances in Northern Ireland: report of the commission appointed by the Governor of Northern Ireland [*Cameron Commission*] (Belfast, 1969)

Bowes Egan and Vincent McCormack, *Burntollet* (London, 1969)

David Evans and Paul Larmour, *Queen's: an architectural legacy* (Belfast, 1995)

John Field, 'Educating active citizens: the contribution of Richard Livingstone', in Martha Friedenthal-Haase (ed.), *Personality and biography: proceedings of the sixth international conference on the history of adult education*, ii (Berlin and Oxford, 1998), 831–45

Peter Froggatt, 'The distinctiveness of Belfast medicine and its medical school', *Ulster Medical Journal*, 54: 3 (1985)

Peter Froggatt, 'Ulster and Trinity: "The end of the affair"?', unpublished quartercentenary address (Belfast, 1992)

A.M. Gallagher, R.D. Osborne, R.J. Cormack, *Attitudes to higher education: report to CCRU and DENI* (Belfast, 1996)

Michael Grant, *My first eighty years* (Henley-on-Thames, 1994)

H.G. Hanbury, 'Introduction', in J.L. Montrose, *Precedent in English law and other essays*, ed. H.G. Hanbury (Shannon, 1968)

R.M. Hartwell, 'Kenneth H. Connell: an appreciation', *Irish Economic and Social History*, 1 (1974), 7–13

R.I.D. Harris, C.W. Jefferson and J.E Spencer (eds), *The Northern Ireland economy: a comparative study in the economic development of a peripheral region* (London, 1990)

Seamus Heaney, Introduction to *Beowolf: a new translation* (London, 1999)

C.H. Holland (ed.), *Trinity College Dublin & the idea of a university* (Dublin, 1991)

K.S. Isles and Norman Cuthbert, *An economic survey of Northern Ireland* (Belfast, 1957),

Alvin Jackson, *Ireland 1798–1998* (Oxford 1999)

Alvin Jackson, 'J.C. Beckett: politics, faith, scholarship', *Irish Historical Studies*, 36: 130 (2002), 129–50.

W. Johnston, E.A. Cheeseman and J.D. Merrett, 'Observations on routine medical examinations of university entrants in Northern Ireland', *British Journal of Preventative and Social History*, 11: 3 (1957), 152–61.

W. Johnston and J.D. Merrett, 'Further observations on routine medical examinations of university entrants in Northern Ireland', *British Journal of Preventative and Social History*, 16: 2 (1962), 152–61.

Robert S. Kidelsky, *John Maynard Keynes*, i, *Hope betrayed, 1883–1920* (London, 1983), 427–8

Ian Ker, *The genius of John Henry Newman: selections from his writings* (Oxford, 1989)

Charles Kinahan, 'Queen's University and the art of development', *Fortnight*, 11 (April 1975), 17–18.

J.J. Lee, *Ireland 1912–22. Politics and society* (Cambridge 1989)

Geoffrey Lockwood and John Davies, *Universities: the management challenge* (Windsor, 1985)

Edna Longley, '"A foreign oasis"? English literature, Irish studies and Queen's University Belfast', *Irish Review*, 17/18 (winter 1995)

Michael McDowell, 'Victoriana vandalised: Queen's University and the art of destruction', *Fortnight*, 21 March 1975, 10–11.

R.B. McDowell and D.A. Webb, *Trinity College, Dublin, 1592–1952* (Cambridge, 1982)

Alex McEwen and Carol Curry, 'Girls' access to science: single sex versus co-educational schools), in R.D. Osborne, R.J. Cormack and R.L. Miller (eds), *Education and policy in Northern Ireland* (Belfast, 1987).

T.W. Moody and J.C. Beckett, *Queen's Belfast, 1845–1949: the history of a university*, 2 vols (London, 1959)

Andrew Motion, *Philip Larkin: a writer's life* (London, 1993), 198.

Antoin E. Murphy and Renée Prendergast (eds.), *Contributions to the history of economic thought: essays in honour of R.D.C. Black* (London and New York, 2000), 3–27.

John A. Murphy, *The College: a history of Queen's University/College Cork, 1845–1995* (Cork, 1995)

Sally Nash and Martin Sherwood, *The University of Southampton: an illustrated history* (London, 2002)

John Henry Newman, *The idea of a university*, ed. I.T. Ker (Oxford, 1976)

Robert D. Osborne, *Higher education in Ireland North and South* (London, 1996)

Gearóid Ó Tuathaigh, 'The establishment of the Queen's Colleges: ideological and political background', in Tadhg Foley (ed.), *From Queen's College to National University: essays on the academic history of QCG/UCG/NUI, Galway* (Dublin, 1999)

Andrew Phang, 'Exploring and expanding horizons: the influence and scholarship of Professor J.L. Montrose', *Singapore Law Review*, 18 (1997), 15–57

Muriel Prichard, *Fullness of life: the story of J.J. Prichard, Professor of Anatomy at Queen's University, Belfast, 1952–1979* (Belfast, 1989)

S. Gourley Putt, 'A packet of Bloomsbury letters: the forgotten H.O. Meredith', *Encounter*, 59 (November 1982), 77–84

Alistair Rowan, 'A perfect university suburb: the Queen's University district, Belfast', *Country Life*, 23 June 1982, 1688–90

Michael Sanderson, *The universities and British industry, 1850–1970* (London, 1972)

A. Brian Scott, 'Classics and Queen's, 1845–1995' (unpublished typescript, 1995)

David Scott (ed.), *Treasures of the mind: a Trinity College Dublin quartercentenary exhibition* (London, 1992)

Michael Shattock and Gwynneth Rigby (eds), *Resource allocation in British universities* (Guildford, 1983)

Harold Silver, 'The making of a missionary: Eric Ashby and technology', *History of Education*, 31: 6 (2002), 557–70

Harold Silver, *Higher education and opinion making in twentieth-century England* (London, 2003)

Donald Southgate, *University education in Dundee: a centenary history* (Edinburgh, 1982)

Lawrence Stone, *The crisis of the aristocracy, 1558–1641* (Oxford, 1965)

B.H. Tolley, *The history of the University of Nottingham*, two volumes (Nottingham, 2001)

Brian Walker and Alf McCreary, *Degrees of excellence: the story of Queen's, Belfast 1845–1995* (Belfast, 1995)

John A. Weaver, 'John Henry Biggart 1905–1979. A portrait in respect and affection', *Ulster Medical Journal*, 54: 1 (April 1985), 1–19

NEWSPAPERS

(There is a an extensive collection of newspaper clippings maintained by the Information Office and the Communications Office and lodged in the University archives.)

Belfast News Letter	*Irish News*
Belfast Telegraph	*Irish Times*
Daily Telegraph	*Northern Whig*
Education Times	*The Times*
Guardian Higher	*Times Higher Education Supplement*
The Independent	

Index

Academic Board 67, 137, 144–5
Academic Council 34, 35, 64–83 passim, 93,
    116, 121, 137, 141–5 passim, 150, 151,
    154, 172, 174, 181, 188
academic planning 20, 24, 69–70, 72, 74, 75,
    81, 83
Academic Registrar 82, 83
accounting 6, 42, 128, 124, 136, 155
Administration Building 91–3, 101–2
administration, proliferation of 20, 63,
    69–71, 83–4, 91, 106, 118, 125–6
Administrative Management Group 71, 74
Administrative Secretary 67, 68, 70–5
    passim, 79, 82, 196
aerospace engineering 157
agricultural education 32, 134
Alanbrooke, Field Marshal Lord 64, 195
anatomy 91, 119
Anderson committee 53
Aquinas Hall 60, 128, 137
archaeology 156
architecture 6, 100, 136, 157
Armagh 24, 33, 104, 172–3, 192
Ashby Building 87, 90, 96, 101, 104
Ashby, Sir Eric 3, 4, 6, 19, 63, 64, 65, 70,
    83, 84, 94, 105, 109, 113, 117, 130, 143,
    149, 179, 195
Association of University Teachers 32, 35,
    53
Atkinson, Professor K 111, 118

BA (General Studies) 23, 130, 134, 153,
    171, 172
Bain, Sir George 24, 44, 75, 82, 188, 195
Barnes, Mr M. 174
Bates, Professor Sir David 35, 109–10, 112,
    116–17
Beckett, Professor J.C. 110
BEd 33, 36, 154–5
Belfast Corporation 28, 95, 191
Belfour, Mr A.O. 107
Bell, Sir Ewart, honorary treasurer 81
Benham, Professor P. 133

Better Equipment Fund 79, 144
Beveridge, Sir Gordon 23, 24, 42, 43, 71–2,
    172, 195
Biggart, Professor Sir J.H. 27, 109, 139,
    178, 195
biochemistry 87,88, 90
biological sciences 32, 41, 88, 120 136
Black, Professor R.D.C. 111, 112, 195
Blacking, Professor J. 117, 154, 162
BMedSc 157
Board of Curators 19, 68, 76, 115, 143
Botanic Gardens gate lodge 101, 102
botany 86, 88
Boyd, Professor M. 109
Braidwood, Professor J. 111
British Academy 7, 112
BSc(Econ) 29, 152
building programmes 17, 20, 36, 61, 86–94,
    98, 99–100, 103–4
built environment 157
Buller, Mr N. 140
Burke, Professor P. 110, 112
Bursar 63, 64, 67, 70, 71, 83, 125, 196
business studies 41–2, 128, 136, 155
Butler working party 41–2, 44, 156

Campbell, Mr J.J. 178
Campbell, Professor C. 114
Canada Room 58, 97
Careers and Appointsments Service 137,
    139–40
Carr, Professor K. 119
Carter, Professor C. 111, 114
Casson, Sir Hugh 88, 90, 91, 95, 102
Catholic University of Dublin 2, 14
Centre for Academic Practice 125, 159, 161
Chancellor 64, 65, 66, 195
Charlesworth, Professor J.K. 109
charter and statutes 64–6, 66–8, 79, 144,
    181
chemistry 41, 86, 88, 120, 136, 156, 157
Chilver review group 37–40, 42, 44, 49, 73,
    152, 155, 172

City Hospital 95, 104
Civil Rights Association 176–7
classics 128, 136, 154
Coleraine 33, 37
College Green Terrace 101, 102
College of Technology 28, 90, 117, 156, 157
colleges as academic units 78–9, 83
Committee of Deans 75, 77, 137, 142
Committee of Vice-Chancellors and
    Principals (CVCP) 51, 73, 159
committee structure 75, 80, 143
Communications Office 126
Computer Centre 99, 101
computer science 6, 128, 136, 156, 162
computing facilities 59, 60
Connell, Professor K.H. 110–11
continuing education (*see also* extra-mural
    studies and Institute of Continuing
    Education) 128, 170–3, 174
Convocation 64, 65–6, 79, 83, 190–1
Cowie, Mr G. 48, 114, 196
Croham report 51
Crossland, Professor Sir Bernard 110, 112,
    195
Cuthbert, Professor N. 163

Dalgano, Professor A. 110, 117
Darragh, Miss A. 126
Deaf and Dumb Institution 87, 89, 90, 101
deans 67, 74–8 passim, 80, 83, 84, 119
Dearing Committee 43–5, 53, 54
degree structures 22, 35–6, 39–40, 134–6,
    151–3, 161
Dennison, Professor S.R. 111, 114
dentistry 18, 128, 136, 151, 152, 157–8
Department of Agriculture, Northern
    Ireland 76
Department of Education, Northern
    Ireland (DENI) 28, 37–42 passim, 49,
    56, 97, 99, 103, 156, 162, 163, 172
departments as units of administration
    67–8, 74, 76
Development and Alumni Office 126
Devlin, Ms Bernadette 176, 177, 184
Director of Human Resources (see also
    Personnel Officer) 79, 120, 125
directors of academic units 76–7, 79
discrimination in employment, allegations
    of 23, 24, 72, 81, 122, 184–8

economics 83, 128, 136, 152
education 18, 154–5, 162
Elmwood Avenue 87, 102

Elmwood Hall 88
Emeleus, Professor K. 109
Emmerson, Mr M. 174
Employment Equality Services (EES),
    report of 72, 123, 187–9
employment legislation 61, 123, 126
engineering 28, 86, 87, 88, 134, 136, 157
English 114, 120, 136, 142, 151, 153, 158
Enterprise Office 125
Equal Oportunities Group 188
Equal Opportunities Commission 122
Equal Opportunities Officer 185, 188
Equal Opportunities Tribunal 192
Equal Opportunities Unit 185
Estates Officer 79
ethnomusicology 117
Evans, Professor E.E. 109, 154
extra-mural studies 17–18, 96, 128, 170–3

faculties 67, 69, 75, 76–7, 80, 83, 128,
    134–6, 149
Faculty of Agriculture (and Food Science)
    27, 33, 35, 65, 76, 78, 117, 118, 120,
    134–5, 142, 149, 156
Faculty of Applied Science and Technology
    27, 33, 35, 36, 39, 134–5, 142
Faculty of Arts (later Humanities) 28, 36,
    64, 91, 117, 134–5, 142, 149, 150, 153
Faculty of Commerce 29, 65, 149
Faculty of Economics (and Social Sciences)
    22, 29, 36, 39, 67, 78, 87, 89, 117, 130,
    134–5, 152, 155
Faculty of Education 36, 76, 78, 117, 134–5,
    154–5
Faculty of Engineering 78, 128, 134–5, 153,
    157
Faculty of Law 28, 36, 39, 64, 78, 117, 120,
    134–5, 149, 150, 153, 156, 179, 183
Faculty of Law, Social, and Educational
    Sciences (LSES) 134–5
Faculty of Medicine (and Health Sciences)
    27, 64, 117, 118, 120, 128, 134–5, 142,
    149, 157–8
Faculty of Science 35, 65, 117, 118, 120,
    134–5, 157
Faculty of Theology 28, 65, 76, 78, 134–5,
    181
Fair Employment Agency (later
    Commission) 185
Fair Employment Tribunal 72, 186–7
female academics 111, 118, 119–22
Festival at Queen's 174, 175
Film Theatre 173, 174

Finance Committee 75
formula funding 50, 52
French 118
Froggatt, Sir Peter 22, 37, 40, 42, 49, 51, 58, 66, 69, 179–80, 191, 195

gender initiative 121–2
General Board of Studies 64, 65, 67, 69
geography 18, 120, 136, 156
geology 87, 104, 156–7
Godin, Professor H. 115, 125, 174
Gown 145–7
Gradule 147
Grant, Dr Michael 21, 35, 48, 118, 195
Great Hall 24, 58, 85, 86, 87, 93–4, 96–7, 99, 104, 111, 173
Greek 2, 135, 151, 154
Green, Professor E.R.R. 158
Guthrie, Sir Tyrone 64, 195

halls of residence 21, 60, 87, 90, 103, 137–8
Hamilton, President Thomas 4, 5
heads of department 67, 69, 74, 75, 76, 79, 83
Heaney Library 93
Heaney, Seamus 111, 112
Henry, Professor R.M. 170
Higher Education Funding Council for England (HEFCE) 43, 51, 103, 162
history and philosophy of science 135
history:
   ancient 118
   economic and social 134, 135
   modern 136, 151, 153, 162
Hobsbaum, Dr P. 111
humanities 6, 7, 31, 56, 114, 117, 120, 128, 134, 158, 162, 167

inflation, effects of on university finances 16, 49, 50, 55, 104
information management 134, 136, 156
information office 74
information technology 75, 77
Institute of Computer Based Learning 78
Institute of Education 36, 154–5
Institute of European Studies 78
Institute of Irish Studies 78, 79, 158, 162
Institute of Life Long Learning 128
Institute of Pathology 87
Institute of Professional Legal Studies 78, 79, 153, 156, 162
Isles, Professor K. 111, 114, 163
Italian 128

Jarratt committee 73, 80, 81
Jarratt working group 73–5
Johnston, Dr W. 139
Joint Authority for Higher Technological Studies 28, 31
Jope, Professor M. 112

Keir Building 20, 85, 87–8, 96, 104
Keir, Sir David Lindsay 18, 63, 195
Kinahan, Mr Charles 101
Kirk, Professor W. 70, 195

language studies 136, 153–4
Lanyon Building 24, 82, 96, 97, 101, 102, 104
Lanyon, Sir Charles 24, 85, 89
Larkin, Mr Philip 115
Latin 2, 151, 154
law 6, 36, 120, 118, 136
league tables 24, 55, 164–5
Lelievre report 155
liberal education 2–3, 5, 6, 8, 21, 149–50, 158, 170–1
Librarian 68, 155, 196
Library 21, 35, 59, 60, 75, 77, 87, 90–1, 97–8, 101, 102, 104, 121, 137, 159
library studies 154–5
Lisburn Road 87, 89, 101
Literary and Scientific Society (Literific) 146, 177
Livingstone, Sir Richard 105, 137, 169
LLB 36
Llubera, Professor I.M.G. 170
Lockwood report 9, 21, 30–7, 39, 42, 61, 65, 91, 129, 154
Londonderry 33, 169
Londonderry, Marquis of 64
Loughry Agricultural College 30
Lowry, Professor C.G. 108
Lyons, Professor F.S.L. 64

Magee University College 30, 37, 40, 107
management studies 83, 134, 155
marine biology 32
mathematics 18, 120, 134, 136, 151, 158
Mawhinney, Dr Brian 42
Maynooth 13, 14
MB, BCh, BAO 152
McAleese, President Mary 111, 119, 178, 195
McCallister, Professor W.J. 108
McCuckian, Mr J., Pro-Chancellor 188
McGeown, Professor M. 111

McGowan, Professor F. 118
Medical Library 91, 100
medicine 6, 23, 36, 128, 134, 151, 153, 157
Meredith, Professor H.O. 107–8, 170
microbiology 87
Ministry of Agriculture 27–8, 32, 57
Ministry of Education 28, 34, 154, 170, 171
Ministry of Finance 46, 155
Mitchell, Senator G. 65, 195
modular courses 40, 130, 153
Molyneaux, Mr J. 190
Montrose, Professor J.L. 108–9
music 18, 104, 173

National Anthem controversy 58, 66,
    188–91
National University of Ireland 14, 116
new Jarratt working group 75–6
New Physics Building 87, 88
New University of Ulster 23, 30, 33, 36,
    37–9, 40, 49, 70, 116, 129
Newark, Professor F.H. 20, 108–9, 150–1,
    195
Newman, Cardinal J.H. 1, 2–3, 5, 29, 126–7
Northern Ireland Higher Eucation Council
    (NIHEC) 43, 165
Northern Ireland Technology Centre 78
Northern Ireland Working Pary (NIWP)
    49, 52, 70, 152
Northern Ireland, economic and social
    conditions in 2, 8–10, 23, 54, 180–1
Nursing, school of 103, 120, 131, 157

Omagh 172–3
Orr, Professor J. 157
Orr, Sir David 65, 195
outreach 103, 170–3
Owen, Professor G. 114, 195

palaeoecology 156
Palley, Professor C. 118
Parkinson, Professor J.R. 111
Pelan, Professor M 118
People's Democracy 177
Personnel Officer (*see also* Director of
    Human Resources) 125, 185, 186–7,
    188
pharmacy 156
Physical Education Centre 89, 101, 125,
    136
physics 18, 41, 88, 120, 134, 136, 158
physiology 88, 90
Policy and Resources Committee 77, 80

Policy Planning Committee 75, 76
political science 67, 83, 128, 134, 136, 155
Porter, Revd Josias 1, 8
postgraduate studies 36, 162–3
premature retirement schemes 50, 61,
    113–14
premises, maintenance of 61
Pro-Chancellors 64, 65
professors 118–19
Pro-Vice-Chancellors 68, 74, 75, 79, 82, 84,
    195
provosts 78–9, 83
psychology 120,
PTQ 146–7
public lectures 173

Q: a literary magazine 147
quadrangle 87, 89, 92–3
QUBIS 57
Qubis 145
Queen's and conservation 100–3
Queen's Chambers 21, 60, 128, 137
Queen's College, Belfast 1, 4, 5, 13, 149
Queen's College, Cork 13, 14
Queen's College, Galway 13, 14
Queen's Elms (new) 87, 104, 128, 137–8
Queen's Elms (old) 90, 101, 102
Queen's Graduates' Association 169
Queen's University, Belfast and the UU,
    relations between 39–40, 41–2
Queen's University at Armagh 24, 172–3,
    192
Queen's University Guild 169
Queen's University in Ireland 1, 12–13, 14
Queen's University, Belfast:
    academic staff, numbers of 15, 17, 19, 22,
        23, 106–12, 197–200
    academic staff, recruitment of 17, 19–20,
        21, 34, 36, 112–18
    administrative staff, numbers of 17,
        105–7
    alleged traditional attitude of 31–2, 33–4,
        39, 41
    as an international university 8, 11, 81–2,
        165, 169–70
    attitudes of to Lockwood committee and
        report 34–7
    expenditure of 58–61
    income of 15–16, 17, 19, 22, 23, 26, 43,
        46–58, 210–12
    non-denominational character 14, 185
    relations with local community 10, 14–15,
        82, 169–70, 179–81, 194

research in 7–8, 18, 24, 41–2, 50, 52–3,
    55–7, 163–7
student numbers in 15, 16, 18, 19, 22,
    23, 31, 34, 36, 201–9
underfunding of 17, 19, 48, 49
undergraduate studies in 134–6, 151–8
QUESTOR 57
Quigley, Sir George 44
quinquennial funding 47–8, 49, 87

Read, Mr E.C. 171
Registrar, post of 64, 68, 69–72, 74, 80, 82,
    188, 196
research assessment exercise (RAE) 23, 45,
    164–7, 168,
research councils 3, 55, 167
research degrees 162–3
research grants and contracts 42, 44, 55–7,
    163–4
Research Office 125, 166
research:
    costs of 16, 163–4
    importance of 7, 50, 52, 55–6, 150–1,
        163–4, 167
    in QUB and UU compared 41, 56–7,
        165–6
Riddel Hall 60, 128, 137, 138
Robbins report 6, 21, 29–30, 35, 44, 61, 128
Roberts, Professor M. 110, 112
Royal Society 7, 56, 112
Royal University of Ireland 8, 14
Royal Victoria Hospital 87, 85, 99–100
Rural College, Draperstown 173
Russian 128

salary costs 58–9
Sayles, Professor G.O. 110
scholastic philosophy 181–2
schools as academic units 76–7
Science Library 91
Secretary of the Academic Council 65, 67,
    68, 69, 70, 71, 79, 82, 125, 150, 163,
    195
Secretary of the University 19, 48, 114, 125,
    196
Senate 20, 22, 24, 34, 40, 48, 50, 64, 65, 66,
    70–83 passim, 87, 88, 91, 118, 119,
    120, 140, 142, 143, 144, 187–90 passim
Shaftsbury, Earl of 64
Shattock and Holmes report 80, 81–2
Smyth, Mr F., appointed as Registrar 71
Snakes Alive 147
social anthropology 117, 154

Social Science Building 93, 174
social sciences 32, 56, 110, 117, 120, 128,
    134, 136, 152–3, 155
social work 134, 136, 155, 162
sociology 83, 128, 134, 136, 155
sources of income:
    fees 44, 46, 53–5, 210–12
    government grants 44, 46–53, 210–12
    other 46, 57–8, 210–12
    sources of income 46, 55–7, 210–12
sports' facilities 60, 136–7, 147
St Joseph's Teaching Training College 30,
    36, 37, 38
St Mary's Teacher Training College 30, 36,
    37, 38, 76
staff training and devlopment 75, 125
staff:
    academic 58–9, 105–7, 124, 126–7
    administrative 59, 105–7, 124, 125–6
    other 59, 105–7, 120–1, 124, 126
    religious composition of 122–4, 126,
        185–6
    research 59–60, 106–7, 124
staff-student committees 137, 142
Stewart, Mr N., honorary treasurer 80, 81
Stormont 1, 3, 21, 26, 47, 48, 170, 179
Stranmillis College 30, 36, 37, 38, 76
strategic review group 80
Student Health Centre *see* University
    Health Centre
student politics 141, 147–8
student/staff ratio 15, 23, 53
students' centre 87, 89
Students' Representative Council 34, 35,
    65, 137, 140–1, 141–2, 158, 175, 178,
    182
Students' Union 60, 89, 96, 101, 104, 128,
    133, 136, 137
    Irish language signs in 81, 189–90, 191
    politicization of 176–9, 182–4
Students' Union Society 140–1
students:
    ages of 131
    female 128, 131–2, 205–8
    geographical origins of, 54, 133–4, 183–4
    students, grants for 53–4, 129–30
    male 128, 131–2, 205–8
    numbers and proportion of in higher
        education 29–30, 26, 37, 44, 45, 50
    numbers of in QUB 128, 129–30
    outflow from Northern Ireland 55
    participation of in University
        management 141–5, 147

students: (*continued*)
    part-time 29, 40, 128, 130, 162–3, 209–10
    Protestant 13–14, 128, 132–3, 148
    research 162–3, 209–10
    Roman Catholic 13–14, 128, 132–3, 148, 175, 185
    social composition of 10, 130
teacher education 31, 32–3, 35, 36, 37–8, 41
teaching companies 57
teaching quality of 23, 45, 55, 56, 129, 142, 150–1, 158–61, 168
technological education 6, 30, 31–2
theatre and film studies 136
theology 5, 28
Thompson, Professor Sir William 117
Todd, Professor J.E. 108, 110, 158
Trimble, Mr D. 112
Trinity College, Dublin 1, 4, 12, 14, 30, 116, 129, 130
Troubles, the, effects of on QUB 16, 22, 23, 25, 95, 98–9, 113–14, 146, 160, 164, 175–84, 192

Ulster Polytechnic 30, 37–9, 40, 70
Union Debating Society 146
universities, purpose of 1, 2–8, 18, 149–51
University Funding Council 43, 51, 56, 181
University Grants Committee 2, 6, 17, 22, 23, 26, 40, 41, 43, 47–51 passim, 55, 69, 73, 86, 87, 88, 90, 95, 97, 98, 100, 153, 154, 161, 164, 169

University Health Service 60, 136–7, 125, 139
University houses 60, 138
University of Ulster 23, 24, 40–1, 49, 69, 73, 116, 155, 156
University precinct 95–6
University Road 91, 96, 128, 183
University Square 17, 87, 96, 100, 102, 128, 136, 140, 141, 183

Vice-Chancellor, duties of 64, 65, 67–8, 69, 74, 193
Vice-President 64, 195
Vick, Sir Arthur 21, 48–9, 177, 195
Visitors' Centre 174
visual arts group 173–4
vocational education 1, 2, 4–6, 8, 21, 40, 149–50, 158, 170

Warren, Professor W.L. 110
Warrender, Professor H. 92–3
Waterhouse, Professor G. 69
Whitla Hall 19, 86, 173, 191
Williams, Professor A. 112, 114, 143, 195
women's forum 122
Women's Students Hall 140–1
Workers' Educational Association 170–1
workstations 59
Wright, Sir Rowland 64–5, 195

zoology 86